CASES LOST
CAUSES WON

CASES LOST
CAUSES WON

THE SUPREME COURT AND
THE JUDICIAL PROCESS

Alice Fleetwood Bartee

Southwest Missouri State University

St. Martin's Press • New York

Deus—Familia—Universitas
"In Lumine Vestro Video Lumen"

Library of Congress Catalog Card Number: 83–61609
Copyright © 1984 by St. Martin's Press, Inc.
All Rights Reserved.
Manufactured in the United States of America.
87654
fedcba
For information, write St. Martin's Press, Inc.,
175 Fifth Avenue, New York, N.Y. 10010

cover design: Paul Conklin
book design: Meryl Levavi

cloth ISBN: 0-312-12336-1
paper ISBN: 0-312-12337-X

PREFACE

The case method for study of the judicial process is both fascinating and dramatic. The analysis of a case as it proceeds through the courts brings to life the participants and their controversy; the context; the attorneys, jurors, and judges; and the law itself. Yet the single case study confines the reader within the boundaries of that case alone, and multiple in-depth studies do not solve the problem of particularism. Moreover, the ongoing, changing nature of the judicial process suggests the need for a broader and more general focus. The question thus becomes, "How can one use the case-study approach to analyze the total workings of the judicial process?"

Good case studies generally include a description, discussion, and analysis of at least five major aspects of a case: (1) the facts, actors, and environmental setting; (2) the movement of the case within the judicial system and the reaction of judicial decision makers; (3) the reasons underlying the case decision; (4) the reactions of the general public to the case decision; and (5) subsequent follow-up cases that either reinforce or modify the case decision.

These five aspects are similar to the parts of a theoretical and analytical framework used by political scientists to study the political system. Known as systems theory, this framework was designed to create a simple model for examining relationships between participants and their environment. Systems theory has a tremendous benefit for those desiring to study the judicial process using the case method. The model organizes data into five major stages known as input, conversion, output, impact, and feedback—categories recognized as important in any good case study. The systems-theory model, however, frees the reader and the researcher both from the confines of the single case study and from the necessity for multiple in-depth case studies. If one first understands the activities that occur within each of the stages postulated by the model, it becomes relatively simple to find appropriate cases that possess the characteristics necessary to document, analyze, and evaluate the workings of the judicial process at each stage.

This book does exactly that. Combining the drama and excitement of the case-study method with the systems approach, I have sought to illustrate and analyze the active workings of each of the major stages in the judicial process of decision making. The Introduction briefly explains and describes the activities that occur within each stage. Chapters 1, 2, 3, and 4 each concentrate on a particular Supreme Court decision, chosen because it well illustrates the activity occurring at a particular stage. Thus Chapter 1 uses *Frohwerk* v. *United States*, 249 U.S. 204 (1919), to illustrate activities at the input stage. Chapter 2 dissects *Minersville* v. *Gobitis*, 310 U.S. 586 (1940), in order to highlight the conversion stage. Chapter 3 describes the interaction and court decision in *Walker* v. *City of Birmingham*, 388 U.S. 307 (1967). Chapter 4 studies *White* v. *State of Texas*, 310 U.S. 530 (1940), as an example of the impact stage. The final stage, feedback, is presented in Chapter 5. Here the output and impact of each of the four cases studied is evaluated in terms of its long-range implications for change through the judicial process.

This approach is unique. Its value is twofold. First, the cases used are classic, landmark decisions that have been drawn from different periods. As illustrations of different stages in the judicial process they will not become dated or inappropriate for study. Second, although in each case the "underdog" party lost, ultimately the constitutional right that had been asserted emerged triumphant. The value of the system, with its openness and its ability to respond to demands for change, is thus affirmed: the system works.

I wish to express my intellectual debt of gratitude to Professor Phoebe Morrison, late Professor of Government, Barnard College, Columbia University, who first aroused my interest in the *Bob White* case; to Professor Louis Lusky of the Columbia University School of Law, whose analysis of World War I cases suggested further exploration of decisions such as *Frohwerk;* and to Professor Alan F. Westin, who, as a professor in the Department of

Public Law and Government at Columbia University and later as my dissertation sponsor, introduced me to the methods of analysis necessary for an understanding of the judicial process.

St. Martin's Press engaged a number of instructors to review various drafts of this book. I am thankful to all of them for their very constructive suggestions. The following reviewers agreed to be listed by name: Robert Toburen, Louisiana Tech University; George F. Cole, University of Connecticut; Erika S. Fairchild, North Carolina State University; Robert A. Carp, University of Houston; and Dr. Larry Berkson, formerly of the American Judicature Society.

Alice Fleetwood Bartee

CONTENTS

CASES LOST
CAUSES WON

INTRODUCTION

Americans have a propensity for settling disputes within a legal framework. The law of the jungle may prevail from time to time and vigilante justice raise its ugly head, yet a preference for a judicial verdict remains rooted in the consciousness of the nation. The courtroom has become the principal battleground, the attorneys with their array of arguments serve as the champions of the opposing parties, and the judges act as referees. As controversies are settled by judicial rulings, the dust of battle begins to settle. Yet, like conflicts decided upon a military battleground, disputes within the legal framework may die temporarily only to be revived in another battle.

This particular openness of the judicial system to continuing battles contributes to the environment necessary for a democratic society. As long as the losers of today can hope to be the victors of tomorrow, there remains a willingness to settle conflict without a resort to arms.

The judicial role in keeping the governmental system open and in providing for an orderly process to handle disputes makes the court a proper object in the study of social and political change. Since the United States Supreme Court is the court of last resort, a study of its process of decision making is of particular value in understanding the role of the judiciary in helping to maintain a responsive yet stable democratic political system.

The Supreme Court in the Political Process: Powers and Limitations

Although only a very small percentage of cases find their way to the Supreme Court, these cases become landmark decisions simply because they do. The Court's ability to hear and decide such cases is related to its position and power within the American judicial system.

The Supreme Court's power is rooted in the Constitution, in congressional statutes, and in conventions and traditions established by the Court. The Constitution provides for only a limited category of cases that the Court hears directly. Known as cases of original jurisdiction, these infrequent controversies may involve two states; ambassadors, ministers, or consuls; and a state and the national government. Most of the cases heard by the Court arise under the appellate jurisdiction specified in the Constitution. These cases come indirectly after being heard in one or more lower courts.

However, the appellate jurisdiction of the Supreme Court is subject to congressional restriction, a power vested by the Constitution in the legislature. Thus Congress, by statute, can prevent the Court from hearing almost any issue it so desires. Congressional power extends not only to defining this appellate jurisdiction but also to determining the size of the Court and to confirming in the Senate the President's nominees. The Court understands that it is prudent to avoid prolonged and bitter controversy with either Congress or the President. Congress's authority to change the size of the Court, to remove certain categories of cases from its review, to impeach Justices, and to seek amendments to the Constitution to overrule decisions all combine to limit the Court's power.

Congress can also *increase* the power of the Supreme Court at the appellate level. For instance, in 1925 Congress granted power of *certiorari* jurisdiction. This permits the Court to exercise its own independent judgment concerning whether to hear a case or not. As a result cases today theoretically can go up to the Court for review either by appeal from a state or federal court or by *certiorari*. The Court, however, treats its so-called mandatory appeals cases exactly as it does *certiorari* cases—it exercises its discretionary power to hear or refuse a case.

The Supreme Court's jurisdiction and power is also rooted in its traditions and norms. The Court can require that a case meet certain judicial standards. For example, cases must present real controversies, they must be brought by parties who have suffered injury, the issue must be one where a decision can make a difference, and the case must be timely. "Concrete controversy," "standing to sue," "ripeness"—these labels designate the judicial standards of procedural and technical rules and requirements a case must satisfy before the Court will hear it.

Finally, the Supreme Court does not act alone in the American judicial process. It must deal with lower federal courts (district courts, courts of appeals, special courts) set up by Congress, state courts, and the other branches of government. It must also be able to persuade public opinion. Presidential support for decisions of the Court is particularly crucial if it is under attack from Congress or vice versa. The Court's control over federal courts is generally greater than over state courts. Support from the public is always tentative. The power of the Court at any moment is thus dependent on a number of factors at work in the system.

Studying the Judicial Process: Methods and Approaches

It can be helpful at the outset to adopt a schematic framework within which the total decision-making process of the Supreme Court can be viewed and analyzed. The method known as systems theory is well suited to this task. First used and applied to the political system in general by David Easton in his landmark studies,[1] systems theory has a number of characteristics that recommend it as a framework or blueprint appropriate for understanding judicial decision making and its role in maintaining an open and democratic political system. Systems theory postulates a model in which data can be organized and analyzed and in which the actors involved in decision making can be identified and their power disclosed. In its simplified form the model identifies five stages in any decision-making process: (1) inputs into the system, (2) conversion (interaction) within the system, (3) outputs (decisions) of the system, (4) impact, and (5) feedback into the system.

Systems Theory and the Judicial Process: Inputs

The input stage in the judicial process develops as members of American society experience "needs, expectations, wants, desires and conflicts."[2] These factors naturally lead to controversies that trigger the judicial system's process of decision making. Demands for judicial action enter the system under a set of constraints that weeds out many of them and structures those that remain. As already noted, procedural and technical rules[3] and requirements can make it difficult for a case to reach the Court. In addition, the Court has developed its own set of prudential[4] self-denying ordinances designed to erect barriers between itself and excessive demands. If, however, a demand can pass all of the procedural, technical, and prudential barriers, the Court will probably allow it to enter the system for judicial consideration and resolution.

Not only the demands themselves but also the persons making

those demands are critical inputs in the decision-making process. The actual parties to a case can have a great deal to do with its ultimate outcome. For instance, a respected interest group with a responsible leadership can be an effective litigant in court against a state having a history of discrimination against the group. The National Association for the Advancement of Colored People (NAACP) has won special respect from courts, as has the American Civil Liberties Union (ACLU). Some courts will be more inclined to listen favorably to "underdog" litigants than to powerful corporations.

The Supreme Court is also affected at the input stage by the representatives of the party in court and their actions. The briefs filed by the attorneys are of singular importance. Attorneys are vested with the responsibility for building a complete record of information relevant to the facts of the case, including signed statements, publications, depositions of witnesses, and irregular and improper procedure at lower court levels. The ability of attorneys, their reputations, and their behavior during oral argument are all factors that can influence decision making by the Justices.

The status of the lower court is also an important input. By developing an impressive record of judicial scholarship and expertise, some courts have been able to enhance their prestige and to command respect from the Supreme Court. This affects the Court's initial approach to the case.

The total environment surrounding a case is an input into the system. Group actions, newspaper accounts and other media coverage, leadership response—all of these factors and many more become part of the input demands made upon the judicial system. As these demands converge into the case presentation before the Supreme Court, it will absorb some, abort others, and move into the second stage.

Systems Theory and the Judicial Process: Conversion and Outputs

The conversion, or interaction, stage is the heart of the decision-making process, during which the inputs or demands on the Court are converted ultimately into a case decision. The conversion stage centers around the conference, at which cases are discussed and debated. Here judicial behavior as well as Supreme Court internal traditions and norms assume critical importance. These include the formal decision-making rules and the informal

College Department
ST. MARTIN'S PRESS
175 Fifth Avenue
New York, N.Y. 10010

PACKING SLIP

Desk Or Examination Copies for

PROFESSOR BYRON E SHAFER
FLORIDA STATE UNIVERSITY

642305 1 240
25340 052285

QTY.	NUMBER AND TITLE
01	12337X CASES LOST — CAUSES WON — PAPER

Your comments on our books help us estimate printing requirements, assist us in preparing revisions, and guide us in shaping future books to your needs. Will you please take a moment to fill out and return this postpaid card?

☐ you may quote me for advertising purposes

☐ will adopt   ☐ have adopted   ☐ am seriously considering it

Course title _____ Enrollment_____

Comments
_____
_____
_____
_____
_____
_____
_____
_____
_____
_____
_____

Fold, tape, and mail

BUSINESS REPLY MAIL
First Class   Permit No. 1147   New York, N.Y.

Postage will be paid by

College Department
ST. MARTIN'S PRESS, INC.
175 FIFTH AVENUE
NEW YORK, N.Y. 10010

group norms concerning "leadership, group consensus, opinion assignment and strategies, role perceptions and strategies of dissenting behavior."[5] Persuasion is the primary tactic used during the conversion stage. Justices seek to influence their brethren, and this interaction is vital to the decision-making process.

The output stage is the result of the intermeshing of input factors and conversion interaction. For the Supreme Court it will take the form of a case decision and "any separate concurrences or dissents which accompany it."[6] The decision is the answer to the demands (inputs) and is the means by which the judicial branch seeks to settle conflicts.

Judicial decisions as outputs legitimize one side or the other, and the members of the Court write their opinions to justify the decision using legal forms, rules, precedents, and traditions. Since the written opinion must stand before the bar of history, Justices seek to ground their decisions in acceptable judicial arguments, legal formulas, and historical examples. Although today Justices may also use sociological data and economic statistics, they do not lose sight of the fact that they are expected to write opinions grounded in clear statements of the law.

The written opinion is thus primarily the justification for the position taken by the Justices at some time between the input stage and the conclusion of the conversion stage. This position emerges when a judicial attitude is triggered and an opinion formed on the basis of the intermeshing of the many input variables and the judicial interactions during conference. Because of the secrecy that surrounds the conference, most studies have been limited to analyses of judicial attitudes and past voting records in their discussion of the conversion stage. However, when other data are available concerning the conference, it is then possible to expand the discussion of judicial attitudes and include the broader context of the decisional output stage.

Systems Theory and the Judicial Process: Impact

Since Supreme Court decisions do not necessarily settle an issue, analysis of judicial decision making does not end there. Behavioral compliance may or may not result from the court order. Private citizens and even public officials may resort to avoidance, evasion, and delay[7] as tactics for resisting the Court's ruling. Thus it is necessary to study the impact of the decision on society. That impact may be quite different from what the Court intended. Since it has limited enforcement power, it relies largely on support from the President, lower courts (federal and state), and public opinion. Some of the Court's outputs are faithfully enforced; others are openly denounced and evaded.

A number of factors account for compliance or noncompliance with Court decisions. Compliance is more likely when the decision is narrow and confined only to the facts in the case than when it is broad. "Decisions also have a cumulative impact."[8] A series of similar cases decided similarly generates greater impact and greater compliance. The degree of unanimity among the Justices is also important with respect to the decision's impact. Generally, a nine-to-zero opinion with no separate concurrences produces a more positive impact leading to greater compliance than a split opinion.[9]

In addition, unambiguous expression increases an opinion's impact. If the opinion's diction is nontechnical, its meaning is harder to distort. However, despite the Justices' intentions a decision can be changed by those charged with communicating it to the public. Lawyers, politicians, the communications media, and scholars can affect the impact of the Court's decision by their analyses.[10]

The general climate of public opinion as well as the reaction of elites and opinion leaders are significant factors in assessing impact. If the public is divided, if opinion leaders respond negatively, if Presidents, congressional representatives, and respected politicians are critical, then the positive impact of the decision and compliance with it are undercut.[11] Court decisions affecting only a limited geographical area and generating an attitude of non-compliance there will need support from other geographical areas in order to pressure compliance from the affected group.[12]

System Response: Feedback

Outputs and their impacts may in turn generate feedback into the judicial process.[13] Feedback here is the "communication from the environment"[14] back to the Justices. Feedback assumes many forms. It can precipitate attacks by Congress, the President, or the general public upon the Court, including threats of impeachment. Irate congressional representatives might introduce legislation to curb the appellate jurisdiction of the Court. Constitutional amendments might be advocated as a means of overturning a decision. Presidential appointments—when they can be made—could be used to change the direction of the Court.

Foremost among feedback devices is additional litigation. In-

corporating professional comment and criticism, the views of prestigious law reviews, the reactions of the communications media,
and sentiments within the political, economic, social, religious,
and educational sections of society, new litigation can be initi-
ated and feedback can thus generate a new input or demand that
will seek a modification of the original decision.

Systems theory thus provides for a study of the judicial process
at five levels: (1) "descriptions and analysis of conditions which
precipitated judicial participation" in a particular case (inputs);
(2) description and analysis of the factors that helped to account
ultimately for the judicial decision (conversion); (3) determination of the "scope and nature of policy decisions which issue from
the judicial process" (outputs); (4) description and analysis of the
"impact of these policies on the resolution of public problems"
(impact); (5) description of the effect of any set of decisions on the
"maintenance of the judiciary as an appropriate and effective
participant in subsequent decisions" (feedback).[15]

Case Studies of the Judicial Process at Work:
Input, Conversion, Output, Impact, and Feedback

Using this model and four landmark Supreme Court decisions, it
is possible to secure a unique perspective on the judicial process
at work. Beginning with the World War I period and *Frohwerk* v.
United States, 249 U.S. 204 (1919), a focus on input variables indicates the critical role of the attorney in the decision-making process. The significance of the conference in the conversion stage is
documented through an in-depth analysis of the first flag-salute
case: *Minersville* v. *Gobitis*, 310 U.S. 586 (1940). Decisional output
and its relationship to judicial attitudes is evaluated in the controversial decision of *Walker* v. *City of Birmingham*, 388 U.S. 307
(1967). The problem of securing compliance during the impact
stage emerges in the study of *White* v. *State of Texas*, 310 U.S. 530
(1940). Finally, the feedback generated by each of these four cases
indicates that continuing Court litigation can turn causes apparently lost in the earlier cases into causes won.

OUTLINE OF THE JUDICIAL PROCESS ACCORDING TO SYSTEMS THEORY.

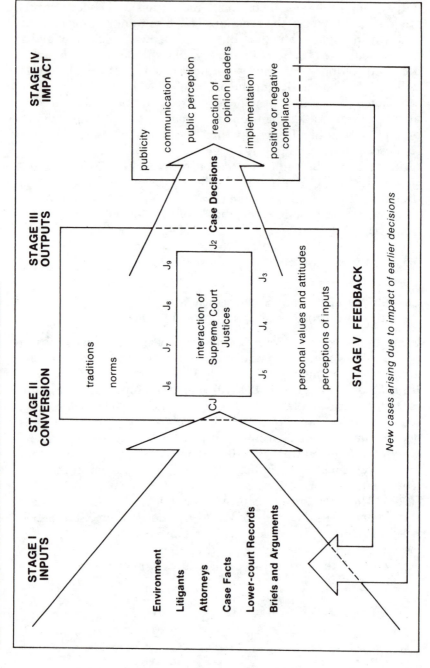

NOTES

1. David Easton, *The Political System* (New York: Knopf, 1964); *A Framework for Political Analysis* (Englewood Cliffs, N.J.: Prentice-Hall, 1965); *A System Analysis of Political Life* (New York: Wiley, 1965).

2. Walter F. Murphy, *Elements of Judicial Strategy* (Chicago: University of Chicago Press, 1964), pp. 37–90.

3. Procedural and technical rules include Article III barriers to court review—the case or controversy requirement—as well as standing to sue, ripeness, and mootness barriers. Cases must overcome these barriers to gain access to the Court.

4. Prudential rules include avoidance of political questions, refusal to make constitutional rulings if statutory ones can settle the issue, and the dispositive adequate-state-grounds doctrine.

5. Joel B. Grossman and Joseph Tanenhaus, eds., *Frontiers of Judicial Research* (New York: Wiley, 1969), p. 418.

6. *Ibid.*, p. 420.

7. Theodore L. Becker and Malcolm M. Feeley, eds., *The Impact of Supreme Court Decisions*, 2nd ed. (New York: Oxford University Press, 1973), p. 100.

8. *Ibid.*, p. 216. See "hypothesis" number 13.

9. Charles H. Sheldon, *The American Judicial Process: Models and Approaches* (New York: Dodd, Mead, 1974), p. 130.

10. Stephen L. Wasby, *The Impact of the United States Supreme Court* (Homewood, Ill.: Dorsey, 1970), pp. 246–68.

11. Charles H. Sheldon, *The American Judicial Process*, p. 133.

12. *Ibid.*

13. Walter F. Murphy, *Elements of Judicial Strategy*, p. 35.

14. Charles H. Sheldon, *The American Judicial Process*, p. 194.

15. Grossman and Tanenhaus, eds., *Frontiers of Judicial Research*, pp. 408–9.

CHAPTER 1

AN INCORRECT INPUT

———

THE SELF-AGGRANDIZING ATTORNEY

The choice of an attorney is one of the few variables in a case over which a defendant has influence, though the choice is subject to the availability of legal talent. The input that the attorney has into the judicial process of decision making has several aspects. An attorney advises his or her clients on how to plead to the charges, questions jurors, cross-examines witnesses, makes motions and objections, argues the case, and files appeals if he or she loses in the first round.[1]

The Role and Power of the Attorney:
Criteria for a Successful Advocate

The importance of the attorney at all stages of the litigation process from the initiation to the final appeal must not be underestimated. Since courts must make their decisions on the basis of materials filed by the attorney in the case, these materials are critical. In fact, the positions taken by the attorney can substantially constrain the decision a judge reaches. Thus the attorney's actions can increase or decrease the range of judicial choice in a case.[2] Briefs, motions, evidence, and oral arguments differ depending upon the nature of the case. However, the skill of the attorney in writing the brief and in making the proper objections and motions at the proper time affects whether the case will be won or lost.

This is especially true of decision making by the Supreme Court. As an appellate court it primarily makes decisions on the basis of the record that the attorney has built in the lower courts, the submitted brief, and the responses given in oral argument. Attorneys confess to apprehension as they prepare for oral argument. They have already had to overcome a number of barriers as the case moved through the lower courts, state or federal. Moreover, they have had to convince the Court to agree to hear the appeal, and this is never an easy task. In the past the Court heard some cases on appeal as a matter of necessity, and it heard others through a procedure known as a writ of error. This method asserted that mistakes had been made in a lower court and sought Court review to correct them. Since 1925 the majority of all cases have come to the Court by the writ of *certiorari*, which replaced earlier methods and allowed the Court greater leeway in deciding which cases to hear. Whatever the method, however, the ability of the attorney to convince the Court of the need to review the case has been critical in the working of the judicial process.[3]

The Influence of Attorneys on Supreme Court Justices

Notable attorneys established reputations as skilled practitioners before the Court in its early days. Generally, these were men who had great oratorical skills. Some were politicians. All were colorful and prominent, and they were allowed almost unlimited time to present their cases. An announcement that Daniel Webster or William Wirt or Henry Clay would be arguing before the Court would bring forth a large audience, including fashionably dressed ladies of quality. During this early period, therefore, there was practically a distinctive bar of the Court. A number of these attorneys resided in the same boarding houses as the Justices, and Justices and attorneys sometimes dined together.[4] Such attorneys were in a position to influence judicial thinking and, in turn, to be influenced themselves by the ideas of the early Justices. Chief Justice John Marshall found some of Daniel Webster's arguments to be so persuasive that he adopted Webster's own words in his opinion. Lawyers of this caliber have even set the verbal parameters for continuing constitutional debate. Carefully chosen words and phrases may be adopted by the Justices and gradually become part of the standard judicial vocabulary. A. H. Garland and J. S. Black are two examples of attorneys who had considerable interaction with and influence upon Justices. Black argued sixteen cases in a four-year period before the Court and lost only three.[5]

Although time and the increased ease of transportation put an end to this particular type of intimate relationship between attorneys and Justices, attorneys today with recurring opportunities for arguing before the Court still have advantages. Although any lawyer who satisfies the simple criteria for practicing before the Court—payment of fee, experience before a state supreme court, sponsorship by a member of the Court bar—is entitled to argue a case, he may find that doing so is not wise.[6] Attorneys who have experience in dealing with the Justices are less likely to be flustered by the constant questions with which the members of the Court interrupt oral argument.[7] Moreover, attorneys who are recognized by the Justices as being renowned advocates or specialists in some particular area of the law will have their prestige to lend to the case. They are therefore in a position to command greater attention. Attorney Abe Fortas was such an expert. He was appointed by the Court to argue the landmark case of *Gideon v. Wainwright*, 372 U.S. 335 (1963), which dealt with the right to have an attorney in state trials of a non-capital nature. The Justices wanted to hear the best legal arguments to assist them in decision making, and Fortas had a high reputation as a civil-liberties advocate.[8]

The Solicitor General of the United States has a greater opportunity than other attorneys to increase his skills as an advocate before the Supreme Court. As counsel for the government, the Solicitor General appears frequently before the Justices. He learns to anticipate their questions and has a greater opportunity to observe particular judicial attitudes and leanings. He also has a better understanding of which issues he should highlight in his brief to appeal to as many of the different judicial views on the Court as possible.[9] The "leading Supreme Court attorney of all time" was John W. Davis, who appeared before the Court 140 times—67 times as Solicitor General and 73 times as a private attorney. Davis's reputation made him a formidable opponent. He was asked several times to accept nomination to the Supreme Court and was a skillful politician, running as the Democratic presidential candidate in 1924. While Solicitor General he was considered unbeatable by many opposing lawyers. His knowledge concerning the attitudes and values of the Justices and their respect for his ability combined to place him in a unique position during argumentation.[10]

The job of any attorney—private or public—is to attempt to win a favorable decision for his client. Attorneys are expected to handle their cases so as to compile a complete record, with every possible argument advanced from the beginning and preserved throughout the various stages the case traverses on its way to the Supreme Court. Since the Supreme Court is primarily an appellate court, it must proceed on the record of the case as it comes up from a lower court. If this record is incomplete, if somewhere along the way counsel failed to assert every possible procedural and constitutional irregularity, the position of his client will be in jeopardy. Attorneys who fail to understand their proper role and who do not observe these norms and traditions of the Court will in all likelihood lose their case.[11]

Attorney, Client, and Case: Joseph D. Shewalter and *Frohwerk* v. *United States*

It would seem to be a self-evident proposition that a defendant or plaintiff would attempt to secure an attorney who met these standards. The attorney certainly should not be personally involved in the case or actually associated with the crime with which the defendant is charged. Neither should the attorney regard the defendant merely as a pawn in his own personal crusade. Yet Jacob Frohwerk chose exactly such an attorney, Joseph D. Shewalter, to represent him in a landmark case dealing with First Amendment freedoms of speech and press.

Frohwerk v. *United States*, 249 U.S. 204 (1919), arose out of the tense environment before, during, and after World War I. Wartime often creates unusual problems both on the battle front and on the home front. World War I was no exception. For the United States those problems included the venerated American policy of isolationism; the unexpected magnitude of the war; the strong pockets of pro-German sympathizers within the United States; the successful attempts of Great Britain in using propaganda to build American sympathy for the Allies; and the emergence of socialistic and communistic ideologies, which helped to topple Czarist Russia and seemed alien and menacing to American citizens.[12]

American attempts to remain neutral were compromised by a genuine identification of many citizens with the British and French cause. Throughout 1914, 1915, and 1916, the United States remained technically neutral. Nevertheless, American sentiment for aiding the Allies grew with each passing month. It became increasingly evident that American involvement could make a difference in determining the outcome.[13]

Within the United States significant settlements of German-

Americans, although loyal and patriotic Americans, retained their love for the Fatherland: its language and culture, its military prowess and glory, and its traditions and history. The fear that the United States might join the Allies to fight the Central Powers was very real for these people. Believing that the Central Powers would be victorious if the United States remained neutral, German-Americans exerted pressure wherever possible to secure this neutrality. Unlike the Allied sympathizers, who understood that positive American action would be necessary to secure a British-French victory, German-Americans believed they needed only to insure noninvolvement. They were unsuccessful.

Two major events set the stage for American preparedness and ultimate entry into the war: the passage of the Conscription Act of May 18, 1917, and the passage of the Espionage Act of June 15, 1917. These pieces of legislation had the backing of President Woodrow Wilson, who, although he had campaigned for his second term under the slogan "He kept us out of war," had become increasingly convinced that an Allied victory was necessary to preserve democracy.[14] German-Americans were incensed by both acts. Under the first they could be drafted to fight, and under the second they could be imprisoned for criticism of governmental policies and actions.[15] Moreover, they perceived in such acts a violation of their First Amendment freedoms of speech, press, and association. The right to criticize government had long been cherished by all patriotic Americans; however, wartime emergencies had often served to place limits upon such rights. This had been true during the American Civil War (1861–65); it was to be true during World War I as well as each succeeding conflict.[16]

The First-Amendment Freedoms and the First World War: The Role of the Supreme Court

However, in the United States World War I was unique in that free and open legal and judicial processes functioned during a wartime emergency to decide the extent of individual First Amendment rights as balanced against the right of government to protect its own interests. Although the First Amendment states that "Congress shall make no law . . . abridging the freedom of speech, or of the press," the exact meaning of this guarantee has been, and is still, the subject of debate. Should the amendment be read so as to bind only the national government and not the state governments? Should the phrase "no law" be taken literally? Could emergencies create situations in which individual freedoms would have to be limited for a time in order ultimately to be preserved?[17]

These were the questions that the Supreme Court would confront in a number of cases growing out of the political and legal environment of World War I. The Court would be the ultimate referee in deciding such issues as the legality of the Conscription Act [*Arver* v. *United States*, 245 U.S. 366 (1918)] and the reach of the Espionage Act. In 1919 the Court decided three cases dealing with violation of the 1917 Espionage Act: *Schenck* v. *United States*, 249 U.S. 47 (1919); *Frohwerk* v. *United States*, 249 U.S. 204 (1919); and *Debs* v. *United States*, 249 U.S. 211 (1919). In addition, amendments that enlarged the scope and reach of the Espionage Act in 1918 resulted in the landmark case of *Abrams* v. *United States*, 250 U.S. 616 (1919). By the middle of the 1920's two other significant First Amendment cases were added: *Gitlow* v. *New York*, 268 U.S. 652 (1925), and *Whitney* v. *California*, 274 U.S. 357 (1927).

The judicial struggle to find guidelines to cope with the problem of constitutionally protected expression in these World War I cases resulted in the development and articulation of a standard known as the clear-and-present-danger test. First stated by Justice Oliver Wendell Holmes in *Schenck* v. *United States*, 249 U.S. 47 (1919), the test has evoked great controversy to this day. Holmes saw it as an answer that avoided extremes. It rejected the idea that political speech could not be restricted—freedom of speech was not an absolute right. The test allowed for protection of speech so long as it did not create some catastrophic crisis endangering individuals as well as government. The precise nature of illegal speech has always been difficult to define, however. As a result, the Court has followed a traditional practice of deciding the issue on a case-by-case basis.

Moreover, in articulating the test for the first time the Court appeared to apply it without reference to case differences. *Schenck, Frohwerk*, and *Debs* were all unanimously decided in the space of two weeks, and in each case the Court's decision cited the new clear-and-present-danger test. As a result it became customary to consider these three cases as a trilogy and so closely linked as to be indistinguishable.[18] Yet the Court itself had not merged the three cases: the cases were not argued together and the Court handed down three distinct decisions rather than one. In fact, there actually were significant differences in the three cases, even though the plaintiffs in each were found guilty of creating a clear and present danger.

The Clear and Present Danger in *Frohwerk:* Attorney Shewalter?

The *Frohwerk* case in particular was different and this difference centered upon the attorney, not the appellant, in the case. Inputs into judicial decision making are many and varied; all affect the ultimate decision. The performance of the attorney in *Frohwerk* deserves particularly close analysis, especially since an attorney's performance has not previously been evaluated in terms of negative input into the Supreme Court's decision. The *Frohwerk* case itself has long occupied a significant place in the study of American constitutional law. A recent prestigious casebook carries an *almost* complete record of the opinion of Justice Holmes, who wrote for the entire Court in *Frohwerk*.[19] However, the sections omitted in the casebook are the very ones that indicate the uniqueness of this case due to the input of Frohwerk's attorney, Joseph D. Shewalter. A Civil War veteran (Confederate), a hot-tempered politician, and a self-appointed authority on constitutional law, Shewalter's greatest claim to fame came through the *Frohwerk* case.

An examination of the entire Court opinion reveals a number of remarks by Justice Holmes indicating that the Court was acutely aware of significant attorney-client-court conflicts. In fact, Justice Holmes stated that it was the existence of these problems that "caused us [the Supreme Court] to consider the case with more anxiety than if it presented only the constitutional question."

The facts in *Frohwerk* can be stated simply. Between 1914 and 1917 Jacob Frohwerk and Carl Glesser were engaged in publishing and circulating a German-American newspaper, the *Missouri Staats-Zeitung*. Gleeser was the owner, editor, and publisher; Frohwerk wrote many of the editorials although his name did not appear in print. As the clouds of World War I formed in Europe and spread to the United States, these editorials became increasingly pro-German. There was a sizable German ethnic community in Missouri, and its ties with the fatherland were very close. St. Louis and Kansas City both had several German-language newspapers with a wide circulation in Missouri, Kansas, and Illinois. The pro-German attitude of these newspapers, particularly of the *Missouri Staats-Zeitung*, quickly brought them into conflict with the United States government after the passage of the Espionage Act of 1917.

Carl Gleeser and Jacob Frohwerk were charged with conspiracy to hinder the war effort through the publication and circulation of twelve specific articles in the *Staats-Zeitung*. Gleeser pleaded guilty and was fined and imprisoned. Frohwerk, however, decided to fight. The attorney he chose to represent him was Joseph D. Shewalter.

Wrong Case, Wrong Attorney

There are at least five excellent reasons why Shewalter should not have had charge of this case. First, he was personally involved in the case. He had written numerous articles for the *Missouri Staats-Zeitung*, and two of his articles were listed as bases (or counts) in the indictments of Jacob Frohwerk.[20] Second, Shewalter looked upon the case simply as a vehicle for advancing, circulating, and publicizing his own political views.[21] His client's best interests were subordinated to this overriding goal. Third, Shewalter's personality and tactics antagonized both the district-court judge and the United States District Attorney to the point that Shewalter was unable to build the kind of record that would have allowed the Supreme Court to consider the case from all angles.[22] Fourth, Shewalter regarded the case briefs as his personal property and, intending them for future publication, was incensed when his client expressed a desire to employ another attorney to argue the case before the Supreme Court. Indeed, Shewalter's outrage led him to institute a suit against his own client and the new attorney. He demanded and secured a court-ordered injunction that stated that the briefs were the property of the author (Shewalter) and prohibited their use in any form by Frohwerk or his new attorney. This strange behavior certainly disrupted the legal processes, since it occurred less than one month preceding oral argument before the Supreme Court.[23] Finally, Shewalter's lengthy brief, which he insisted on filing with the Supreme Court, was an incredible manuscript filled with emotional, acrimonious, and personal attacks on the President, the Congress, and the Justices themselves. It was not an appropriate legal document.

The behavior of this attorney turned *Frohwerk* v. *United States* into a horror story of "Joseph D. Shewalter: Self-Aggrandizing Attorney." Thus *Frohwerk* becomes the case *par excellence* for studying the disruptive effect that an attorney can have on the smooth working of the judicial process, the negative input that such an attorney can create, and ultimately the adverse impact he or she can have on judicial decision making.

Attorney Shewalter: A Proper Subject for Prosecution under the Espionage Act?

The personal involvement of Shewalter with the *Missouri Staats-Zeitung* and with Frohwerk is clearly documented as early as Feburary 16, 1917, when the front page of the newspaper was given over to an article by Shewalter.[24] He was introduced to the readers of the paper as a "legal authority" and a "true American, dating his ancestry to revolutionary times."[25] His connection with the paper occurred because he held many of the beliefs of the German-American community and in particular those of the editorial staff of the *Staats-Zeitung*. While German nationalism and patriotism motivated the stand of the paper, Shewalter was moved not by love of Germany but by hatred of England. Shewalter's emotion toward England went beyond ordinary hatred,[26] and he turned all of his talents into a personal crusade to oppose any action that could conceivably help his foe. Shewalter also bitterly detested a strong national government and extolled the virtues of state government. He was an unreconstructed Southerner who had fought for states' rights and had never abandoned his belief in this theory of government.[27] Thus, moved by love and hate combined, Shewalter joined forces with the *Missouri Staats-Zeitung*. The paper was overjoyed to have his assistance. First, Shewalter had the advantage of not being a German, which gave his anti-interventionist views, shared by the paper, greater creditability.[28] Moreover, he was able to give a legal aura to the anti-British position of the paper. Shewalter could advance arguments based on history and filled with legal precedents. His brief tenure as a special circuit judge and a probate judge in Lafayette County, Missouri, allowed him to use the title "Judge" to add respectability to his arguments.[29] The *Staats-Zeitung* was more than happy to use such a man in its effort to prevent the United States from going to war with Germany. Shewalter in turn was delighted to find a public forum in which he could air his grievances, publish his political views, and gain personal attention.

Over eight months Shewalter contributed eight articles.[30] They were printed in English on the front page and in German on page two. His articles were always prominently highlighted. They were usually printed in the middle of the page, set aside by wide, black margins, with titles in heavy, black capital letters. The author's name and title (Judge Joseph D. Shewalter) were centered directly below the title of the article.

The article titles indicated clearly the philosophy that Shewalter and the *Staats-Zeitung* advanced. A content analysis of the articles reveals to the reader the legal and historical approaches used by Shewalter to give credibility to his views. His first article was entitled "On International Law and Submarine Blockade," and he declared in it that the "American public had been deceived by the Administration upon practically all the questions of International Law."[31] The newspaper welcomed such an approach, and it extolled "Judge" Shewalter and urged its readers to send ten cents for a complete copy of the judge's pamphlet. Thus Shewalter gained publicity and praise from the German-Americans who subscribed to the paper, while at the same time the paper got a new argument to assure its readers that one could be a patriotic American while maintaining sympathy for the German cause.

During February and March of 1917 the *Staats-Zeitung* stepped up efforts to keep the United States from joining the Allies. In an article of March 9, 1917, entitled "The Law Against Mr. Wilson," Shewalter used his own interpretation of international law to support the German declaration of a blockade and his interpretation of constitutional law to protest any act that President Wilson might take to involve the country in war.

However, on April 6, 1917, the United States did declare war on Germany. Shewalter, nevertheless, continued to insist that such a war was unconstitutional, and the *Staats-Zeitung* of April 20, 1917, offered its readers an opportunity to order the judge's pamphlet "War with Germany: Concerning the Rights of Belligerents and the Rights of Neutrals." Once war was actually declared, however, arguments that the United States should not become involved became superfluous. Instead, new problems arose from the passage of the Conscription Act and the Espionage Act. Actually the two issues were related, and for the *Staats-Zeitung* and its publishers the problem could be stated in the following question: Did the newspaper have the constitutional right to urge young men to refuse to comply with the conscription law? Shewalter insisted that the paper was protected under the First Amendment and that the Conscription Act was invalid and unconstitutional.[32]

During May 1917 the *Staats-Zeitung* gave prominent coverage to Shewalter's actions to have the judicial system declare the law unconstitutional. Shewalter had agreed to represent one Thomas Sullivan, who had been imprisoned for resisting the draft. The case began as a *habeas corpus* proceeding; Shewalter hoped to turn it into a test case in which the Supreme Court not only would declare the new army bill unconstitutional but also would reprimand the

President. The *Staats-Zeitung* appealed to its readers to contribute money to help the judge in his fight to "save our sons, prevent militarism, and preserve the Constitution." This appeal appeared in the paper of May 18, the very day the Conscription Act became law. Throughout June 1917 the newspaper assured its readers that Judge Shewalter was vigorously fighting the constitutional battle against the draft. Shewalter himself boasted that the careless wording of the bill would be sufficient to have it overturned by the Court.[33] The paper also gave tremendous publicity to a brief that Shewalter had sent to Governor Gardner of Missouri and that had been forwarded to Washington.[34] The paper asserted that the judge's brief had forced President Wilson to confer with his military lawyers, and as a result the President was "not sure of his ground on the Draft Bill."[35]

On June 15, the day the Espionage Act was passed, Shewalter appealed through the *Staats-Zeitung* for money to help him carry forward his case to have the draft law declared unconstitutional. Shewalter worded his appeal as an "Open letter to Patriots and not English Tories." Readers of the *Staats-Zeitung* were thus assured by this "most American and patriotic" of judges that *they* were true patriots and that by opposing the draft they were actually helping to save the Republic. Even the passage of the Espionage Act failed to deter Shewalter and the *Staats-Zeitung*, and the paper of June 29 carried Shewalter's "Open Letter to President Wilson," which was a vicious, personal attack on the President and his genealogy. According to Shewalter, Wilson's grandfather had refused to serve in the War of 1812 and instead had published an antiwar newspaper. Using Wilson's books and other writings as evidence, Shewalter asserted that Wilson, like his grandfather, was really an English Tory and *not* an American patriot. Thus the President was portrayed as a criminal and those who resisted "Mr. Wilson's War" were patriots.

Apparently the *Staats-Zeitung* believed that it could continue to print material of this nature, and Shewalter believed he could continue to write such articles and make public speeches against the war and conscription. He used an Independence Day invitation to address the German-American Alliance of Kansas City, Kansas, as another occasion to attack England in an oration titled "England's Farsighted Attempt to Rule America Exposed (From a Legal Standpoint)." The *Staats-Zeitung* faithfully reported this event and then praised his wisdom by voicing the wish that "Judge Shewalter were in the Senate or President." He was, in the words of a reader, "one brave judge," the kind of man in whose hands the country would be safe.[36]

The love affair between attorney and newspaper reached its highest point during August and September of 1917. The paper publicized Shewalter's legal and historical arguments against conscription, reported the admiration given his briefs by attorneys throughout the United States, and urged readers to send five dollars to secure copies of the judge's briefs and manuscripts. In return, Shewalter decided to support wholeheartedly the editorial policies of the *Staats-Zeitung*, even its anti-Prohibition position. Desiring to be in step with his new friends and also to continue the emphasis on his anti-English and pro-states'-rights goals, Shewalter came up with the ingenious argument that a Prohibition amendment would centralize power in Washington and create a Wilsonian monarchy, destroying the Tenth Amendment and states' rights.[37]

However, the relationship between attorney and newspaper would soon enter a new phase. In December 1917 the Supreme Court heard oral argument in a case testing the constitutionality of the Conscription Act. On January 7, 1918, the Court's decision in this case—*Arver* v. *United States*, 245 U.S. 366 (1918)—upheld the constitutionality of the draft.

The Case Against Jacob Frohwerk and the *Missouri Staats-Zeitung*

By April 1918 the *Missouri Staats-Zeitung* found itself in court under indictment based on the Espionage Act. A thirteen-count indictment was brought against the two men in charge of the paper—Gleeser and Frohwerk—for the content of its editorials. Frohwerk protested that his editorials were subject to change by Gleeser and that he himself had no power to put anything in the paper or keep it out. Since the editorials were never signed, it was difficult to pinpoint authorship. Thus all of the editorials were held to be the responsibility of *both* Gleeser and Frohwerk and both men were held accountable. They were indicted under Sections 3 and 4 of the Espionage Act; the indictment was returned by the Grand Jury in the United States District Court for the Western Division (Western District) of Missouri on April 23, 1918. Gleeser entered a plea of guilty to the charges contained in the indictment and was given a five-year prison sentence in the United States Penitentiary at Leavenworth, Kansas. He testified for the government against Frohwerk, who refused to plead guilty. Frohwerk insisted that since he was only an employee of Gleeser and received a mere salary of ten dollars per week, he should be exempt from prosecution. Moreover, he had decided to fight the charge of "conspiracy to commit espionage," and he hoped to win his case with the assistance of counsel, Shewalter.[38]

Two of the counts on which Frohwerk was indicted were based on articles that Shewalter had written—"The Truth in a Nutshell"[39] and "Come Let Us Reason Together."[40] Although Shewalter's name did not appear with the articles, it was affixed to the "Letters to the Editor" that immediately followed. Moreover, Frans Lindquist, Frohwerk's second attorney, claimed in both his brief and in oral argument before the Supreme Court that Shewalter had written both articles. Shewalter did not deny this.

A logical question to raise at this point might be, "Why wasn't Shewalter indicted also?" The basic reason was that the government was concerned with putting the *newspaper* out of business, and Gleeser and Frohwerk were in charge of the paper. The Espionage Act had specified three offenses: (1) "to make or convey false reports . . . with intent to interfere with the . . . military forces of the United States or to promote the success of its enemies," (2) "to cause or attempt to cause . . . refusal of duty in the military," and (3) "to . . . obstruct the recruiting or enlistment service." The penalty for these offenses was a "fine of not more than $10,000 or imprisonment for not more than twenty years, or both."[41]

Shewalter had contended from the beginning that American entry into World War I was unconstitutional, that the Conscription or Selective Service Act was illegal, and that the Espionage Act would be quickly struck down by the Supreme Court once it was presented to them in a case.[42] He had stated these opinions repeatedly, and Frohwerk believed him.

Shewalter was a respected lawyer and politician. He had practiced law in Lexington, Independence, and Kansas City, Missouri. He had served as a probate judge and a special circuit judge in Lafayette County, Missouri. Always a strong party man, he had served on state and national committees of the Democratic Party. In 1910 he had conducted a colorful but unsuccessful campaign to secure the Democratic Party's nomination for United States Senator from Missouri. The campaign showed something about Shewalter's personality. He insisted on traveling around the state mounted on a huge black horse. Dressed in the appropriate attire of a Southern gentleman, he was a commanding figure. However, his campaign was out-of-date in 1910, as was his political rhetoric.

Nevertheless, Shewalter was still respected as a leading civil and criminal lawyer in Missouri. Local newspaper editors described him as a fine trial lawyer, an expert on issues of constitutional law, and a legal and political speaker of great force.[43] Apparently, Jacob Frohwerk believed that he would be well represented by such counsel. However, an old axiom says, "The lawyer who represents himself has a fool for a client." In one respect this was the situation in the *Frohwerk* case. Shewalter was so closely entangled with the *Staats-Zeitung* and in such complete agreement with the attitudes and beliefs expressed in the paper that in representing Frohwerk he was really representing and defending himself.

The Legal Philosophy of Shewalter: His Attitude Toward the *Frohwerk* Case

Shewalter's determination to use the *Frohwerk* case to advance, circulate, and publicize his own legal and political views was another important hindrance to Frohwerk's defense. Shewalter had failed to get *his* case on conscription, the Sullivan *habeas corpus* case, before the Court, which had heard arguments on that issue in *Arver* v. *United States*, 245 U.S. 366, on December 13 and 14, 1917, and had decided on January 7, 1918. At stake was the constitutionality of the Conscription Act. Joseph Arver and five other young men had refused to register for the military draft. They had been prosecuted under the statute and convicted in district court and had appealed under a writ of error. They argued that the Constitution did not give Congress power to compel military service by a selective draft. The government was represented by Solicitor General John W. Davis. The Supreme Court at that time was presided over by Chief Justice Edward White and included Justices Brandeis, Clarke, Day, Holmes, McKenna, McReynolds, Pitney, and Van Devanter. The Court sustained the constitutionality of the law, citing congressional powers under Article I§8 and Article VI. The unanimous opinion incorporated almost *in toto* the statistics and authorities cited in Davis's brief. Thus *Frohwerk* became increasingly important for Shewalter. He hoped that he could use it to persuade the Supreme Court to reverse their *Arver* decision and declare the Espionage Act and the Conscription Act unconstitutional.

Moreover, in his seventy-two years Shewalter had never before had an opportunity to argue before the Supreme Court. Since the Court hears landmark cases, lawyers generally consider it an honor if it agrees to hear their case. Joseph Shewalter believed that *Frohwerk* would be the high point of his career. He saw his appearance not only as a personal triumph but also as a political triumph for the doctrines of individual and states' rights. Convinced that President Wilson was a megalomaniac and that Congress had abandoned its legislative duties, Shewalter saw the Court as the last bulwark against unconstitutional encroachments upon civil liberties. He perceived himself as a prophet sent to explain the law to the Court.

Naturally, Shewalter was somewhat concerned with saving his client from a possible twenty-year jail sentence and a $10,000 fine. It was, however, a question of priorities. Should he give first priority to getting Jacob Frohwerk acquitted or to arguing the constitutional issue? In a case of much later date, *Gideon* v. *Wainwright*, 372 U.S. 335 (1963), Attorney Abe Fortas debated with himself the question of his primary duty. Should his goal be simply to get Gideon off, or should he concentrate on proving that the Sixth Amendment's guarantee of counsel extended to all state trials? Since Fortas had been appointed by the Supreme Court to argue the case, and since Gideon had no special circumstances that Fortas could use, Fortas concentrated on the overriding constitutional issue. He was successful on both scores.

In the *Frohwerk* case Shewalter apparently believed that by giving priority to the constitutional issues he could secure the acquittal of his client. Moreover, he assumed that Frohwerk understood the necessity of placing issues ahead of personal welfare and that he was willing to have his attorney proceed in this way.

Shewalter's View of National Power

Shewalter wanted to present many legal and political ideas to the Court. First, he wanted to argue that First Amendment freedoms were absolute. He believed that the national government could not legislate in this area because doing so would violate the police powers of the state under the Tenth Amendment. Moreover, in Shewalter's view there were no national police powers.[44] This was not the accepted legal or judicial position, however. The belief that freedom of speech and freedom of the press were absolute— that any legislation touching on them was unconstitutional—had never been accepted by a majority of the Supreme Court. Instead, the Court generally balanced competing interests. Moreover, it implicitly recognized from earliest times that the national government had to be allowed to claim and exercise certain national police powers even though they might touch upon or effect the valid, recognized, and traditional state police powers in the areas of health, education, welfare, safety, and morals. The Court concluded that the national government could not *ipso facto* be excluded from legislation and rule making in these areas.

Shewalter's second major objective was to secure a strongly worded Court opinion limiting the so-called war powers of the President. Early American Presidents such as Washington, Adams, Jefferson, and Madison had carefully respected Congress's authority to initiate war. However, even then, Presidents could and did commit military forces to combat acts of piracy and terrorism; in many instances congressional authorization was wanting. During the Civil War President Lincoln created his own doctrine of presidential war powers by combining his power of commander-in-chief (Article II§2), his constitutional duty to "faithfully execute" the laws (Article II§1), and the Presidential oath of office. However, Lincoln was always careful to secure appropriate congressional legislation to approve his conduct, and the Supreme Court accepted this ex-post-facto action. Some Presidents, notably Polk, Grant, and McKinley, interpreted their war powers broadly; others, such as Buchanan and Cleveland, were scrupulously deferential to the war powers of Congress. The use of the armed forces against sovereign nations without authorization by Congress became common practice in the 20th Century. Presidents Theodore Roosevelt and William Howard Taft both sent armed forces into combat in Latin America without congressional authorization.[45]

A third goal that Shewalter hoped to achieve through the *Frohwerk* case was a court decision stating that the "necessary and proper" clause of the Constitution did not expand national power. The debate over the "necessary and proper," or elastic, clause (Article I§8c.18) had never been settled. In general the argument had involved two extreme positions. One had insisted that the clause not only failed to add power to Congress but also actually limited congressional power by requiring that laws be essential to the implementation of an enumerated power in the Constitution. The other view had held that the clause should be construed as a positive grant of power to Congress and the word "necessary" interpreted as "helpful." Shewalter held the first view and was determined to win the Court's support for it.[46]

A fourth objective was to use the Thirteenth Amendment, which prohibited involuntary servitude, to secure Court endorsement for the compact theory of American government—the basis of states' rights.[47] Shewalter argued that the "involuntary servitude" phrase of the Thirteenth Amendment had been violated by the passage of the Conscription Act: a draft created a type of slavery. This argument has continued to resurface from time to time since the passage of the Thirteenth Amendment in 1865. For Joseph Shewalter it would have been a sweet victory if the very amendment that had deprived his beloved Southland of its property in slaves served ultimately to limit federal governmental powers.

Finally, Shewalter wanted the Supreme Court to state categorically that the powers of all branches of national government, itself included, were limited to express powers granted in the Constitution, and that one branch could not venture into the area belonging to another. This statement would secure strict separation of powers.[48] The immediate purpose was to place limits on President Wilson. Shewalter's brief in *Frohwerk* indicated his vicious attitude toward Wilson. He first attacked Wilson's prestige as a scholar:

> Professor Wilson wrote two large volumes of about 400 pages each. 'Constitutional Government' and 'Congressional Government.' He quotes in neither a clause of the Constitution; no American records; no proceedings of the Constitutional Convention; the opinion of none of the statesmen of the Revolutionary period as to the character of our Government. The only author he quotes is Mr. Baghote [sic], a silly English story writer upon the English Constitution.[49]

In other paragraphs Shewalter warned the Court of the growth of presidential power under Wilson. After pointing out that "the President has ordered the clocks to be turned up one hour and thus changed the meridian," Shewalter concluded:

> Now let it be asked what single measure is lacking in order that the President may become an absolute ruler? Name one other power necessary to be given the President to enable him effectually to destroy the Constitution and enslave the people. All these powers now reside with the President. A few years ago, there was no humbler citizen than Mr. Wilson—*too poor to buy a piano* says a member of his family. Today he has more power than any ruler living in the world, or that ever lived.[50]

Shewalter's Ego: A Major Problem for Frohwerk

Shewalter's objectives thus placed his own constitutional theories and his personal desire for glory above the direct and clear needs of Frohwerk. As a result Shewalter's brief was filled with material that he hoped would overwhelm the Court and demonstrate his own legal acumen. To demonstrate his talents as a historian he included a "short" discourse on the history of conscription from the Roman Empire to the American Civil War. He sought to show his mastery of literature by quoting from Milton, Sheridan, and Erskine. He used authoritative statements of great political writers such as Jefferson, Hamilton, Madison, Tocqueville, and Hume to try to add prestige to his own political theories. Finally, he resorted to the unanswerable authority of heaven, quoting freely from the Bible. For example, in his attack on conscription he stated that "the thoughtful citizen will ask if there is any name under Heaven given among men whereby they may preserve their liberty" (Acts 4:12). The supposed defense of Frohwerk also turned into a laudatory tribute to Shewalter, who bragged of his academic achievements and expounded on his ancestors: one a "distinguished officer in the American Revolution," another a commander in the War of 1812. He related his personal and military triumphs in the Confederate Army as well as his early training at the Lafayette Military Institute in Missouri. Concluding with a grandiose waving of his LL.B. diploma from the University of Virginia School of Law,[51] Shewalter himself had become the principal character in the legal brief supposedly defending Frohwerk. Supreme Court support for his views of history, government, and political theory would bring him personal glory, free his client, and return the country to true constitutional democracy.

Given that Shewalter wanted to have his case heard by the Supreme Court, it would be logical to assume that he would lay the proper foundation for it in district court. If he had won there, the government would certainly have appealed, and the Court would have granted review, since the constitutionality of a federal statute was at stake. If Shewalter lost, however, he needed a record that would present issues to attract the attention of the Court and persuade it to hear the case. It is ironic that while the Court did agree to hear the case, it was not because Shewalter had built a solid record. In fact, it was in part the very reverse— because the record was so sparse. In particular, the case record was devoid of a bill of exceptions,[52] which is a formal statement in writing drawn up by the attorney and presented to the judge and opposing counsel.[53] It asserts that certain errors occurred in the trial, presents a list of complaints, and explains why the defendant "takes exception" to them. This then becomes an integral part of the appeal process, since it gives a clearer picture of what actually occurred during the first trial.

Shewalter did write a voluminous bill of exceptions. However, he had so alienated trial judge Frank A. Youmans and District Attorney Francis M. Wilson that they refused to accept it and it never became part of the record. Instead, Judge Youmans wrote out a different bill of exceptions. Shewalter then stated that this bill was not proper, contained none of the major points, and was not acceptable to the defendant. As a result the official record before the Supreme Court lacked a bill of exceptions and thus was scanty and incomplete.

The clash of opinions and personalities of judge and attorney in district court made compromise impossible and resulted in this incomplete record. Shewalter accused Judge Youmans of bias, of deciding the case before hearing oral argument, and of failing to follow proper legal procedure. He insisted that the judge had to rule on the constitutionality of the Espionage Act before he could empanel a jury. Youmans refused to do this and Shewalter became incensed. Moreover, Shewalter's oral argument, which raised old issues of states' rights, secession, and nullification, irritated the judge. He was, therefore, in no mood to accept Shewalter's list of exceptions.[53]

After the Supreme Court had heard the case, it refused to reverse on any procedural ground, asserting that it had "to take the case *on the record* as it is," and that the record showed "nothing . . . that makes it possible to say that the judge's discretion was wrongly exercised."[54] An incomplete record had attracted the attention of the Court and caused it to hear the case; but the record had also given them a technical argument for dismissal.

The loss of the case before Judge Youmans in district court affected the two central characters in the case differently. Shewalter increased his efforts to organize his brief and to have it printed. His goal was to overwhelm the Supreme Court with his legal ability and force it to bow to the wisdom of his interpretation of history and political philosophy. Frohwerk began to lose interest in issues and to think seriously about self-preservation. He was fifty-four years old, jobless, and apparently on his way to prison. The paper that had been his love had been sold on February 8, 1918, to Val J. Peter, who had merged it with his *Kansas City Press*.[55] The Kansas German-American Alliance, which Frohwerk had headed, was in disarray. Therefore, he revised his priorities. His new goal was that of winning his freedom and avoiding prison and fines by whatever means necessary. Friends suggested that he secure additional counsel and recommended Frans E. Lindquist of Kansas City, Missouri. Lindquist was a bright young attorney, a member of the bar of the Supreme Court who had been following the events in the *Frohwerk* case and was well informed. In fact, he had introduced himself to Shewalter and offered to help file a mandamus petition to get Judge Youmans to send up a complete bill of exceptions. Such a petition, if granted by the Supreme Court, would have resulted in the Court's sending a direct order to the judge to deliver to them all of the case-related documents, whether part of the official record or not.

Shewalter had brushed aside this offer of help and scornfully remarked that Lindquist obviously did not understand the problems involved. When Frohwerk insisted that Lindquist enter the case, Shewalter exploded, and it became clear that the case had become a personal crusade to establish his own reputation. Retaining his position as Frohwerk's attorney, however, he commenced an action for an injunction to prevent Lindquist and Frohwerk from interfering with his manuscripts, proofsheets, and briefs. Shewalter accused Frohwerk and Lindquist of entering into a secret conspiracy to get possession of his briefs. The Circuit Court of Jackson County, Missouri, responded favorably to his appeal and issued a permanent injunction on December 28, 1918, awarding Shewalter complete possession of his materials.[56] It was ironic that Frohwerk, already convicted of conspiracy under the Espionage Act, was now charged with the same offense by his own attorney. Using the title "of counsel" Shewalter filed a 334-page brief, with seven pages of explanations concerning "How Mr. Lindquist Enters Case" and a twelve-page "Supplemental and Reply Brief" in which he responded to specific questions raised by the Supreme Court Justices during oral argument.[57] Shewalter was not to be deprived by his client of his day in court: he was, in fact, so excited that he drafted and wrote out his last will and testament.[58] He stated at the beginning of the document that he was writing it "at this particular time" because he was preparing to embark on a long journey. The will was written, dated, and witnessed on January 21, 1919, only six days before the oral argument in *Frohwerk*. The intensity of Shewalter's belief that this was to be his crowning hour is demonstrated by the fact that he had never made a will prior to this time, although he was seventy-two years of age.

Thus Frohwerk had two attorneys representing him before the Supreme Court. Shewalter filed his monumental brief and prepared to argue before the Court. Lindquist also wrote and filed a brief of ninety-nine pages and journeyed to Washington for the oral argument. With the two attorneys shooting verbal arrows at each other, *Frohwerk* v. *United States* was presented to the Supreme Court on January 27, 1919.

The Supreme Court's Response: Briefs, Oral Arguments, and Court Decision in *Frohwerk*

The Court at this time was presided over by Chief Justice Edward White and included Justices Brandeis, Clarke, Day, Holmes, McKenna, McReynolds, and Van Devanter. It heard oral argument in *Debs* v. *United States* as well as *Frohwerk* on January 27, 1919. The opinions in both cases were handed down on March 10, 1919. Justice Holmes was the spokesman for the Court in these cases, as he had been in *Schenck* v. *United States*, decided the week before *Frohwerk* and *Debs*. Although Holmes's opinion in *Frohwerk* was short—only seven pages—he referred three times to Shewalter specifically. It is thus obvious that an inquiry into Shewalter's brief and argument before the Court is necessary for a better understanding of the decision.

Holmes's first reference to Shewalter was in connection with the case record. The Justice stated that the Supreme Court had heard the case because it was concerned about the absence of the bill of exceptions and was "anxious" to ascertain if the defendant had had a proper trial.[59] Although Lindquist's petition for a mandamus had not been granted by the Court, the petition had made the Court aware that Judge Youmans and Shewalter had clashed so violently that a complete record of the case had not reached the Supreme Court.[60] Holmes referred to this as a set of "unfortunate differences." Ultimately, however, the Court stated that it could not change the record and would be forced to decide the case on that record. Implicit here is a severe criticism of Shewalter's handling of the case in the district court.

Holmes's second reference to Shewalter was in connection with the articles published in the *Staats-Zeitung* for which Frohwerk was indicted and convicted. In outlining these articles, Holmes, after describing the first article, said, "Then comes a letter from one of the counsel who argued here."[61] In the district court proceedings, where Shewalter had conducted Frohwerk's case alone, nothing had been said about the attorney's own involvement in the case. Lindquist's brief before the Supreme Court, however, had emphasized this point. Lindquist had held up two articles and a letter, all written by Shewalter, and had pointed out that if the Court upheld Frohwerk's conviction, then it ought to direct some action against Shewalter. Moreover, Lindquist told the Court that Shewalter had assured Frohwerk that the articles were protected under the First Amendment and that Frohwerk (knowing Shewalter's reputation as a "learned" attorney) had believed him.[62] Lindquist's statements were not ignored by the Court, and Holmes made it clear in his opinion that the Justices had taken judicial notice of this unusual connection between client and attorney.

In the third reference to Shewalter Holmes barely concealed his annoyance with the attorney. Noting the arguments advanced in Shewalter's written brief, Justice Holmes then referred to "counsel's argument (here) . . . that the present force is a part of the regular army raised illegally . . . a matter (also) discussed at length in his voluminous brief, on the ground that before its decision to the contrary the Solicitor General misled this court as to the law."[63] Shewalter had devoted over ninety-two pages of his brief in *Frohwerk* to an attack on the Supreme Court's opinion upholding the Conscription Act in the *Arver* case. He had coupled this with a vehement attack on Solicitor General Davis, who had briefed and argued the case. The language used in these attacks was not the language of persuasion, but was characterized by venom, sarcasm, and gratuitous name calling.

The attorney had reprimanded the Court for "rushing in to decide the case" and condemned their action, which, he said, had produced "the most unfortunate consequences." He then proceeded to portray Davis as a sort of Pied Piper, with the nine Justices of the Supreme Court acting like children as they followed his piping. Shewalter was actually trying to get the Court to overturn its recent *Arver* decision. This is acceptable legal strategy for an attorney to use, assuming that he advances well-reasoned arguments delivered in an appropriate manner. For example, in *Gideon v. Wainwright* (1963) Attorney Abe Fortas asked the Court to overrule *Betts v. Brady*, 316 U.S. 455 (1942), and to establish a new doctrine concerning right to counsel. Fortas used appropriate intellectual persuasion and was successful. The Court generally prefers merely to distinguish cases. By this strategy the Court highlights differences between cases, thus allowing the old decision to stand, although narrowed to its own specific facts.[64] However, on many occasions the Court has reversed earlier opinions, even where the precedent was recent and reversal would leave the Justices open to the charge of acting like a legislature or changing their personal attitudes.

Unfortunately for his client Shewalter was not content to use logical and unemotional arguments to persuade the Court. Instead he lectured the Court on its misuses of history and legal precedent and its failure to resist the temptations of a clever Solicitor General and denounced their decision as "only an opinion." "What does it matter what members of the Supreme Court think?" wrote Shewalter. "They must first show *their* power before they can interpret." In Shewalter's view the Constitution was so clear and precise that there was very little room for interpretation. This is the mechanistic-jurisprudence approach to, or slot-machine theory of, decision making, which was given its classic formulation by Justice Roberts in *United States* v. *Butler*, 297 U.S. 1 (1936):

> When an act of Congress is appropriately challenged in the courts as not conforming to the constitutional mandate the judicial branch of the Government has only one duty—to lay the article of the Constitution which is involved beside the statute which is challenged and to decide whether the latter squares with the former.[65]

Shewalter had fully expected the Court to agree with him in the *Arver* case. He had been positive that the Court would declare conscription invalid. When the Justices failed to rise to his expectations, he ridiculed them and then set out to explain to them their error and to give them a chance to reverse *Arver* in the *Frohwerk* decision. Conscription was so clearly unconstitutional to Shewalter that he could not understand why the Justices had such difficulty in interpreting the simple language of the Constitution. Annoyed with their "stupidity," he could not refrain from a vicious attack at the very time when gentle persuasion was needed.

Shewalter's attack on Davis was equally uncalled for, in bad form, and more destructive of Shewalter himself than Davis. The Justices knew Davis personally; moreover, by 1919 Davis had already made a name for himself in the legal world. During his five years as Solicitor General, he argued sixty-seven cases orally and won forty-eight. He was praised by bench and bar alike, and members of the Supreme Court declared that he forced other lawyers to improve their arguments and that his briefs and arguments challenged the Justices themselves to a better performance. Davis ultimately would win the title "lawyer's lawyer" and become one of the wealthiest and most successful and prestigious lawyers of the Twentieth Century.[66] Shewalter's vicious, petty attack on Davis did nothing to help his client; instead, it clearly indicated to the Court that it was dealing with a pompous, peevish, smug attorney who exhibited traits of paranoia.

In his discussion of *Arver* (which Shewalter continually misspelled "*Avers*") Shewalter insisted that Davis's argument was "ingenious" and deliberately "calculated to deceive the court." He accused Davis of misunderstanding one of the cases used as precedent, *Prigg* v. *Pennsylvania*, 16 Peters 539 (1842), and stated that this case actually decided the reverse of what Davis had asserted. The *Prigg* case had involved the controversial Fugitive Slave Act of 1793. Justice Joseph Story wrote the majority opinion, holding that a Pennsylvania law interfered with the proper enforcement of the act. All the members of the Supreme Court agreed with the holding; however, Chief Justice Taney and Justices Thompson and Daniel had written separate concurring opinions sharply disagreeing with Story's assertion that federal power over the rendition of fugitive slaves was exclusive, therefore prohibiting state laws that either obstructed or aided federal enforcement. Davis cited *Prigg* during his argument in the *Arver* case as an "authority to prove that the current act [the Conscription Act] is *not* unconstitutional on the ground that state officials aid in its enforcement."[67]

Shewalter insisted that Davis had misunderstood *Prigg* either because he had "only read the headnote," which was misleading, or because he had not researched it at all and had left it to his clerk. While Shewalter referred to Davis as "distinguished," "intellectual," and "astute," he managed to give a derogatory aura to these complimentary words. This type of heavy-handed sarcasm and irony pervaded his entire brief. He concluded by calling Davis a "case lawyer" who had no knowledge of, or respect for, "history and principle" and who was thus a "great curse" on the legal profession.[68]

Given the differing opinions in *Prigg* it was possible for both Davis and Shewalter to use it as an authority; however, Shewalter's method of attack on Davis's brief lacked either a logical or a proper legal tone. He allowed a respectable argument, based on historical analysis of legal precedent, to degenerate into a personal attack accompanied by malicious name calling.

Shewalter also turned his vitriolic pen and tongue on the Court opinion that had upheld conscription. The "logic" used by the Justices was "silly," he claimed; their reasoning was "immature, sophomoric, and downright destructive." Moreover, any Court that could uphold the constitutionality of a conscription bill and of an espionage bill was obviously a "child like" Court, hood-

winked and bamboozled by a slick Solicitor General. He concluded that the Justices should remember that they were "fallible
men" and should now use the *Frohwerk* case to strike down the
espionage and conscription bills. Thus they could regain their
honor and prestige.[69]

Given this sort of language, these accusations, and this attack
on the collective intellect of the Court and a prestigious Solicitor
General, it is not surprising that Justice Holmes found it appropriate to cut Shewalter's arguments down to size. Indeed, the
restraint shown by the Court was remarkable in light of such an
attack.

Justice Holmes Answers Shewalter: A Revealing Court Opinion

Shewalter had devoted seventy-three pages of his brief to the
argument that freedom of speech and press was absolute and that
Congress could not legislate in that area in any fashion whatso-
ever. Citing Jefferson, Madison, and Hamilton as authorities,
Shewalter asserted that even in wartime Congress had no power
to pass legislation dealing with speech or press.[70] Only states
could legislate in these areas.

Justice Holmes dismissed this argument in a few lines. "With
regard to that argument," said Holmes, "we think it necessary to
add to what has been said in Schenck . . . only that the First
Amendment . . . can not have been, and obviously was not, intended to give immunity for every possible use of language. We
venture to believe that neither Hamilton nor Madison, nor any
other competent person, then or later, ever supposed that to make
criminal the counselling of a murder within the jurisdiction of
congress would be an unconstitutional interference with free
speech."[71] In this fashion Justice Holmes cut down the "absolute"
argument advanced by Shewalter in response to a question posed
by Justice Pitney during the oral argument. Apparently Shewalter realized immediately after the close of argument that he had
gone too far. In his "Supplemental and Reply Brief" filed two
days afterward he attempted to hedge his position, but it was too
little and too late.

In his original brief Shewalter had also argued the legal issues
of "intent" and "means and purpose" as a method of clearing
Frohwerk of the charge of conspiracy. He argued that the government had not proved criminal intent nor shown that the publications were false.[72] Justice Holmes, writing for the unanimous

Court, dismissed this seven-page argument in a two-page rebuttal, closing with the following statement:

> It is said that the first count is bad because it does not allege the means by which the conspiracy was to be carried out. But a conspiracy to obstruct recruiting would be criminal even if no means were agreed upon specifically by which to accomplish the intent. It is enough if the parties agreed to set to work for that common purpose. That purpose could be accomplished or aided by persuasion as well as by false statements, and there was no need to allege that false reports were intended to be made or made. It is argued that there is no sufficient allegation of intent, but intent to accomplish an object cannot be alleged more clearly than by stating that parties conspired to accomplish it.[73]

Another argument claiming that the acts for which Frohwerk had been indicted were by definition acts of treason and hence could be punished only as such or not at all was summarily dismissed by Justice Holmes with the response, "These suggestions seem to us to need no more than to be stated."[74] Finally, all of Shewalter's arguments concerning the procedural irregularities of the trial were answered by the Court thus: "There is nothing before us that makes it possible to say that the judge's discretion was wrongly exercised."[75]

Had the Court desired, it could have lectured Shewalter on his numerous improprieties, in particular his inappropriate reference to his personal life in a legal brief. For instance, the Court could easily have taken exception to the following long and elaborate peroration:

> I carry the blood of men who shed blood and wore chains on the British prison ships to establish this right [freedom of press], and I shall not remain silent, and especially at the command of men [President Wilson] who carry no revolutionary blood and who hold to no revolutionary principles.[76]

In yet another place Shewalter returned to this favorite theme, claiming:

> One of my ancestors, a distinguished officer of the Revolution, wore chains on the prison ship to establish this liberty. And God be praised, I have inherited the principles and courage to raise my voice in protest, and to say that every intelligent man, whatever his position KNOWS that no such despotic power [to pass a conscription act] was given to the general Government.[77]

In concluding his brief Shewalter could easily have antagonized even the most benevolent of Justices by his warning of the dire consequences awaiting any Justice who failed to be convinced by his logic. His own self-exaltation was demonstrated in his final paragraph:

> The writer of this Brief, though called to live an humble life has taken care of those principles, as best he could. He has done so in this Brief, when he knew it must bring down upon him the hatred of the ignorant and vicious, and when he knew that his years precluded any earthly profit to be derived. And he well knows—which will be full compensation—that he will receive a glad welcome on the other shore from Revolutionary ancestors and from all who aided in that cause.[78]

A modern Supreme Court would not likely have passed over in silence such lengthy discourses on genealogy and such self-glorification based on education and social status. Thus, it was not surprising that Justice Holmes in the majority opinion also found it necessary to point out the problems created by Frohwerk's attorney. These problems were not only personal ones that had developed due to Shewalter's behavior in court and his vicious attacks in his brief on the patriotism and legal expertise of the Justices and the Solicitor General; there was also the critical problem produced by the philosophical and legal views that Shewalter was advancing. The political theory of an extremely limited national government, limited in this case by First Amendment claims of individual rights of speech and press and advanced by a zealous states'-rights advocate like Shewalter, was quite sufficient to cause the Court to perceive that a clear and present danger most certainly existed. Holmes's own background would have made him peculiarly aware of the real danger that lurked behind the civil-liberties claims put forward by Shewalter. Holmes had been raised in a patriotic Yankee family. A poem of his father's had helped to save the *U.S.S. Constitution*. Holmes, like Shewalter, was a Civil War veteran—a Union volunteer from Massachusetts—and had once been left for dead on the battlefield. He had been appointed to the Court in 1902 and was five years older than Shewalter when *Frohwerk* was argued and decided in 1919. Preservation of the Republic was, therefore, part of Holmes's heritage,[79] and as the record in *Frohwerk* unfolded he perceived the issues against this background. Shewalter's objectives—if achieved—would have greatly reduced all national power. His appeal to the First Amendment for absolute protection of speech and press appeared in a sinister light to the Court. Was the First Amendment's protection of speech and press being used as a pretext to secure approval for the states'-rights theory of government? If so, this could create a clear and present danger, a conspiracy against which government had a right to protect itself. The close philosophical link between the German-American editorial writer, Jacob Frohwerk, and his Southern, states'-rights attorney, Joseph Shewalter, was sufficient for Justice Holmes to pronounce the situation as one constituting a clear and present danger.[80]

Thus Shewalter failed in his attempts to persuade the Court to declare the Espionage Act or the Conscription Act unconstitutional; he also failed to secure Court endorsement for the absolute rights of freedom of speech and press; finally, he failed to convince the Court to adopt the states'-rights theory of a limited and circumscribed national government. His client paid the penalty. Shewalter himself remained free, continuing to write, make speeches, and give legal advice for the next six years until killed by an automobile. Frohwerk, on the other hand, was sent to prison at Fort Leavenworth, Kansas; the *Staats-Zeitung* disappeared from the annals of publications. Like many parties involved in Supreme Court cases, Frohwerk found himself overwhelmed and lost. It was unfortunate for him that he had hired as counsel the epitome of the self-aggrandizing lawyer.

Yet the constitutional issues of freedom of speech and press remained to prick the conscience of the Court, Congress, and community. The open workings of the judicial process would make it possible for many others to raise the same issues in the context of new cases. Feedback at work would require re-examination of the issues. As we shall see, this feedback would ultimately lead to a modification of the *Frohwerk* decision: a lost case did not represent a lost cause. The judicial process was still working.

NOTES

1. Alan F. Westin, *The Anatomy of a Constitutional Law Case* (New York: Macmillan, 1958), p. 26. See also Samuel Krislov, *The Supreme Court in the Political Process* (New York: Macmillan, 1965), pp. 51–54.

2. Stephen L. Wasby, *The Supreme Court in the Federal Judicial System* (New York: Holt, Rinehart and Winston, 1978), pp. 125–28.

3. Glendon Schubert, *Constitutional Politics: The Political Behavior of Supreme Court Justices and the Constitutional Policies That They Make* (New York: Holt, Rinehart and Winston, 1964), p. 89.

4. Samuel Krislov, *The Supreme Court in the Political Process*, pp. 51–54.

5. Glendon Schubert, *Constitutional Politics*, pp. 87–88.

6. Walter F. Murphy and C. Herman Pritchett, eds., *Court, Judges, and Politics: An Introduction to the Judicial Process*, 2nd ed. (New York: Random House, 1974), p. 128. These were the standards for joining the Supreme Court bar in the 1970's.

7. John M. Harlan, "The Role of Oral Argument," in Alan F. Westin, ed., *The Supreme Court: Views from Inside* (New York: Norton, 1961), pp. 57–61.

8. Anthony Lewis, *Gideon's Trumpet* (New York: Vintage, 1964).

9. Stephen L. Wasby, *The Supreme Court in the Federal Judicial System*, pp. 128–29. See also Samuel Krislov, *The Supreme Court in the Political Process*, pp. 48–51.

10. William H. Harbaugh, *Lawyer's Lawyer: The Life of John W. Davis* (New York: Oxford University Press, 1973).

11. Underhill Moore and Gilbert Sussman, "The Lawyer's Law," in Glendon Schubert, ed., *Judicial Behavior: A Reader in Theory and Research* (Chicago: Rand McNally, 1964), pp. 77–83.

12. Arthur S. Link, *Woodrow Wilson and the Progressive Era* (New York: Harper, 1954), pp. 145–73.

13. Samuel Flagg Bemis, *A Diplomatic History of the United States*, 5th ed. (New York: Holt, Rinehart and Winston, 1965), pp. 590–616.

14. Arthur S. Link, *Woodrow Wilson and the Progressive Era*.

15. Josephus Daniels, *The Wilson Era: Years of War and After* (Westport, Conn.: Greenwood, 1974), pp. 15–40.

16. Carl B. Swisher, "Wartime Curtailment of Civil Rights," *The Taney Period: 1863–64*, Paul A. Freund, ed., *The Oliver Wendell Holmes Devise History of the Supreme Court of the United States*, vol. 5 (New York: Macmillan, 1974), pp. 901–30.

17. Gerald Gunther, *Constitutional Law: Cases and Materials*, 10th ed. (Mineola, N.Y.: Foundation, 1980), pp. 1105–48.

18. Jonathan D. Casper, *The Politics of Civil Liberties* (New York: Harper and Row, 1972), pp. 25–34. See also Paul Murphy, *World War I and the Origin of Civil Liberties in the United States*, (New York: Norton, 1979).

19. Gerald Gunther, *Constitutional Law: Cases and Materials*, pp. 1121–22.

20. Philip B. Kurland and Gerhard Casper, eds., *Landmark Briefs and Arguments of the Supreme Court of the United States: Constitutional Law*, vol. 19: *Frohwerk v. United States* (Arlington, Va.: University Publications of America, 1975), p. 7. Hereafter cited as *Landmark Briefs and Arguments. The United States Law Week* (Washington: Bureau of National Affairs) presents portions of oral arguments, as does the *New York Times*. In 1980 the University Publications of America also began printing oral arguments delivered before the Court.

21. *Ibid.*, pp. 461, 463.

22. *Ibid.*, pp. 129–33, 136–37.

23. *Ibid.*, pp. 102–3, 460–64.

24. *Missouri Staats-Zeitung*, 16 February 1917.

25. *Ibid.*

26. *Ibid.*, 13 July 1917.

27. *Ibid.*, 10 August 1917.

28. *Ibid.*, 16 February 1917.

29. *Ibid.*, 1 June 1917.

30. *Ibid.*, February 1917–July 1917.

31. *Ibid.*, 16 February 1917.

32. *Ibid.*, 6 July 1917.

33. *Ibid.*

34. *Ibid.*, 1 June 1917.

35. *Ibid.*

36. *Ibid.*, 13 July 1917.

37. *Ibid.*, 10 August 1917.

38. *Landmark Briefs and Arguments*, pp. 6–11.

39. *Missouri Staats-Zeitung*, 5 October 1917.

40. *Ibid.*, 6 July 1917.

41. The Espionage Act of June 15, 1917, c. 30, §3, 40 Stat. 217, 219.

42. *Missouri Staats-Zeitung*, 1 June 1917, 15 June 1917, 6 July 1917, 21 September 1917, 2 November 1917.

43. "Joseph D. Shewalter Succumbs to Injuries," *Lexington* (Missouri) *Intelligencer*, 25 December 1925. See also "Judge Shewalter Dead," *Independence* (Missouri) *Examiner*, 23 December 1925.

44. *Landmark Briefs and Arguments*, pp. 154–244.

45. Gerald Gunther, *Constitutional Law*, pp. 212–18, 1105–17.

46. *Landmark Briefs and Arguments*, pp. 246–82. See also Gerald Gunther, *Constitutional Law*, pp. 92–112.

47. *Ibid.*, pp. 398–99. See also Alice Fleetwood Bartee, "States' Rights: A Rationale for a Particular State Action" (M.A. thesis, Columbia University, New York City, 1961).

48. *Ibid.*, pp. 176–79.

49. *Ibid.*, p. 350.

50. *Ibid.*, p. 448.

51. *Ibid.*, pp. 228, 380, 390, 451, 457. See also William Young, *History of Lafayette County Missouri* (Indianapolis, Ind., 1910), vol. 1, pp. 273–74.

52. *Frohwerk v. United States*, 249 U.S. 204 (1919).

53. *Landmark Briefs and Arguments*, pp. 135–40.

54. *Frohwerk v. United States*, 249 U.S. 204 (1919), 210. Italics added by author.

55. *Neue Kansas Staats-Zeitung*, 8 February 1918.

56. *Landmark Briefs and Arguments*, pp. 102–4.

57. *Ibid.*, pp. 125–466, 494–506.

58. Last Will and Testament of Joseph D. Shewalter, No. 5131, Probate Court of Jackson County, Independence, Missouri.

59. *Frohwerk v. United States*, 249 U.S. 204 (1919).

60. *United States ex rel Frohwerk v. Youmans*, 248 U.S. 540 (1918).

61. *Frohwerk v. United States*, 249 U.S. 204 (1919), 207.

62. *Landmark Briefs and Arguments*, pp. 46, 84–85.

63. *Frohwerk v. United States*, 249 U.S. 204 (1919), 207.

64. Glendon Schubert, *Constitutional Politics*, p. 224.

65. *United States v. Butler*, 297 U.S. 1 (1936).

66. William H. Harbaugh, *Lawyer's Lawyer: The Life of John W. Davis*, pp. 89–109.

67. *Arver* v. *United States*, 245 U.S. 366 (1918).

68. *Landmark Briefs and Arguments*, pp. 358, 363, 383 , 422, 427, 440.

69. *Ibid.*, pp. 358–85, 392–93, 395–96.

70. *Ibid.*, pp. 154–55, 179–82, 188–214, 238–40.

71. *Frohwerk* v. *United States*, 249 U.S. 204 (1919), 206.

72. *Ibid.*, pp. 127–28, 138, 140, 496–97.

73. *Frohwerk* v. *United States*, 249 U.S. 204 (1919), 209–10.

74. *Ibid.*, p. 210.

75. *Ibid.*

76. *Landmark Briefs and Arguments*, p. 228.

77. *Ibid.*, p. 390.

78. *Ibid.*, p. 457.

79. Catherine Drinker Bowen, *Yankee From Olympus: Justice Holmes and His Family* (Boston: Little, Brown, 1944), pp. xii, 149–197.

80. Fred D. Ragan, "Justice Oliver Wendell Holmes, Jr., Zechariah Chafee, Jr., and the Clear and Present Danger Test for Free Speech: The First Year, 1919," 58 *Journal of Americal Legal History* 24 (1971). Ragan points out that in *Frohwerk* Justice Holmes had not mentioned the clear-and-present-danger test, although he had said that the purpose of that decision was to "add to *Schenck*." In *Frohwerk* Holmes "employed another suggestive phrase, 'a little breath' that could 'kindle a flame' and arrived at the same conclusion." Ragan believes that by November 1919 Holmes had accepted the position that the "First Amendment established a national policy favoring a search for truth while balancing social and individual interests."

CHAPTER 2

CONFUSION IN THE CONFERENCE

JUDICIAL MISPERCEPTIONS AND
BREAKDOWN IN COMMUNICATION

It is essential in conducting post-mortem examinations of why a case was lost before the Supreme Court to look not only at the input stage but also at the second stage of judicial decision making—the conversion or interaction stage.[1] For the Supreme Court the conversion stage is the conference at which the case is discussed, Justices vote, and opinion writing begins. Studies focusing on the conference are relatively new, perhaps because of the extreme difficulties involved; however, political scientists and students of the judicial process are engaging in concentrated efforts to document the workings of the conference.[2] Thus far they have made inroads first by defining and describing the conference setting; second, by producing and applying hypotheses concerning leadership roles and small-group interactions that are developed during the conference; third, by discovering and expanding data sources to increase knowledge concerning decision making at the conference.

A brief summary of the existing knowledge in each of these three areas can help to provide the background necessary for an understanding of the relationship between the conference and a case win or a case loss before the Court. In addition, through an actual case study of a conference these theories can be made concrete, and generalized statements and descriptions about this area of decision making can be specifically applied. Even greater insight can be gained by analyzing an unusual case loss where confusion reigned during the conference period. The first flag-salute case—*Minersville School District* v. *Gobitis*, 310 U.S. 586 (1940)—was such a case, and a study of the conference at which the decision was made can be helpful in demonstrating the kind of conference that one does not want to have.

The Decision-Making Environment of the Conference

The conference is a confidential Friday (formerly Saturday) meeting in which the nine Justices of the Supreme Court meet to discuss the cases heard in oral argument during the week as well as to decide which cases to hear or not to hear later. These two major types of decisions are called decisions on the merits and jurisdictional decisions. Jurisdictional decisions are much more numerous—at least ten times as many as decisions on the merits—and dealt with quickly. In a jurisdictional decision the Court is generally deciding whether to hear the case or not; decisions on the merits involve the Court's ruling in cases that have been presented and argued. A decision on the merits is based on the strict legal rights of the parties to the case.[3]

Many of the jurisdictional decisions are made when the Chief Justice puts together a consent list, in which he enumerates those cases that, in his opinion, the Court need not hear. During the conference the Justices will express agreement or disagreement with the listing. Unless at least four Justices dissent from this listing the Court will automatically refuse to hear the case. This procedure, known as the Rule of Four, is possible because of the Court's power under *certiorari* jurisdiction granted by Congress in the Judiciary Act of 1925. Most of the Court's cases are petitions that ask for a writ of *certiorari;* whether the Court grants it or not is completely discretionary, and the Court is not obliged to explain its refusal to hear a case. Generally it is assumed if the Court gives no other reason that denial of *certiorari* was due to the fact that there were not at least four Justices wanting to hear the case. If the Court does agree at the conference to hear a case, then it will reappear at a later conference, generally after oral argument, and will be discussed and decided on the merits. After hearing argument in a case, however, the Court may then decide that it lacks jurisdiction and thus refuse to rule on the merits. During the nine months when the Court is in session (October–June) oral argument is heard on the first four days of alternate weeks and the conference is held on the following Friday. Jurisdictional decisions are usually handed down during the early fall, while decisions on the merits are announced in the late spring.[4]

The physical environment and setting in which the conference takes place is attracting more attention than ever before. Many political scientists, sociologists, and psychologists believe that decision makers are affected by factors such as furniture and seating arrangements, the size and mystique of a room, and the traditions and procedures associated with a particular place.[5] Thus an examination of the room in which the conference is held may be helpful in understanding judicial decision making.

Located across the corridor from the courtroom proper, the conference room is connected to the office of the Chief Justice. Its main door, however, opens onto the central corridor. The room has been little changed since Chief Justice Charles Evans Hughes held the first conferences in it in 1935. Its size is unchanged, it is still lighted by a magnificent crystal chandelier, and it retains its three large floor-to-ceiling windows. The heavy rug, elaborate drapes, book-lined walls, oak paneling, and massive furniture combine to reduce the impression of size of the room and make it more conducive to small-group discussion. The marble fireplace, brass accessories, and imposing portrait of Chief Justice John Marshall add to the overall sense of dignity and tradition imparted by the room.[6]

The focal point of attention remains the same: a massive twelve-foot-long Honduran mahogany conference table. Around the table are nine high-backed leather swivel chairs, each with the brass nameplate of a Justice. Built into the table are shallow drawers, one for each Justice, each fitted with a lock and key. This conference table became the source of much speculation during the 1970's. Little attention had been given to the table in 1940 when the Justices met around it to discuss the *Minersville* case. At that time the table was apparently centered under the chandelier, with Chief Justice Hughes sitting at the head of the table and the eight Associate Justices grouped around it in order of seniority. This arrangement was only traditional and subject to changes by succeeding Chief Justices, yet it remained stable until the appointment of Warren E. Burger as Chief Justice in 1969. It was then that conflicting reports began to emerge concerning the arrangement of the furniture in the conference room and, specifically, the conference table itself. It was reported that Chief Justice Burger had had the table sawed into three pieces and fitted together into an inverted "U" shape, an alteration designed deliberately to eliminate the second "end" and "along with it . . . the possibility of legitimizing by special position the role of leadership" of the senior Associate Justice who traditionally sat at the foot of the table, facing the Chief Justice. Apparently, Chief Justice Burger wanted to make changes designed to increase his influence over the Court.[7] However, these reports to the contrary, the conference table itself is still intact. While Chief Justice Burger did move an antique desk into the room, it is not placed in a "T" with the conference table, as was also reported;[8] it sits in splendid isolation some distance from the conference table.[9]

The preoccupation with the shape of the conference table and the grouping of the Justices around it has developed due to the theories of small-group analysis. Sociologists and psychologists espousing these theories hypothesize that the positions at which people are seated at a table tend to have an important effect on how they interact.[10] According to these theories, the Chief Justice sitting at one end of the conference table is potentially in a position of great power. Moreover, by tradition he opens the conference and has control of the agenda. Once the jurisdictional decisions are disposed of, he leads into the discussion of the cases argued before the Court. Thus the Chief Justice's opinions and the arguments that support his views are advanced first. Discussion generally proceeds in order of seniority, although there have been deviations from this tradition from time to time.[11] The length of time allowed for the discussion of each case depends on the Chief Justice's personality, leadership skills, and control over the Court.

The Power of the Chief Justice at the Conference

Chief Justice Hughes has become the model by which other Chief Justices are measured. His imprint upon the traditions and procedures of the conference continues even today. Hughes replaced Taft as Chief Justice in 1930, and five years later, when the Supreme Court moved into its "Marble Palace," Hughes became the first Chief Justice to sit at the head of the conference table in the now-traditional conference room. When he became Chief Justice in 1930, his associates included Justices Holmes, Van Devanter, McReynolds, Brandeis, Sutherland, Butler, Stone, and Roberts. In 1935 when the first conference was held in the new Supreme Court Building the Hughes Court consisted of the same Justices with the exception of Holmes, who had been replaced by Justice Cardozo in 1932. Hughes had almost total control of the conference, including its agenda, discussion, and voting. He was able to keep the Court abreast of its work. He had a unique ability to control conference discussions and to stop discussions that had degenerated into bickering and were no longer serving to persuade. Apparently he would simply interrupt the conference discussion with the crisp statement, "Gentlemen, the time has come to vote." His prestige stood so high even among those who disagreed with him that he could do this. Believing that the Chief Justice had to be the leader, Hughes opened the conference by stating the problems of the case clearly and concisely and then presented his own opinions based on his analysis of the facts and on precedent. He had a tremendous ability to marshal facts, and his use of stacks of law books all conspicuously marked and placed on the table before him made it difficult for another Justice to disagree. It seemed impossible for anyone to be better informed on a case than Hughes.[12]

Hughes has been called the model "task" and "social" leader of the Court. A "task" leader is defined as one who uses "intellectual persuasion" to influence other Justices to vote with him. The "task" leader must be able to demonstrate his mastery of the case. He or she must be better informed on the facts, have a thorough knowledge of legal precedents that might apply, and be able to sum up and analyze the arguments that have been advanced. Such a role also calls for the ability to speak persuasively and authoritatively. Hughes succeeded in this role. In addition, Hughes also dominated his Court through the role of "social" leader, using tactics of courtesy, friendship, and kindness to build good will for himself and hence for his policy goals. Sending birthday cards, visiting sick Justices, showing genuine concern for the personal lives of the other Justices—in all of these ways a Justice can build good will for himself. Chief Justice Taft as well as Hughes was a masterful "social" leader.[13]

Other Chief Justices, however, have been unable to control their Courts this way. Chief Justice Stone found it most difficult to cut off discussion and demand a vote. As an Associate Justice, Stone had resented Hughes's method of pushing discussion along and cutting off debate. He believed in having all issues fully explored, and as Chief Justice he was slow to end debate. Frequently the Saturday conference would continue over into Monday, Tuesday, or even Wednesday of the following week. Having spent a number of years as a dissenter himself, Stone was not in a position to "whip a majority into line." Such behavior was alien to his personality and beliefs.[14]

Voting and Opinion Assignment:
  #### The Desire for Unanimity

If the Chief Justice should think that there is a consensus among the Justices, he might not call for a vote. At any rate a vote at the conference does not necessarily bind the Justices. They may be persuaded to change their vote even after the conference is over. However, the initial vote in the conference is important because it helps determine who will be assigned the job of writing the opinion. Voting has usually started at the bottom of the seniority ladder with the most junior Associate Justice voting first. This procedure is the reverse of the case-discussion order, which begins with the Chief Justice. One purpose behind this tradition is to prevent the newest member of the Court from being placed in the awkward position of breaking a tie. In addition it is thought that voting first will place the junior Justice under less pressure and allow him or her to be more independent.[15] The discussion and voting procedure are both merely traditions. When Warren E. Burger became Chief Justice he refused to be bound by these traditions and decided to vote first as well as open the discussion.[16]

Some political scientists believe that the sequence of discussion and voting has a direct bearing on the ability of one Justice to influence another. Using concepts of game theory developed by international-relations experts,[17] these political scientists hypothesize that the voting in conference can be critical to the disposition of the case.[18]

When the Chief Justice votes with the majority, he assigns opinion writing for that group; if, however, the Chief Justice votes with the minority, then the senior Associate Justice voting with the majority makes the assignment. An astute Chief Justice can use his opinion-assigning power to increase his influence. He can assign the opinion to the most moderate member, hoping to prevent defections or even gain adherents. He may assign the opinion to a wavering Justice, hoping to strengthen the Justice's commitment to the opinion.[19] Chief Justice Warren E. Burger has apparently shifted his vote in some cases so that he could be in the majority, assign the opinion to himself, and write a "watered-down" decision. However, this practice eventually encourages separate concurrences, as Burger has discovered.[20]

Whoever is assigned the opinion will usually attempt to write one that will satisfy his or her group, perhaps even persuade another Justice to switch, and prevent separate concurrences. Thus most opinions will, of necessity, be compromise opinions and relatively broad. The Court realizes that if every Justice writes his or her own opinion or if there are several separate concurrences as well as dissents, then the decision will carry much less weight. Therefore, the conference discussion takes on added significance, as the nine Justices attempt to reach agreement.[21]

The Court can agree from the beginning on how to dispose of a case—that is, on the judgment to be handed down affecting the parties involved—but divide on the theoretical grounds. If this happens, a conference discussion may turn into an extended debate. For a case to be sound precedent Justices need to unite not only on the decision but also on the legal and constitutional theory supporting it. A modern, dramatic illustration of this problem is *United States* v. *Guest*, 383 U.S. 745 (1966). In this highly publicized case the Court handed down a unanimous verdict but split into blocs on the reasoning behind the voting. The *Guest* case had raised a question concerning the power of Congress to enact legislation (18 U.S.C. §241) to prevent private conspiracies aimed at destruction of an individual's civil rights. In *Guest* six white men had been charged with acting to "deprive Negro citizens of their rights," thus violating 18 U.S.C. §241. The Court ruled for the United States and against the defendants, but the Justices could not agree on their reasons. Justice Stewart, speaking for the "majority," held that the Court did not have to decide the issue of the reach of congressional power under Section 5 of the Fourteenth Amendment. Justices Clark, Black, and Fortas agreed, but insisted that Section 5 gave Congress power to reach *private* conspiracies, even if there were no state action connected with the conspiracy. Justice Harlan concurred in part and dissented in part because he did not want to extend 18 U.S.C §241 to reach private action—only state. Finally, Justices Brennan and Douglas and Chief Justice Warren concurred in part and dissented in part, finding in Section 5 of the Fourteenth Amendment a "positive" grant of ample, discretionary power to Congress. Thus *Guest* left many problems unanswered and indicated that the Court was experiencing severe internal problems. Persuasion during the conference had obviously been ineffective.

The Secrecy of the Conference: Preserving the Judicial Myth

The difficulties in piecing together the events during the conference arise because the meeting has always been shrouded in such secrecy. The Justices are alone in the room; a record is not kept, although the Chief Justice may make notes about votes; no one comes into the room; and the junior Associate Justice (in terms of seniority) guards the door. If materials or documents are needed from outside the room, a written request is given to the junior

Justice, who in turn gives it to the page outside. The item is then secured and handed in to the junior Justice. Thus no one enters or leaves the room. This junior Justice is sometimes referred to as the "highest paid doorkeeper in the world."[22]

It has taken a long time for political scientists to put together even this general picture of the workings of the conference. Given the secrecy and mystique that surrounds it, one might well ask how the information that we do have was secured. Basically, it has come from the published papers of deceased Justices or from their biographies; from a Justice's law clerk who blabbed intentionally or unintentionally; and from leaks within the Court itself. Unfortunately, some Justices are now making a practice of destroying conference memoranda. Justice Owen Roberts destroyed many of his papers, and Justice Hugh L. Black vehemently insisted from his hospital bed that his son burn his papers.[23]

Case and Conference: The First Flag-Salute Case

It is always difficult to separate truth from rumor in evaluating the information about the conference proceedings. The best technique for gaining reliable information is to use the personal papers of several Justices who participated in the conference, supplementing this material with data derived from interviews with law clerks and secretaries. Published biographies of the Justices may also contain material relevant to decision making and interaction during a conference. Unfortunately, not all of these data sources are available in every case. In some cases only the recorded vote has been noted; in others, the final, written opinion. Finding a case in which many different data sources are available for an in-depth analysis of judicial decision making during the conference is not easy. It is for that reason that *Minersville School District* v. *Gobitis*, 310 U.S. 586 (1940), is of particular value.

Five Justices left accounts of that conference; their personal papers provide detailed pictures of judicial interaction. One law clerk gave an extensive written interview describing the situation as he had perceived it at that time. Three judicial biographies and two autobiographies contain discussions of the attitudes and perceptions of the Justices involved in the decision. Thus *Gobitis* is an excellent case study for gaining insight into judicial interaction in the conference and its impact on judicial decision making.[24]

This case arose when Lillian Gobitis, age twelve and in the seventh grade, and her brother William, age ten and in the fifth grade, refused to participate in the flag-salute ceremony in their Minersville, Pennsylvania, public school.[25] The reason for their refusal derived from their beliefs as Jehovah's Witnesses. Their parents had converted to this sect in 1931 and followed the teachings of its leader, Judge J. F. Rutherford, who taught that the flag salute violated the first two of the Ten Commandments, which forbids the creation and worship of "graven images."[26] Other religious groups had opposed the flag-salute ceremony long before the Jehovah's Witnesses. However, a number of these groups, such as the Mennonites, were unable to fight for their belief in court; this would have offended some of their other doctrines. Jehovah's Witnesses did not have this problem, and they were ready and eager to take their cases to court.

Moreover, the ceremony used in the United States in 1935, when Jehovah's Witnesses decided to take their stand against it, was quite similar to the Nazi salute used in Germany at that time. In 1935 the flag-salute ceremony began with the participants standing and facing the flag with arms at their sides. They would recite in unison, "I pledge allegiance to the flag . . ." and at that point they would extend their right hand toward the flag with arm stiffly outstretched and palm upward.[27] This position was maintained during the remainder of the pledge, which was identical to the present pledge except that it did *not* include the phrase "under God."

The Minersville School District had established the tradition of the daily flag salute in 1914. While there was no formal written rule requiring participation, no pupil had ever refused to take part. Moreover, in many states public schools were required by state law to give instruction in American government and history and also to provide occasions and ceremonies designed to "inculcate patriotism." The power of states to do this was based on the Tenth Amendment to the Constitution (reserved powers to the states) and on state police powers to protect and promote the health, education, welfare, safety, and morals of its citizens. Different states adopted different measures to encourage patriotism. The flag-salute ceremony, which originated in 1892, was frequently used. States would pass a general statute relative to the "need to encourage patriotism"; implementation of the statute would then be left in the hands of local school boards and superintendents.[28] Thus the Minersville school system was not out of line with other school systems.

The Legal Background of the *Minersville* Case

When the Gobitis children made an issue of the flag salute in their school, the local school board hurriedly met and passed a resolution ordering the School Superintendent to make a daily flag-salute ceremony mandatory for all teachers and pupils. Lillian and William Gobitis continued to refuse, and they were expelled from the school. The struggle was almost immediately translated into the legal arena. Walter Gobitis, with the assistance of the legal staff of the Jehovah's Witnesses and that of the American Civil Liberties Union, filed a bill of complaint with the United States District Court for the Eastern Division of Pennsylvania. This was the appropriate procedure, because in this type of initiatory pleading the plaintiff (Gobitis) presented to the defendant (the school system) the information concerning the material facts he was relying upon to support his demand for reinstatement of his children. The bill of complaint is a legal document designed to state clearly and concisely the facts "constituting the cause of action" and the relief sought. In this case Gobitis charged that the Minersville rule deprived his children of First and Fourteenth Amendment rights. On the opposite side, counsel for the Minersville School District urged the district court to dismiss the complaint "for want of jurisdiction and lack of a substantial federal question." This meant that the court could not hear the case because it lacked the legal power and because no federal (First and Fourteenth Amendment) issues arose from the facts.

However, on December 1, 1937, the district court denied the motion to dismiss, declared that it did have jurisdiction, and set the trial for February 1938. The case was then argued on its merits, and on June 18, 1938, the district court found in favor of the Jehovah's Witnesses. The Minersville School District immediately voted to appeal the decision to the Third Circuit Court of Appeals in Philadelphia, and the case of *Minersville* v. *Gobitis*, 108 F. 2d 683 (3d. Cir. 1939), was argued before a three-judge court on November 9, 1938. A year later, on November 10, 1939, the Circuit Court of Appeals unanimously affirmed the decision of the district court. The school board then decided to seek a Supreme Court ruling, and a petition for *certiorari* was filed on January 30, 1940. On March 4, 1940, the Court granted the petition and issued a writ of *certiorari* to the lower court. This appellate proceeding, which is used for re-examination of action of an inferior tribunal, is a substitute for an appeal and is the most common method today of taking a case to the Court.

Jehovah's Witnesses Before the Supreme Court

Oral argument in *Minersville* v. *Gobitis* was scheduled for April 25, 1940, and was heard by a full Supreme Court presided over by Chief Justice Hughes and including eight Associate Justices— McReynolds, Stone, Roberts, Black, Reed, Frankfurter, Douglas, and Murphy.[29] A number of these Justices had confronted the problems created by flag salutes in earlier cases. The first flag-salute appeal had reached the Court in 1937, when it dismissed the appeal in *Leoles* v. *Landers,* 302 U.S. 656 (1937). Using a *per curiam* decision (implying that the decision proceeded from the whole Court rather than being written by any one Justice), the Court stated that there was no substantive federal question. Apparently in this case at least, the Court did not believe that an issue affecting a federal constitutional right—such as freedom of religion—had been raised or presented to them for decision. In 1938 the Court had done the same thing in *Hering* v. *Board of Education,* 303 U.S. 624.

The following year the Court again used a *per curiam* order to affirm a lower-court decision upholding a compulsory flag salute. The Court did this through a summary affirmation, which meant that the Court acted immediately (peremptorily) and entered its order without reaching the arguments on the merits of the case, *Johnson* v. *Deerfield,* 306 U.S. 621.

Six of the Supreme Court Justices who heard *Minersville* v. *Gobitis*—Chief Justice Hughes and Justices McReynolds, Stone, Roberts, Black, and Reed—had also participated in *Leoles, Hering,* and *Johnson.* Justice Frankfurter had participated in the *Johnson* case, so only two Justices—Douglas and Murphy—were voting for the first time in a flag-salute case. However, none of the three earlier cases had had a full hearing, including oral argument before the Supreme Court. Therefore, *Minersville* v. *Gobitis* would have the dubious distinction of being called the first flag-salute case. Moreover, in the three earlier cases the Jehovah's Witnesses had lost their cases in the lower courts and the Court had used *per curiam* decisions to summarily dismiss the Witnesses' appeal. However, in *Minersville* v. *Gobitis* the Witnesses had won in two lower courts, which had distinguished the earlier Court rulings.[30] These lower courts had employed this judicial strategy of distinguishing precedents so that they could avoid an apparent conflict with the earlier decisions. This method confined each case to its own peculiar set of facts and made the decision so narrow that it could not apply in future cases.[31]

Since two federal courts had ruled in favor of the Gobitis children and had set aside three Supreme Court decisions in the process, it seemed to some of the Justices that a clear, authoritative statement needed to come from the nation's highest tribunal. Apparently Chief Justice Hughes and Justices Roberts and Frankfurter believed that the only reason for hearing *Minersville* v. *Gobitis* was to "clinch"[32] what they believed to be a "settled issue." They wanted to lay the issue of the flag salute "to rest."[33]

Inside the Conference Room: Judicial Interaction

The conference at which *Minersville* v. *Gobitis* was decided is remarkable for what was *not* done and *not* said; it presents a case study in judicial misperceptions and breakdown in communication among the Justices. In order to understand what happened we need to see the conference with the eyes of the Justices involved and to hear the discussion with their ears. At least four totally different versions emerge from four Justices—Chief Justice Hughes and Justices Frankfurter, Stone, and Murphy.

Chief Justice Hughes approached the conference in his usual manner. Sitting at the head of the table, he always presented an imposing figure, in both charisma and intellectual genius. His blue eyes were penetrating in their directness; his white hair and bristling beard gave dignity to his physical appearance. Every Justice in the room was well aware of Hughes's powerful intellect and dominant personality. Hughes had displayed his genius during his childhood, during his college days at Colgate and Brown universities, and as a law student at the Columbia University School of Law. He had passed the difficult New York bar examination with a record score.[34]

Chief Justice Hughes's Domination of the *Minersville* Conference

Hughes's approach to any case was intellectual, and he employed to its highest degree the judicial strategy known as "persuasion on the merits," in which intellectual arguments are advanced and bolstered by legal precedents and historical data.[35] As usual, he came to the conference armed with many legal volumes, each carefully and visibly marked with white paper slips. Surrounded by these authorities he proceeded to open the conference by stating his own opinion in clear, precise, and forceful terms, citing precedents without even having to open the volumes in front of him.

Hughes was blessed with that rare quality—a photographic memory. Thus the books were merely for show, should any Justice challenge his facts; few ever did.[36] This is not to say that the other Justices always agreed with Hughes; they merely found it extremely difficult to oppose him in a verbal exchange in conference. Hughes's method of speaking generally reduced his opponents to silence. He spoke rapidly, but clearly and precisely; he apparently never had to search for words.[37] According to contemporaries he could "pose polar opposites" and make them appear to agree. However, Hughes always denied that he dominated his Court. He pointed out that men like Black, Douglas, and Frankfurter were extremely independent and no one could dominate them. Hughes would admit only to attempts at intellectual persuasion.[38]

In *Minersville* v. *Gobitis* Hughes had apparently already made his decision before he went to conference. He later stated that he believed the case was minor and that the Court had heard it simply to put an end to any more cases of this nature. Moreover, he had apparently concluded that religious freedom was not an issue in the case. He considered himself to be a civil libertarian in the highest sense of the term. Indeed, he had encouraged the Court to take and hear *in forma pauperis* cases, which was a boon to indigent defendants. In addition, Hughes had built a solid reputation for himself in the area of guaranteed procedural due-process rights for blacks accused of crimes.[39]

However, Hughes had demonstrated in *Lovell* v. *Griffin*, 303 U.S. 444 (1938), that when possible he would decide a case on almost any issue except freedom of religion. The *Lovell* case had involved the conviction of a Jehovah's Witness for refusal to secure a permit before distributing her religious literature. Alma Lovell insisted that her freedom of religion was violated by such an ordinance. Hughes ruled that the ordinance was invalid because it "struck at the very foundation of the freedom of the *press*." The fact that Hughes himself was the only child of a Baptist preacher and had been raised to pursue a ministerial calling may have had a bearing on his reluctance to rule on an issue of freedom of religion. Hughes's college career at Colgate and Brown had been financed by scholarships awarded partly because he was a Baptist minister's son. Moreover, religion had been a vital element throughout his life. Thus, perhaps unconsciously, Hughes avoided questions of religious liberty and sought to settle a case like *Minersville* v. *Gobitis* without raising the issue of free exercise of religion or establishment of religion. In evading the religious issue Hughes could avoid any charges of prejudice; settling a case on the intellectual argument of state police powers was less open to the criticism of personal predilections.

In his opening statement at the conference Hughes apparently first pointed out that the flag-salute issue had been decided by the Court three times in the previous five years. In each instance it had adopted the so-called secular-regulation rule, which stated that "there is no constitutional right to exemption on religious grounds from the compulsion of a general regulation dealing with non-religious matters."[40] If one defined the flag salute to be nonreligious, then the Court would obviously have to hold for the Minersville School Board and against the Jehovah's Witnesses. Thus Hughes's opening statement was "strongly negative."[41] He stressed the broad powers of a state over its own public schools. It was, Hughes stated, clearly an issue of the states' police power under the Tenth Amendment to provide for the education of its citizens.[42]

Having already defined the flag-salute issue as non-religious and having denied any infringement of freedom of religion, Hughes then termed the issue at stake to be one of educational policy only. This strategy allowed Hughes to avoid both references to religion in the First Amendment: the "establishment" clause that prohibits laws "respecting an establishment of religion" and the "free-exercise clause" that forbids laws "prohibiting the free exercise thereof." "Establishment" problems usually arise when religious matters intrude into governmental activities, particularly the problem of religious exercise in public schools and governmental aid to religious organizations. "Free exercise" problems arise when a freedom-of-religion claimant argues that general governmental regulation resting on state interests not related to religion either interferes with behavior allegedly dictated by religious belief or compels conduct forbidden by religious belief. Obviously the two clauses are interrelated. The provisions protect overlapping values; however, they also can exert conflicting pressures.[43]

If the flag salute did not fall within the rubric of the First Amendment but instead fell under the Tenth Amendment's guarantee of "reserved powers to the states," then the ultimate conclusion was inescapable: the Court should exercise judicial self-restraint and find the case to be one "inappropriate for judicial meddling."[44] The Court has often adopted this strategy of limiting its own power to avoid confrontations that might ultimately hurt its power and prestige. This restraint is deliberate and self-imposed. Its objective is to protect the Court from attack.[45]

The judicial-self-restraint argument advanced by Hughes was

calculated to appeal to Justices like Frankfurter, Black, Reed, Douglas, Murphy, and Stone who, for differing reasons, supported the doctrine of judicial self-restraint. At this time and throughout the New Deal, judicial self-restraint primarily referred to the belief that the Supreme Court should not try to act as a "super legislature" or to rule on the wisdom of legislative statutes, only on the power of Congress to enact them. President Roosevelt had determined upon his "court-packing plan" primarily because he felt the pre-1937 Court had not restrained itself and had attempted to dictate economic policy. When FDR had an opportunity to appoint Justices, he looked for men who understood the need for a Court that would not try to be a legislature. Black and Reed had both been in the thick of FDR's fight to reorganize the Court. Stone had early urged his brethren on the Court not to vote their "policy predilections" and to restrain themselves, fearing that if they did not do so, "someone else will do it for us." Professor Felix Frankfurter also supported this view.[46]

Hughes did not think it was necessary to find arguments to persuade Justices Roberts and McReynolds. Their voting record clearly indicated that they would not see the flag salute as a religious issue. In fact, Hughes did not anticipate that there was or could be any opposition to his decision to reverse the lower court's rulings and to establish the flag-salute ceremony as clearly non-religious, appropriate for state regulation, and not appropriate for Court interference. After stating his opinion the Chief Justice presumably waited for discussion, which, according to tradition, would have proceeded in descending order of seniority. McReynolds would have been the next Justice entitled to discuss the case, followed by Stone, Roberts, Black, Reed, Frankfurter, Douglas, and finally Murphy. After Hughes's opening statements there was apparently a period of silence. As it came their turn to speak, Justices McReynolds, Stone, Roberts, and Reed each remained silent. Justice Frankfurter did speak, although not in the manner one might have expected. Frankfurter persuasively and openly encouraged his brethren to support Hughes's position. Such support from Frankfurter in particular was critical. Frankfurter was considered the leader of the liberal group on the Court at this time. In fact, civil libertarians had rejoiced when he had been appointed by FDR in 1939. Frankfurter had a long history of support for unpopular causes and defendants, many of whom were believed to be anarchists, socialists, or communists. A Jewish immigrant himself, Frankfurter was expected to identify with persecuted minority groups. He had certainly defended such groups and causes in the past by upholding the Fifth and Sixth Amendments' guarantees of due process and a fair trial as well as the First Amendment rights of speech and belief. While a professor at Harvard Law School Frankfurter had been acknowledged as the country's leading authority in American constitutional law. Yet in the *Gobitis* conference Frankfurter did not espouse the pro-civil-libertarian point of view. Instead, he joined Hughes.

Justice Frankfurter: The "Liberal" Leader Supports the Flag-Salute Requirement

Frankfurter explained in detail why he thought it essential that the Court uphold the Minersville School Board's flag-salute requirement. First, Frankfurter argued, the flag salute was inspired by the highest public purpose—"inculcation of loyalty in the young citizen of the country." Second, public schools were appropriate instruments for encouraging patriotism, while courts—not elected and not accountable—should remember the necessity of judicial self-restraint. When Frankfurter concluded his speech, silence descended again. Douglas and Murphy said nothing.[47] Hughes later stated that there was no opposition in the conference and that the Justices seemed to be unanimously in favor of reversal. Apparently, he was so sure of his position and the agreement of the other Justices with him that he did not find it necessary to take a formal vote.

Upon the conclusion of the conference Justices Frankfurter and Roberts walked out with the Chief Justice and remarked that they hoped Hughes himself would write the Court's decision. Generally Hughes made opinion assignments only after very deliberate considerations. He would return to his office after the conference and, using a bulletin board and cards inscribed with the names of the Justices, he would arrange the Justices' names on the board according to their vote and the opinions they had expressed during the conference discussion. Hughes mentally evaluated the value preferences of the different Justices (employing a strategy known as the "voting paradox"—a rank ordering of judicial values in any given case) and then assigned the opinion to that Justice who appeared most likely to be able to win over dissenters and still hold the majority together. The Justice who had not taken an extreme position and was closest to the center would usually receive the case assignment.

Hughes took for himself those cases that he believed the public expected the Chief Justice to write. In *Gobitis*, however, Hughes departed from his ordinary practice. He immediately told Justice Frankfurter that he wanted him to write the opinion. Frankfurter's support for Hughes's position had pleased the Chief Justice. He commended Frankfurter for his "moving statement . . . [during the] conference on the role of the public school in instilling love of country in our pluralistic society." As a result, Hughes said, the opinion was "properly Frankfurter's to write."[48] Both Hughes and Frankfurter believed that all of the Justices had concurred with Hughes's statement and disposition of the case. They were wrong.

The Unexpected Dissent: Justice Harlan Fiske Stone

Justice Harlan Fiske Stone was the Justice second in seniority on the Court. His relationship with Chief Justice Hughes had never been entirely happy on Stone's part. He *may* have believed that Hughes had taken the position of Chief Justice away from him. There had been a rumor that President Hoover had offered the Chief Justiceship to Hughes out of courtesy, expecting Hughes to refuse on the basis of his age and the fact that his son was Solicitor General. Some believed that Hoover really intended to make Stone the Chief Justice in 1930. Ultimately, upon Hughes's retirement in 1941, Franklin Roosevelt, acting partly on Hughes's recommendation, elevated Stone to the Chief Justiceship. Differences of personality and temperament divided the two Justices, and Stone particularly resented the dominance that Hughes exerted over the conference. Stone himself was an experienced and well-educated Justice and a master of written opinions. A graduate of Amherst College, he, like Hughes, had studied law at Columbia University and had later become dean of the law school.[49]

Justice Stone's Position on the Flag-Salute Requirement

In verbal exchanges with Hughes, however, Stone was at a disadvantage. He functioned best in a seminar where time was not a factor and there was opportunity for lengthy debate. Hughes did not run the conference this way, and as a result Stone said much less in the conference and much more in his written opinions. Stone apparently went to the conference discussion of *Minersville* v. *Gobitis* with his mind already made up. According to his law clerk at that time Stone had decided to uphold the right of Jehovah's Witnesses to refuse to participate in the flag-salute ceremony.[50] He had reached this position gradually and he was aware that the other Justices might well wonder why, having supported the flag salute in previous cases, he should now change.[51] The explanation was simple and clear to Stone. Two years earlier in *United States* v. *Carolene Products*, 304 U.S. 144 (1938), Stone, writing for the majority, had included a now famous footnote that, although actually drafted by his law clerk, Louis Lusky, was representative of Stone's beliefs.[52] This footnote had indicated that when "discrete and insular" minorities—religious, racial, ethnic—appealed to the Court claiming violations of their civil rights, it should examine the circumstances carefully, subjecting them to an "exacting and searching judicial scrutiny," particularly if the "ordinary political processes" were not sensitive to the needs of these groups. The three paragraphs of the footnote indicated under what circumstances the Supreme Court might depart from its self-imposed restraints and enter the policy-making arena:

> There may be narrower scope for operation of the presumption of constitutionality when legislation appears on its face to be within a specific prohibition of the Constitution, such as those of the first ten amendments, which are deemed equally specific when held to be embraced within the 14th.
>
> It is unnecessary to consider now whether legislation which restricts those political processes which can ordinarily be expected to bring about repeal of undesirable legislation, is to be subjected to more exacting judicial scrutiny under the general prohibitions of the 14th Amendment than are most other types of legislation. On restrictions upon the right to vote . . . on restraints upon the dissemination of information . . . on interferences with political organizations . . . and peaceable assembly.
>
> Nor need we enquire whether similar considerations enter into the review of statutes directed at particular religious . . . national . . . or racial minorities . . . ; whether prejudice against discrete and insular minorities may be a special condition, which tends seriously to curtail the operation of those political processes ordinarily to be relied upon to protect minorities, and which may call for a correspondingly more searching judicial inquiry. *United States* v. *Carolene Products*, 304 U.S. 144, 152–153n. (1938)

This footnote was very much on Stone's mind as he considered the flag-salute case. Moreover, his former law clerk, who had helped to articulate this new role for the Supreme Court, also played a role in *Minersville* v. *Gobitis*. Louis Lusky did most of the spadework for the *amicus curiae* brief filed by the American Bar Association's Committee on the Bill of Rights.[53] *Amicus curiae* briefs can be filed by groups that are vitally concerned with a case's outcome, although not actual parties to it. Consent to file is needed from the court, the Solicitor General, and the party involved. The groups desiring to submit such a friend-of-the-court brief must demonstrate a concrete, substantial interest in the decision of the case, and the proposed brief must assist the Court by presenting relevant arguments or materials that would not otherwise be submitted.[54] After reading this brief on behalf of the Jehovah's Witnesses and the other records and materials in the case, Stone concluded that the Jehovah's Witnesses were precisely the sort of minority he had had in mind in his *Carolene Products* footnote.[55]

The Communication Breakdown in the Conference

Stone had discussed *Minersville* v. *Gobitis* with his current law clerk, Allison Dunham. Dunham later stated that he knew that Stone had gone into the conference resolved to vote against the state's case.[56] But Stone did not, apparently, have an opportunity to cast a vote during the conference. Hughes had taken the lack of general discussion at the conclusion of his summary of the case plus Frankfurter's strong endorsement to mean that he had unanimous consent from the other Justices, and so did not call for a formal vote.[57] Stone was not quick in oral argument, and, moreover, he had assumed that a vote would be taken. Unable to adjust quickly, he lost the opportunity to voice his opposition or to state his opinion, which closely followed the brief of the American Bar Association Bill of Rights Committee.[58] The conference concluded without anyone in the room knowing that Stone was opposed to the decision. Only his law clerk knew. Upon returning to his chamber Stone began the long, laborious process of deciding what to do now that the case had been decided.[59] At no point did he consider voting with the other eight Justices, who, he assumed, were solidly united with Hughes. He would later bemoan the lack of "one just man" to support him.[60] At that moment Stone was a very lonely man.

It was not surprising that Stone should feel alone. His closest allies were gone from the Court by 1940. Justice Holmes had resigned in 1932 at the age of ninety. Stone's great admiration and respect for Holmes had not diminished over the years of their association, and they had often been together in dissent.[61] Stone felt a similar sense of comradeship with Holmes's replacement, Justice Cardozo. Unfortunately, Cardozo had suffered from a heart condition that resulted in a long illness and left him totally helpless before his death in July 1938. Stone again had lost a close comrade.[62] Cardozo's place was taken by Professor Felix Frankfurter from the Harvard Law School, but Stone never had the same close and harmonious relationship with Frankfurter that he had had with Holmes and Cardozo. This was a particularly keen disappointment for Stone, since Frankfurter, during his years as a professor at Harvard Law School, had supported many of Stone's dissents in the bleak days of the early and mid 1930s when he was seldom with the majority. As a result he had paid closer attention to the attitudes of academia toward his opinions. Legal scholars became his reference group—the people he looked to for approval and support. He had particularly valued comments from Frankfurter, whose letters encouraged Stone, kept him from despair, and helped prevent him from resigning when it seemed that he was in a permanent minority on the Court. Throughout the 1930's Stone depended upon Frankfurter's praise to reinforce his belief in the correctness of his own views.[63] However, when Frankfurter came to the Court this relationship disappeared and the *Minersville* v. *Gobitis* decision pitted the two men against each other, with Frankfurter writing for the majority and with Stone in lone dissent.

Justice Louis D. Brandeis had retired from the Court in 1939. He had been one of Stone's close allies from the beginning of Stone's career on the Court. When Stone joined the Court in 1925 Holmes was a veteran of twenty-three years' service and Brandeis of nine years' service. Stone had not immediately joined the Holmes-Brandeis liberal bloc, which Chief Justice Taft had found so annoying, and Taft had hoped to persuade Stone to ally himself with the conservative bloc on the Court. Although Stone was fundamentally a conservative he soon joined Holmes and Brandeis in what the Chief Justice considered to be radical constitutional opinions. Taft could not understand that Stone was attracted by the intellectual and social companionship of Holmes and Brandeis. Almost a year to the day after Stone's appointment, the Holmes-Brandeis-Stone bloc made its appearance and lasted until 1932, when Cardozo replaced Holmes. It then became the Brandeis-Stone-Cardozo bloc.[64] However, in 1940 when *Minersville* v. *Gobitis* was decided Cardozo had been replaced by Frankfurter and Brandeis by Douglas. While Stone would later find an ally in Douglas, in 1940 he perceived Douglas primarily as his former student at Columbia and as one of FDR's Young Turks. The existing conditions on the Court, therefore, did not appear to Stone to be conducive to a bloc development, such as he had known with Holmes, Brandeis, and Cardozo.[65]

Keenly aware of what he believed to be his isolated position, Stone did not look for allies. It did not occur to him that there might be other Justices sitting around the conference table who also wanted to decide *Minersville v. Gobitis* differently. Preoccupied with his own resentment of the Chief Justice's handling of the case and with the question of what he personally should do, Stone missed his opportunity to use the conference effectively. He exerted no leadership in the conference discussion and as a result had a completely erroneous perception of the attitudes of some of the other Justices—particularly that of the newest Justice, Frank Murphy.[66]

Since Stone was not looking for allies, it is not surprising that he found none. Instead, he spent the time after the conference debating whether he should merely note his dissent or write one. In noting dissent Stone would simply have refrained from saying anything about the majority opinion. Justices may do this if they believe that no purpose would be served by exposing court differences to the public. However, it does at least allow a Justice to assert his disagreement and thus serves as a personal escape valve while not damaging Court prestige. Stone discussed these two alternatives with his law clerk, Allison Dunham, but apparently no one else was aware of his position until he failed to initial Frankfurter's opinion.[67]

Frankfurter, having been assigned the task of writing the majority opinion, had completed his draft and was circulating it among the Justices for comments and suggestions. This was and is standard practice. The opinion writer has the task of producing a written decision that will carry as many Justices as possible and avoid separate concurrences and dissents. Some Justices may approve the opinion and affix their initials to the draft. Others may request changes and modifications before agreeing to initial the draft opinion. What every opinion writer ideally hopes for are eight sets of initials plus brief notes of praise. Justice Holmes was famous for his laudatory notes, which he sometimes wrote in Latin or adapted from a Shakespearean or Biblical quotation.[68] In the circulation of his draft opinion in *Minersville v. Gobitis*, Frankfurter collected seven sets of initials—only Stone's was missing.

However, it was not until after the circulation of Frankfurter's opinion that Stone was able to complete his written dissent.

Stone had hesitated for so long that the other Justices did not have an opportunity to read his arguments before initialing Frankfurter's opinion. By the time Stone's dissent was written and circulated it was too late for him to win allies. The opportune moment for this had been in the conference and Stone had lost it. Douglas later confirmed this. Writing about the conference later Douglas claimed that while Frankfurter's opinion had circulated for some time, "no one knew for sure where Stone stood." According to Douglas, Stone's dissent did not appear until May 31, 1940, the Friday before the Saturday conference. At that time Frankfurter's opinion was routinely cleared for release and announcement the following Monday, June 2, 1940. Douglas complained that he "didn't have a chance to fully consider [Stone's dissent]." Moreover, he could not understand why Stone had not "campaign[ed] for it."[69]

Justices Roberts and Reed remained unperturbed by Stone's dissent. Whether they were surprised is not known. At any rate, discussion of the flag-salute issue in the conference would not have influenced them; three years later they continued to uphold the flag salute and noted dissent when the Supreme Court overruled *Minersville* v. *Gobitis*. Justice McReynolds was also an unlikely candidate for persuasion in the conference, since he was strongly allied to the position of Chief Justice Hughes and Justice Frankfurter. His vote in all of the earlier Jehovah's Witnesses cases eliminated him as a possible convert to the anti-salute position.[70]

Stone, seeing a winning bloc of five Justices (Hughes, McReynolds, Roberts, Frankfurter, and Reed), probably assumed that his position was lost and saw no need to argue for it. The fact that it took a great deal of persuasion on the part of his clerk to get him to write his dissent seems to indicate that Stone regarded the prospects for his view as hopeless.[71] He probably had never even looked for allies in the persons of Justices Black, Douglas, and Murphy, particularly when Justice Frankfurter rushed to support Hughes. Stone in all likelihood felt personally chagrined at the alliance of Frankfurter with the Chief Justice. Seeing Frankfurter's quick acceptance of Hughes's opinion Stone assumed that no one else would argue with the Chief. Yet Black, Douglas, and Murphy were known to be opposed to any form of oppression of the poor and helpless. Moreover, none of them had faced a "hard" civil-liberties case on the Court and none was really committed on the flag-salute issue.[72] Black had been on the Court for only three years, Douglas for only one, and Murphy for a mere four months.

Three years later Black, Douglas, and Murphy would prove that a *true* conference discussion of *Minersville* v. *Gobitis* might have changed their votes. In *West Virginia State Board of Education* v. *Barnette*, 319 U.S. 624 (1943), these three Justices joined Stone in helping to overturn the very case they decided in 1940. The majority in *West Virginia State Board of Education* v. *Barnette* was composed of Justice Robert Jackson (who had taken Stone's place as Associate Justice when Stone assumed the Chief Justiceship vacated by Hughes) and Justice Wylie Rutledge (who was appointed to McReynolds's position). Justices Black, Douglas, and Murphy completed the majority. Justices Roberts and Reed noted dissent, leaving Frankfurter alone to write a bitter dissenting opinion. Justices Black, Douglas, and Murphy had changed their minds and *publicly* requested an opportunity to change their votes. In *Jones* v. *Opelika*, 316 U.S. 584, 623–24 (1942), Black, Douglas, and Murphy dissented together and openly invited the Jehovah's Witnesses to bring up another flag-salute case for the purpose of challenging the earlier decision. In brief, they stated that

> this decision [*Jones* v. *Opelika*] is but another step in the direction which . . . *Gobitis* took against the same religious minority. . . . Since we joined in the opinion in *Gobitis*, we think this is an appropriate occasion to state that we now believe that it also was wrongly decided.

This somewhat extraordinary confession and solicitation assured the Jehovah's Witnesses of the four votes necessary to grant *certiorari*, and the Jehovah's Witnesses pushed forward with the new flag-salute case that would ultimately overturn *Minersville* v. *Gobitis*. Thus, even though Stone could not have changed the majority of five in *Gobitis*, given hindsight we can suspect that at least a minority of four Justices could have been mustered to oppose the Minersville flag salute. An eight-to-one opinion might have been five-to-four had Stone attempted persuasion in the conference. The decision would have appeared much weaker even from the beginning, and the wave of cruel anti-Witness persecution that immediately swept the country might have been lessened. Mobs in one Maine town attacked a Jehovah's Witness Kingdom Hall as well as the home of an elderly Witness. In Illinois, Wyoming, Nebraska, Arkansas, Michigan, Massachusetts, and New Hampshire, beatings, shootings, and burnings occurred.[73]

Justice Frank Murphy: The Problem of the "Freshman Attitude"

Even if Stone had been unable at the time of *Minersville v. Gobitis* to mobilize Justices Black and Douglas to support his position, there is little doubt today that he could have had the support of the newest Justice on the Court, Justice Frank Murphy. On the basis of Murphy's papers as well as interviews, it is apparent that from the beginning he was opposed to Chief Justice Hughes's handling of the flag-salute issue. Murphy would have been in complete accord with Stone's position if Stone had articulated his views in the conference.

Murphy, by his own account, left the conference in a most unhappy state of mind. He would later describe Hughes's handling of the *Gobitis* conference as dogmatic. Moreover, although Hughes insisted that he himself had had very little to say about the case (since it was so minor), Murphy claimed that Hughes had had a great deal to say.[74] In a detailed, handwritten memo, dated April 25, 1940, Murphy described the *Gobitis* conference and gave his "Observations of Chief Justice Hughes." Murphy insisted that from the time of the oral argument in the case, he personally adhered to the position of the Jehovah's Witnesses and agreed that for them at least, a "compulsory flag salute *was* offensive to the First Amendment."[75] He wanted to state his position during the conference, he claimed, but Hughes so dominated the Court that Murphy hesitated to speak up. Moreover, Murphy claimed that Hughes was really bothered by the case and was overly authoritarian for this very reason. According to Murphy, the Chief Justice opened the discussion at the conference with the remark, "I came up to this case like a skittish horse to a brass band"; he continued in this vein by admitting (according to Murphy) that he was profoundly disturbed by the case. Hughes then declared that "there was no legitimate impingement on religious belief. . . . The flag salute *is* a legitimate object for the exercise of state power. . . . The only question which the court can decide is whether there has been a proper exercise of state power." Hughes concluded by telling the other Justices that while he did not want to be dogmatic, he did firmly believe that the state *could* insist on "inculcations of loyalty" and had the power to secure this "social objective which has nothing to do with religion."[76]

When none of the other Justices openly disagreed with the Chief

Justice, Murphy apparently assumed that *he* was alone, and kept silent during the conference. However, after the conference he debated with himself—as Stone also was doing—concerning the need to dissent. In the end Murphy decided to vote with the majority. He was not sure of any acceptable *legal* argument that he could use. He was afraid of being accused of voting his "personal policy predilections." This particular phrase and its accompanying indictment were well known to the Justices of this period, and it was not surprising that Murphy expressed concern at the possibility of its being levelled at him.

The four conservative Justices of the early New Deal period had been accused by their brethren in the minority (Stone in particular) of voting their "personal policy predilections" to strike down both state and federal regulations designed to control the economy. During 1936 and 1937 Stone had used this phrase as he begged the Court to stay out of political and economic decisions that he believed should be left to the executive and legislative branches of government. Stone had realized that the conservative pre-1937 Court was out of step with economic reality and the demands of the public, and he believed, as did Justice Holmes, that the Court should not try to enforce its own policy views on the country. In a dissenting opinion in *Morehead* v. *New York ex rel. Tipaldo,* 298 U.S. 587 (1936), Stone had accused the Court majority of reading into the Constitution their own "personal economic predilections" in order to strike down the New York minimum-wage law. FDR had seized upon the phrase for use in legitimizing his "court-packing plan" of 1937.[77] It would be natural for Justice Murphy—a supporter of FDR and the New Deal legislation invalidated by the pre-1937 Court—to seek to avoid any appearance of judicial self-aggrandizement.

There were additional reasons for Justice Murphy's silence during the conference discussion of *Minersville* v. *Gobitis.* Murphy was well aware that the other Justices considered him to be legally inferior; in fact, he felt that way about himself. In letters to friends and relatives and even to President Roosevelt, who had appointed him to the Court, Murphy admitted his limited qualifications to sit on a "Supreme Court of illustrious justices." He begged FDR for a different job, claiming that he was really a politician and not a judge. Murphy's law-school record at Michigan was less than brilliant and the university apparently worried about the harm he might do to their prestige.[78] Stone himself would later declare that Murphy lacked that legal intelligence necessary for a Justice and described him as a "weak sister."

Murphy's appointment to the Court was a shock to many, himself included. He had been a strong supporter of FDR, and when Murphy was defeated for re-election as Governor of Michigan, everyone expected Roosevelt to find a place for a loyal party man. However, it came as a surprise when Roosevelt first named Murphy to be Attorney General. Murphy actually aspired to be Secretary of War and apparently FDR had constructed an elaborate scheme in which Murphy would finally get this post and Robert Jackson would become Attorney General. However, FDR changed his mind and offered an Associate Justiceship to him. Murphy did not want to accept the appointment and tried desperately to evade Roosevelt's demands. In the end he accepted the role reluctantly. He did not want to go against FDR's desires and, moreover, he had nowhere else to go. He needed the job and the money. When his appointment was announced on January 4, 1940, even his friends remarked concerning his unconcealed "anguish."[79]

Thus, it is not surprising that Murphy—only in his fourth month on the Court—would fail to voice his opposition to the position stated by the Chief Justice. Even Stone, a veteran of fifteen years on the Court and a Justice of impressive legal talents, remained silent. In fact, both Justices were so silent that they never suspected that they were in agreement; the other seven Justices also had no inkling of the opposition of these two men to the majority position.

Stone could have provided Murphy with the acceptable legal arguments to use; his own dissent in *Gobitis* was impressive. However, by the time it reached Murphy, the Court was almost ready to announce its opinion. According to one on-the-spot observer, Murphy rushed in to see Chief Justice Hughes barely an hour before the Court was to read its opinion and begged to be allowed to change his vote and to join Stone. Apparently Hughes was able to dissuade him.[80] But Murphy would grow more sure every day that Stone's dissent was correct. The "picture of the *Gobitis* children haunted him," and the same image shadowed the thoughts of Black and Douglas.[81]

Frankfurter and Stone: Differing Interpretations of the Role of the Court

Thus the conference stage in *Gobitis* was without doubt a breakdown in judicial communication. It was also marked by judicial misperceptions. Frankfurter and Stone take center stage at this point, with each having a different perception of the meaning of Footnote Four from *Carolene Products*. Frankfurter was shocked when Stone refused to initial his draft opinion; he was even more shocked when Stone refused to be persuaded by what Frankfurter contended was the logical and appropriate approach to the case. Frankfurter took the initiative after the conference in appealing personally to Stone and attempting to convince him that the majority opinion was really based on Stone's own ideas as expressed in his *Carolene Products'* Footnote Four, paragraph two. In a personal letter to Stone, Frankfurter insisted that he was but following Stone's statement that the Court should exercise great restraint, leaving all doubtful statutes to the test of the political process except when the process itself was endangered.[82] Justice Frankfurter noted that both paragraphs one and two of Footnote Four of *Carolene Products* had carefully identified the conditions necessary for the Court to become involved. The laws or actions challenged had to violate specific guarantees of the Bill of Rights; they also had to be aimed at racial, religious, or national groups.[83]

Stone sharply rebuked what he considered Frankfurter's misuse of this footnote. He called Frankfurter's attention to its paragraph three. This paragraph had defined an unknown minority, described as "discrete and insular," and had provided for an active and interventionist role for the Supreme Court should political avenues such as voting or the formation of interest groups fail to provide the guarantees of minority rights that are essential for the working of a true democracy. Stone declared that the *Gobitis* case presented a case of "prejudice against a discrete and insular minority" that created a "special condition" because it "seriously curtailed the operation of those political processes ordinarily to be relied upon to protect minorities"; thus there was a need in *Gobitis* for a "correspondingly more searching judicial inquiry."[84]

Stone thus used his interventionist paragraph three, while Frankfurter used Stone's deferential paragraph two. Persuasion was impossible. After *Gobitis* neither of these Justices would ever feel quite the same about each other. Frankfurter would later insist that Stone's attitude was the result of his law clerk's influence. Claiming that Dunham had "fierce feelings" on the flag-salute issue, Frankfurter asserted that Dunham pushed Stone first into writing a dissent and then into delivering it orally. Dunham naturally denied any such influence.[85]

Was *Gobitis* lost in the conference stage? Perhaps in one sense it was, even though an eight-to-one vote seemed to indicate otherwise. Discussion and debate in the conference might have produced a five-to-four split, definitely a weaker decision. The break-down in communication among the Justices as well as mispercep-tions of attitudes and beliefs contributed significantly to this case loss and helps to demonstrate the critical nature of this stage of judicial decision making.

NOTES

1. Glendon Schubert, *Judicial Policy Making* (Glenview, Ill.: Scott, Foresman, 1974), pp. 134–35.

2. Walter F. Murphy, *Elements of Judicial Strategy* (Chicago: University of Chicago Press, 1964), pp. 32–35.

3. Glendon Schubert, *Constitutional Politics: The Political Behavior of Supreme Court Justices and the Constitutional Policies That They Make* (New York: Holt, Rinehart and Winston, 1964), pp. 89–94.

4. William J. Brennan, Jr., "How the Supreme Court Arrives at Decisions," Peter Woll, ed., *American Government: Readings and Cases*, 7th ed. (Boston: Little, Brown, 1981), pp. 545–55.

5. John N. Hazard, "Furniture Arrangement as a Symbol of Judicial Roles," *ETC.*, 19 (1962), pp. 181–88.

6. Wesley McCune, *The Nine Young Men* (New York: Harper, 1947), pp. 4–5. See also Richard L. Williams, "The Supreme Court of the United States: The Staff That Keeps It Operating," *Smithsonian*, vol. 7 (Spring 1977); Richard L. Williams, "Justices Run Nine Little Law Firms at Supreme Court," *Smithsonian*, vol. 7 (Fall 1977). See also Tom C. Clark, "Inside the Court," Alan F. Westin, ed., *The Supreme Court: Views from Inside* (New York: Norton, 1961), pp. 45–50. In 1947 McCune stated that the portrait was that of Chief Justice Salmon P. Chase; in 1956 Justice Tom Clark stated that it was a portrait of Chief Justice John Marshall. This illustrates the secrecy and mystery surrounding the conference—both the room itself and the proceeding. After Warren E. Burger became Chief Justice he added three pictures to the decor of the room. Impressionistic in style with hot pink and bright chartreuse the dominant colors, they seem alien in the otherwise traditional and formal room. (Observations of the author made during a private evening reception hosted by Chief Justice Warren E. Burger, American Society of Legal Historians, Supreme Court Building, Washington, D.C., October 23, 1981)

7. Howard Ball, *Courts and Politics: The Federal Judicial System* (Englewood Cliffs, N.J.: Prentice-Hall, 1980), p. 254.

8. Bob Woodward and Scott Armstrong, *The Brethren: Inside the Supreme Court* (New York: Simon and Schuster, 1979), pp. 21–32.

9. Observations of the author made during a private evening reception hosted by Chief Justice Warren E. Burger, American Society of Legal Historians, Supreme Court Building, Washington, D.C., October 23, 1981. See also John R. Schmidhauser, *Judges and Justices: The Federal Appellate Judiciary* (Boston: Little, Brown, 1979), pp. 190–91. Schmidhauser bases his conclusion on the following article: Associate Justice Lewis Powell, Jr., "Myth and Misconceptions about the Supreme Court," *American Bar Association Journal* 61 (November 1975), p. 1344.

10. S. Sidney Ulmer, *Courts As Small and Not So Small Groups* (New York: General Learning, 1971), p. 11. See also Robert E. Bales, *Interaction Process Analysis: A Method for the Study of Small Groups* (Cambridge, Mass.: Addison-Wesley, 1950).

11. David Danelski, "The Influence of the Chief Justice in the Decisional Process," Murphy and Pritchett, eds., *Courts, Judges and Politics* (New York: Random House, 1961), pp. 497–508.

12. Glendon Schubert, *Constitutional Politics*, pp. 116–25.

13. David Danelski, "The Influence of the Chief Justice in the Decisional Process," pp. 497–508.

14. Alpheus T. Mason, *Harlan Fiske Stone: Pillar of the Law* (New York: Viking, 1956), pp. 790–99.

15. William J. Brennan, Jr., "How the Supreme Court Arrives at Decisions."

16. Roger Hilsman, *To Govern America* (New York: Harper and Row, 1979), p. 145.

17. See Thomas Schelling, *The Strategy of Conflict* (Cambridge, Mass.: Harvard University Press, 1960).

18. Glendon Schubert, *Constitutional Politics*, pp. 155–68.

19. Walter F. Murphy, *Elements of Judicial Strategy*, pp. 39–78, 82–85.

20. Bob Woodward and Scott Armstrong, *The Brethren*, pp. 33–36.

21. Walter F. Murphy, *Elements of Judicial Strategy*, pp. 37–78.

22. Richard L. Williams, "Justices Run Nine Little Law Firms at Supreme Court," p. 88. This particular phrase is attributed to Justice Tom Clark.

23. Arthur S. Link, "The Historian and the World of Documents," paper given at the Southern Historical Association, 46th Annual Meeting, November 13, 1980, Atlanta, Ga.

24. Alice F. Bartee, "Judicial Biography and the Judicial Process" (Ph.D. dissertation, Columbia University, 1976), pp. 313, 329–41. Also Professor Lewis J. Edinger, "Colloquium on Leadership," Columbia University, February 1972. There is a recognized need for an eclectic approach to data gathering and for scholars trained in different disciplines to cooperate.

25. David R. Manwaring, *Render unto Caesar: The Flag Salute Controversy:* (Chicago: University of Chicago Press, 1962), pp. 1–147.

26. Exodus 20: 1–5 (King James version).

27. David R. Manwaring, *Render unto Caesar: The Flag Salute Controversy.*

28. *Ibid.*

29. *Minersville School District* v. *Gobitis,* 310 U.S. 586 (1940).

30. David R. Manwaring, *Render unto Caesar,* pp. 133–34.

31. Glendon Schubert, *Constitutional Politics,* p. 224.

32. Merlo J. Pusey, *Charles Evans Hughes* (New York: Macmillan, 1951), vol. 2, pp. 728–29.

33. David R. Manwaring, *Render unto Caesar,* p. 134.

34. Merlo J. Pusey, *Charles Evans Hughes,* vol. 1, pp. 2–7, 15, 24–62, 69–73.

35. Walter J. Murphy, *Elements of Judicial Strategy,* pp. 43–45.

36. Edwin McElwain, "The Business of the Supreme Court As Conducted by Chief Justice Hughes," *Harvard Law Review,* vol. 63 (1949), pp. 6, 12–20.

37. Merlo J. Pusey, *Charles Evans Hughes,* vol. 1, pp. 55–56.

38. *Ibid.,* vol. 2., pp. 675–77.

39. *Ibid.,* pp. 727–28.

40. David R. Manwaring, *Render unto Caesar,* p. 115.

41. J. Woodford Howard, *Mr. Justice Murphy: A Political Biography* (Princeton, N.J.: Princeton University Press, 1968), pp. 250–51, 287–88.

42. Merlo J. Pusey, *Charles Evans Hughes,* vol. 2, p. 729.

43. Gerald Gunther, *Constitutional Law: Cases and Materials,* 10th ed. (Mineola, N.Y.: Foundation, 1980), pp. 1546–47, 1581.

44. David R. Manwaring, *Render unto Caesar,* p. 135.

45. Gerald Gunther, *Constitutional Law: Cases and Materials,* pp. 1668–76, 1680, 1688, 1694. See also Glendon Schubert, *Constitutional Politics* pp. 179–80, 206–16.

46. Gerald Gunther, *Constitutional Law: Cases and Materials,* pp. 151, 288.

47. James F. Simon, *Independent Journey: The Life of William O. Douglas* (New York: Harper and Row, 1980), pp. 200–7. See also Joseph P. Lash, *From the Diaries of Felix Frankfurter* (New York: Norton, 1975), pp. 68–69.

48. James F. Simon, *Independent Journey,* p. 207. Douglas is quoting Chief Justice Hughes. See also Merlo J. Pusey, *Charles Evans Hughes,* vol. 2, pp. 728–29.

49. Alpheus T. Mason, *Harlan Fiske Stone,* pp. 56–61, 67, 83, 267–71,

336–37. See also Merlo J. Pusey, *Charles Evans Hughes*, vol. 1, pp. 66, 69, 74; vol. 2, pp. 648–62.

50. Alpheus T. Mason, *Harlan Fiske Stone*, pp. 525–28.

51. *Ibid.*

52. *Ibid.*, pp. 513–15.

53. David R. Manwaring, *Render unto Caesar*, p. 146.

54. Glendon Schubert, *Constitutional Politics*, pp. 76–77.

55. David R. Manwaring, *Render unto Caesar*, p. 146.

56. Alpheus T. Mason, *Harlan Fiske Stone*, pp. 527–28.

57. Merlo J. Pusey, *Charles Evans Hughes*, vol. 2, pp. 728–29. David R. Manwaring, *Render unto Caesar*, p. 135. Alpheus T. Mason, *Harlan Fiske Stone*, p. 526.

58. David R. Manwaring, *Render unto Caesar*, p. 144.

59. Alice Fleetwood Bartee, "Judicial Biography and the Judicial Process," pp. 320–27.

60. *Ibid.*

61. Alpheus T. Mason, *Harlan Fiske Stone*, pp. 326–29, 334.

62. A. Dunham and P. Kurland, eds., *Mr. Justice* (Chicago: University of Chicago Press, 1965), pp. 251, 278.

63. Alpheus T. Mason, *Harlan Fiske Stone*, pp. 251–62.

64. *Ibid.*

65. Walter F. Murphy, *Elements of Judicial Strategy*, pp. 53, 78–79.

66. J. Woodford Howard, *Mr. Justice Murphy*, pp. 250–51.

67. Alpheus T. Mason, *Harlan Fiske Stone*, p. 528.

68. Walter F. Murphy, *Elements of Judicial Strategy*, pp. 56–67.

69. William O. Douglas, *The Court Years, 1939–1975: The Autobiography of William O. Douglas* (New York: Vintage, 1981), pp. 44–45. See also James T. Simon, *Independent Journey*, p. 12. In addition, see Alpheus T. Mason, *Harlan Fiske Stone*, p. 527.

70. David R. Manwaring, *Render unto Caesar*, p. 134.

71. Alpheus T. Mason, *Harlan Fiske Stone*, p. 526.

72. David R. Manwaring, *Render unto Caesar*, pp. 134–35.

73. *Ibid.*, pp. 163–92.

74. Alice Fleetwood Bartee, "Judicial Biography and the Judicial Process," pp. 324–25.

75. J. Woodford Howard, *Mr. Justice Murphy*, pp. 250–51, 287.

76. *Ibid.*

77. Alpheus T. Mason, *Harlan Fiske Stone*, pp. 405–26, 444.

78. J. Woodford Howard, *Mr. Justice Murphy*, pp. 198, 215–16, 228, 236.

79. *Ibid.*, pp. 117–216.

80. Wesley McCune, *The Nine Young Men*, p. 214.

81. *Ibid.*

82. Stone Papers, vol. 65, Manuscript Division, Library of Congress, Washington, D.C.

83. Alpheus T. Mason, *Harlan Fiske Stone*, pp. 525–30.

84. *United States* v. *Carolene Products Company*, 304 U.S. 144 (1938).

85. Alpheus T. Mason, *Harlan Fiske Stone*, pp. 527–28.

CHAPTER 3

TO DECIDE AND HOW TO DECIDE

SUPREME COURT DECISIONS AS OUTPUTS

One of the goals of systems analysis, when applied to the judicial process, is to analyze the output, or decision, of the Court. Case decisions as reported in the *United States Reports* and other publications are a clear statement of this output. Citing the name and number of the case, its origin, record, and facts, the Justices proceed to decide for one party and against another. The written opinion or opinions are published to say to all who would read, "This is our decision."

It would appear on the surface that examining outputs of the judicial process would, therefore, be relatively simple. Yet behind the written words that constitute the decision are many factors that must be analyzed and evaluated before the decision can be meaningful. The view that judges simply "found" the law and then announced it in their decision has been shown to be a myth.[1] Although couched in legal phrases and peppered with earlier case precedents and examples as well as appeals to history and tradition, judicial decisions are nevertheless "functions of attitudinal variables."[2] Stated simply these outputs reflect the personal values, beliefs, and attitudes of the Justices involved in the case decision. Understanding a decision or output thus requires a knowledge of judicial preferences and ideologies.[3]

Judicial Attitudes and Judicial Decisions

The Justice brings to every case his own individual attributes and attitudes, developed during his formative years and out of his background experiences and pre-court career. His perception of his own role as well as the proper role of the Supreme Court also contribute to his reaction to a case and to its facts, issues, and defendants. These multiple reactions intermesh and contribute to the development of a Justice's decision. Background and pre-court-career experiences, professional socialization within the Court itself, and the particular case inputs combine to trigger a set of attitudes and values that will affect decision making.

Any analysis of the output stage must attempt to answer the question, "Why do Justices decide the way they do?" Such an analysis must include among other things an attitudinal profile of each member of the Court, a study of the voting record of each of the Justices, and an appraisal of the written record in the particular case in order to determine the degree of coincidence between private attitudes and public decision making.[4]

To know how and why Justices decide as they do is to know the very essence of the judicial process. If one scrutinizes a case in which the Justices were sharply divided, an even clearer and more detailed picture of decision making can be drawn. When Justices resort to separate concurrences or dissents as they vote to decide who wins or loses in a case, they raise the curtain shrouding the mystery of judicial decision making and give to the spectator an opportunity for gaining a better understanding of the total process. One such case is *Walker* v. *Birmingham*, 388 U.S. 307 (1967), a case loss for civil-rights leader Rev. Martin Luther King, Jr., and his associates. The Justices split into blocs and a five-to-four decision resulted. Four separate opinions were written (three were dissents), demonstrating the intensity of the conflicting attitudes of the Justices. Thus an analysis of *Walker* is appropriate for understanding a case loss by focusing on one set of critical factors in the output stage of the judicial decision making process—the attitudes of the nine Justices who made the decision.[5]

Walker v. *Birmingham:* A Case Study in Judicial Attitudes and Decisions

The *Walker* case can best be described as a civil-rights-demonstration case in which black civil-rights leaders had attempted through the use of demonstration marches on the streets of Birmingham, Alabama, to pressure the city merchants to abandon their segregated lunch counters in various downtown department stores. Under the sponsorship of the Southern Christian Leadership Conference (SCLC) in conjunction with the Alabama Christian Movement for Human Rights (ACMHR), plans had been made to hold marches and conduct sit-in demonstrations in Birmingham during the week preceding Easter Sunday in April 1963.[6]

Background Events in the *Walker* Case

Birmingham had been selected because of its adamant commitment to the maintenance of segregation policies in spite of the Supreme Court decision in *Brown* v. *Board of Education*, 347 U. S. 483 (1954), which had struck down segregated schools. As late as 1963 everything in Birmingham was still rigidly segregated— schools, recreation facilities, motels, restaurants. The National Association for the Advancement of Colored People (NAACP) had come under severe attack by the Attorney General of the state of Alabama in 1956, and as a result that organization had to spend nearly nine years in court litigation.[7] This meant that other groups had to take the lead in Alabama during these years. The ACMHR was one such group. It was led by Rev. Fred L. Shuttlesworth, the pastor of the Bethel Baptist Church in Birmingham. Shuttlesworth had approached the SCLC, an organization of individual black leaders and groups, for help in breaking the hold of the white segregationist leadership in Birmingham. Although the SCLC was a relatively young organization, having been organized in 1957, it had charismatic leadership in the person of its president, Rev. Martin Luther King, Jr., as well as other officials, such as Rev. Wyatt T. Walker and Rev. Ralph Abernathy.[8]

The discriminatory policies of the state of Alabama were well understood by SCLC. In particular, the attitudes of the City Commissioners of Birmingham were a matter of public record. Their response to the Supreme Court ruling requiring integration was "Never!" As a result of this situation, SCLC and ACMHR decided upon a strategy of protest-demonstration marches and accompanying picketing and sit-in actions; their first targets were segregated lunch counters in downtown department stores in Birmingham.

The first in the succession of events involved in *Walker* v. *Birmingham* occurred on April 3, 1963. Two black leaders, Mrs. Lola Hendricks and Rev. Ambrose Hill, went to the Birmingham City Hall to apply for a permit to picket and to parade. Under the rules of a city ordinance such a request had to be made to the entire City Commission. However, the two civil-rights workers only saw and spoke with one member, the Public Safety Commissioner "Bull" Connor. Their oral request was immediately refused by Connor, who had already established his reputation as a die-hard segregationist. On Friday, April 5, Rev. Shuttlesworth sent a telegram to Connor requesting on behalf of the ACMHR a permit to picket against the segregation policies in effect in Birmingham. Such a request technically should have been directed to the entire City Commission, but Shuttlesworth knew that the ordinance had never been administered that way. In practice, parade permits were granted by the city clerk on the recommendation of a subor-dinate of Connor. Connor responded with a telegram of his own to the effect that the ACMHR would have to seek permission from the entire commission. No further efforts were made to secure the permit and on the following day Shuttlesworth led the first pro-test march. Pickets were organized at the downtown stores and sit-ins at various lunch counters; these continued on Monday, Tuesday, and Wednesday of the following week, April 8–10. By this time the leadership of SCLC—King, Walker, and Abernathy—had arrived in Birmingham to participate in the scheduled Easter-weekend demonstration.[9] On Wednesday, April 10, at-torneys for the city of Birmingham applied for a temporary re-straining order directing these leaders of the demonstration to cease their activities. This order, issued by State Circuit Judge William Jenkins, Jr., directed the black leaders to halt their ac-tivities or face a contempt-of-court charge. Alabama law permit-ted judges to issue such a restraining order upon the application of one party alone; this meant that the leaders of SCLC and ACMHR were unable to argue against the granting of the order. Known as an *ex parte* injunction, this particular court order would be *the* critical variable in the ultimate decision reached by the Supreme Court in *Walker*.[10]

The injunction writ was served on King, Walker, Abernathy, and Shuttlesworth early on Thursday morning, April 11. They announced immediately, however, that they would proceed with the Easter-weekend demonstration. They asserted their belief that the injunction was based on an invalid and unconstitutional city ordinance and was therefore itself unconstitutional. Thus on Good Friday, April 12, King and Abernathy led fifty volunteers from the steps of the Sixteenth Street Baptist Church. They were immediately joined by more than 500 followers. The Birmingham police force was waiting for them, and the police intercepted the leaders before they had travelled many blocks. King and Aberna-thy were arrested and quickly rushed to jail.

Walker had not been part of this group. He first tried to secure intervention by the federal government, but failed when the Civil Rights Division of the Justice Department stated that there had been no state action that infringed federal rights. Walker then proceeded to organize the Easter Sunday demonstration march. He was assisted by Rev. Albert Daniel King, brother to Martin Luther King, Jr. The scenario that followed resembled the Good Friday arrests.[11]

Walker Before the Alabama State Courts

Events moved quickly from the streets to the courtroom. On Monday, April 15, lawyers for the civil-rights leaders filed an application to dissolve the injunction on the basis that it violated due process and was an unlawful prior restraint on First Amendment freedoms of speech and expression. Attorneys for the city of Birmingham filed a charge for contempt of court, based on the undisputed fact that the jailed civil-rights leaders had led demonstration marches in spite of the court's temporary restraining order forbidding them to do so. The case was docketed with Judge William A. Jenkins, Jr., who had issued the order in the first place, and the hearing was scheduled for 9:30 A.M. Monday, April 22.

The legal issues raised in this first trial were of critical importance in building a record for appeal. Since the attorneys for the accused civil-rights leaders did not expect to win in the Alabama courts, it was essential for them to raise every issue that could be used in later appeals. In all they raised five issues: that the injunction was invalid (eleven reasons were given); that the case should be removed to a federal court on the grounds that the state prosecution had been instituted solely to prevent persons from exercising their First Amendment rights; that the demonstration or protest marches were "peaceful walks" and not "parades" within the meaning of the Birmingham parade-permit ordinance; that the conduct engaged in by the civil-rights leaders was protected by the First and Fourteenth Amendments; and that the city's parade-permit ordinance was administered in an arbitrary and discriminatory fashion and thus should be held void as applied.

On Friday, April 26, just two weeks after the Easter-weekend parades the civil-rights leaders were found guilty of contempt of court. Judge Jenkins held that Birmingham's parade-permit ordinance was not "invalid upon its face" and that the defendants had not proved that it had been administered arbitrarily or capriciously. The temporary restraining order issued to prevent a march for which no permit had been granted was also, according to Judge Jenkins, a valid exercise of the power of the court. Since the defendants had knowingly and willfully violated this injunction, they were in contempt of court. The sentence was a fine of fifty dollars and five days in jail.

Lawyers for the civil-rights leaders immediately announced that they would appeal; in the meantime bail was posted and the black leaders remained free pending the appeals. The case should have passed through two levels of state appellate courts. However, under Alabama law persons convicted of contempt of court could bypass the first-level appellate court and petition the Alabama Supreme Court to exercise its discretion to review the trial-court proceedings. This is what occurred in the *Walker* case. On May 15, 1963, the court granted the petition of the civil-rights leaders for a writ of *certiorari* asking for review of their contempt-of-court convictions. During the following two months both parties wrote and filed their briefs. There was no request for oral argument. On August 22, 1963, the Alabama Supreme Court officially accepted the *Walker* case on briefs and transcripts alone. It would be almost two-and-one-half years before a decision would be handed down. The Alabama court was well known for its inability to keep abreast of its docket of cases, and in this particular case the opinion had been assigned to Justice Coleman, who suffered from pen paralysis—the inability to produce a written opinion on time.[12]

Thus the decision of the court was not announced until December 9, 1965.[13] Again the civil-rights leaders were found guilty and their convictions were affirmed. The Alabama Supreme Court focused on two issues: that no permit had been obtained to hold the parades and that the leaders had knowingly violated a court order directing them not to demonstrate. However, the court did not address the constitutional question, "Was the injunction an abridgement of First Amendment rights made applicable to states on the basis of the Fourteenth Amendment?" Neither did the court consider the validity of the parade-permit ordinance of the city of Birmingham as applied in this case.

Persuading Justices: *Walker* Before the United States Supreme Court

The attorneys representing the civil-rights leaders had been preparing from the beginning of the *Walker* case for an appeal to the

United States Supreme Court. Once the Alabama court had spoken they quickly marshalled their arguments and petitioned the Supreme Court for a writ of *certiorari*. The Court granted the writ and scheduled the case for oral argument on March 13, 1967.[14]

The issues that confronted the Supreme Court were basically spelled out in the briefs submitted by the attorneys representing the civil-rights leaders. First, there was the issue of the parade-permit ordinance. It was essential that the convicted ministers prove that the ordinance had been administered in an arbitrary manner by city officials. Approximately ten pages were devoted to this in the brief filed by the attorneys for the civil-rights leaders. The attorneys attempted to convince the Court that the trial court's ruling had made it impossible for the ministers to prove that they could not have obtained the parade permit, which the injunction required them to have. They argued that evidence could have been introduced that would have shown that the permit ordinance had been administered so as to discriminate against blacks. This evidence was not included in the lower-court record, because the trial judge had ruled narrowly and had excluded it. Included in this evidence was the history of the parade-permit ordinance showing that permits had never been granted by the entire City Commission; that at least two limited efforts to secure a permit had been made by Rev. Shuttlesworth and his co-workers; and that Public Safety Commissioner Connor had told these workers not to try to apply for a permit. The vague wording of the ordinance allowed it to be administered so as to enforce unconstitutional racial-segregation policies characteristic of Birmingham. In addition the ordinance allowed for overdelegation of authority and uncontrolled discretionary decision-making power; total unfettered discretion had been vested in the city officials.

The attorneys for the civil-rights leaders also presented evidence from the lower-court record to show the peaceful nature of the marches and to emphasize that none of the marchers themselves had been involved in any disorders; the city police had not called in the local sheriff's office nor the state police. The Good Friday and Easter Sunday marches had not been situations requiring police intervention to protect persons or property.

A second issue centered on the validity of the temporary restraining order (injunction) issued by Judge Jenkins ordering the civil-rights leaders not to engage in demonstration marches. The attorneys for the convicted leaders stressed the fact that the injunction had been issued *ex parte*, thus denying the black ministers any opportunity to argue against it before it was issued. Counsel for the civil-rights leaders considered this a violation of the Fifth Amendment's guarantee of due process of law and also as a prior restraint upon the First Amendment's guarantee of freedom of speech and expression. States are bound by these Bill of Rights provisions through the Fourteenth Amendment.

A third issue involved the power and jurisdiction of the Supreme Court. Although the Court had agreed to hear the case, this did not necessarily mean that a majority of the Justices believed that they had the right to decide the issues; it only meant that four Justices had voted to hear the case under the discretionary jurisdiction power granted them by Congress in the Judiciary Act of 1925.[15] It was absolutely essential for the civil-rights leaders' attorneys to convince the Court that Alabama law was not dispositive of the constitutional issues. The attorneys needed to prove that federal constitutional issues such as the First Amendment's guarantee of freedom of speech and expression were central to the decision and that Alabama law could not alone and independently settle the issues.[16]

This legal argument is referred to as the adequate-and-independent-state-grounds barrier to Supreme Court review of state-court decisions. The issue is whether or not the state court's reliance on an issue of state law bars Supreme Court review. If state-court judges mainly use their own state-constitutional provisions in their decision so that intervention of federal courts could not change that decisional output, then the Court would decide not to rule. Even if the state court had discussed federal guarantees and given them a wrong interpretation, the Court would still not intervene if the outcome of the decision would not be changed. In addition, if the state-court decision relied solely on the state-law ground and held that non-compliance with the state procedural requirement precluded an adjudication of the federal issue, the Court might well refuse to intervene. The Court itself must decide whether to review the decision and then to reach the question, "Are the state grounds adequate to support the conviction?" The Court also must decide whether to entertain the federal issue despite a state-court ruling that it could not be properly raised.

While the Supreme Court generally prefers to defer to state procedures, this deference has never been total because the Court has remained conscious of its role as protector of the federal rights of all citizens. How then does the Court decide? A comprehensive answer has been given by Justice Tom Clark writing in dissent in *Williams* v. *Georgia*, 394 U.S. 375 (1955):

> A purported state ground is not independent and adequate in two instances. First, where the circumstances give rise to an inference that the state court is guilty of an evasion—an interpretation of state law with the specific intent to deprive a litigant of a federal right. Second, where the state law, honestly applied though it may be, and even dictated by the precedents, throws such obstacles in the way of enforcement of federal rights that it must be struck down as unreasonably interfering with the vindication of such rights.

In *Walker* the attorneys for the civil-rights leaders sought to convince the Court that there was no barrier to review since the state law had been applied to deprive blacks of their federal rights, specifically their right to freedom of speech. There were also two major precedent-setting cases associated with the adequate-and-independent-state-grounds barrier that the attorneys sought to distinguish from *Walker*. Both of these decisions were the opposite of the position the black leaders' attorneys wanted the Court to adopt. In *Howat* v. *Kansas*, 258 U.S. 181 (1922), the Supreme Court had refused to review a Kansas state-court decision that had held that the constitutional validity of an injunction could not be attacked in a contempt proceeding. The Court here deferred to the state court's ruling because federal issues were not involved. In *United States* v. *United Mine Workers*, 330 U.S. 258 (1946), the Court restated the doctrine announced in *Howat* and in additional dicta stated that in all *federal* courts the validity of an injunction should not be decided in a contempt proceeding. These two precedents could be distinguished from *Walker* on the basis of factual differences. Specifically, free-speech rights were not an issue in these cases, as they were in *Walker*.

The Supreme Court that would hear the *Walker* case was presided over by Chief Justice Earl Warren and Associate Justices Black, Douglas, Clark, Harlan, Brennan, Stewart, White, and Fortas. Oral argument in *Walker* began late in the afternoon of March 13, 1967, and the Court decision was announced on Monday, June 12, 1967. The marble courtroom in which oral argument is presented and in which the Court's decisions are announced is impressive. Across the back of the courtroom are dark-red velvet drapes through which the Justices pass as they step onto the raised platform where the Court sits. Nine leather swivel chairs—

each of a different size and custom-made to suit individual judicial preferences—are located behind a high, curved bench. Originally this bench had been rectangular—it was in 1967 when *Walker* was decided — but under the direction of Chief Justice Warren E. Burger (appointed in 1969) the bench was remodeled to be slightly curved. The alleged purpose for doing this was to produce better eye contact between lawyers and the Justices.[17]

Elaborately carved marble pillars and columns encircle the room and a large clock is centered directly above the judicial bench. All the furnishings of the courtroom are made of mahogany: these include the tables directly in front of the judicial bench as well as the pews at the back of the courtroom, where visitors may sit. The combination of marble, mahogany, velvet, leather, and heavy, intricately designed ironwork in a room of lofty proportions produces a sense of awe in the spectator. The somber black robes of the Justices serve to emphasize the dignity, respect, and deference that the entire courtroom is designed to inspire. Yet the Justices are not gods, but only men and women. Their "Marble Palace"[18] is not a sacred temple, only an impressive building. And the Washington hilltop is not the Mount Olympus of the Greek gods.

Why Justices Decide As They Do

Indeed, an analysis of the background, heredity, and experience of the Justices who participated in *Walker* would quickly demonstrate that decisions are made, not found. Each Justice involved in the *Walker* decision had his own unique set of attitudes and ideologies that had developed due to his social, economic, political, and religious background and his hereditary attributes and professional experience. As a result each Justice perceived the *Walker* case differently and related to the issues on the basis of these perceptions. While each Justice is quite different from his colleagues, similarities do exist. These similarities predispose some Justices to align themselves with others while refusing to cooperate with still others. This predisposition is known as bloc behavior.[19]

By 1967 when the decision in *Walker* was handed down by the Supreme Court, several blocs had emerged on the Court. Glendon Schubert has divided the Warren Court into two periods: the early Warren Court (1953–1962) and the later Warren Court (1962–1969). Since *Walker* occurred during this latter period, an analysis of it is appropriate for an understanding of the voting patterns, judicial-bloc behavior, and decisional outputs that provided the background for the *Walker* decision.

In attempting to describe, understand, and analyze judicial voting Schubert also devised a framework for study. His theory postulates three major attitudinal components (political, social, and economic) for each Justice and attempts to classify Justices as liberal or conservative on the basis of their voting records in the cases that fall into each of the three areas. Political liberalism is defined by Schubert as the "belief in and support of civil rights and liberties"; political conservatism as the "upholding of law and order and the defense of the status quo." Social liberalism and conservatism focus on issues such as equality of access to government, economy, and society; economic liberalism and conservatism revolve around the rights of private property.[20] In *Walker* it could be argued that all three attitudinal components were involved and that some of the Justices chose to emphasize one over the others. In addition, each Justice's classification of the case as one of political, economic, or social issues helped to determine whether he exhibited a liberal or conservative attitude.

Judicial Voting Behavior in Pre-*Walker* Demonstration Cases

An examination of some of the major demonstration cases that preceded *Walker* documents the various blocs and voting alignments that emerged at that time as well as the judicial attitudes expressed. Beginning in 1963 and concluding in 1966 on the threshold of *Walker*, the Supreme Court considered no fewer than eight significant cases dealing with the rights of demonstrators.[21] Facts differed from case to case and as a result the decisions also differed. Moreover, various coalitions emerged in response to the differing case elements.

In 1963 the Court dealt with a situation in which 187 black student demonstrators had been convicted of breach of the peace. These students had held their protest against racial discrimination on the grounds of the South Carolina statehouse. By a vote of eight to one the Court in *Edwards* v. *South Carolina*, 372 U.S. 229 (1963), reversed these convictions. Justice Stewart wrote the opinion for a majority composed of Chief Justice Warren and Justices Black, Douglas, Brennan, White, Goldberg, and Harlan; only Clark was in dissent. Stewart based his opinion on his interpretation of the Fourteenth Amendment, which, he believed, South Carolina had violated by making "criminal peaceful expression of unpopular views." There had been no violence. Moreover, South Carolina's law was not "a precise and narrowly drawn regulatory statute." Clark, however, based his dissent on his belief that racial feeling was high and disorder and violence could have occurred at any moment.

The following year brought *Hamm* v. *City of Rockhill*, 379 U.S. 306 (1964), to the Court. At issue here was the validity of state convictions under local trespass statutes of blacks participating in sit-ins at lunch counters of department stores. The actions had occurred *before* the passage of the Civil Rights Act of 1964 and as a result several opposing lines of reasoning emerged. The Court divided five to four, as it was to do in many sit-in and demonstration cases; Justice Clark wrote for the five-man majority, which overturned the state convictions for trespass. Clark held that the Civil Rights Act of 1964 had clearly prohibited discrimination in places of public accommodations. Since a federal law is superior to state law under the supremacy clause (Article VI) of the Constitution, the state trespass charges had to be dismissed and the state judgments vacated. Justices Douglas and Goldberg concurred separately, basing congressional power on the Fourteenth Amendment rather than Article VI.

However, four Justices dissented from the majority holding. Justices Black, Harlan, Stewart, and White wrote separate dissents, each highlighting his own particular view. Black focused on the students' behavior, which he characterized as "taking the law into their own hands." He insisted that sit-ins were illegal and violated property rights. Justice Harlan based his dissent upon what he perceived as a doctrine destructive of the federal system. In his opinion the Civil Rights Act of 1964 could not legally set aside state trespass convictions that had occurred before the passage of the act. Moreover, he did not think that it was the proper role for the Supreme Court to "attribute to Congress a purpose to preempt state law in such instances." Justices Stewart and White agreed with Harlan's position.

The Court's ambivalence in demonstration cases was obvious in 1965 in the divided votes accompanying opinions in two related cases: *Cox* v. *Louisiana* [*Cox I*], 379 U.S. 536 (1965), and *Cox* v. *Louisiana* [*Cox II*], 379 U.S. 559 (1965). A Field Secretary of the Congress of Racial Equality (CORE), Rev. Cox, had led a demonstration march to protest the jailing in the courthouse jail of twenty-three black college students who had been arrested and incarcerated for picketing stores that maintained segregated lunch counters in Baton Rouge, Louisiana. Cox was arrested for violating three Louisiana statutes: a breach-of-the-peace statute, an obstructing-public-passages statute, and an ordinance that prohibited picketing before a courthouse. The sharp division of the nine Justices resulted from their perception of the issues, facts, and events involved as well as from their legal analysis of the Louisiana laws. For example, all nine Justices voted to reverse the state's conviction of Cox for disturbing the peace, eight Justices voted to reverse the obstructing-public-passages conviction (Justice White dissented here), and only five Justices voted to reverse the conviction for picketing before a courthouse. The four Justices in dissent—Black, Clark, Harlan, and White—stressed the importance of protecting a courthouse and its accompanying jail from mob demonstrations. Moreover a number of issues were not settled in *Cox*. These included the constitutionality of the Louisiana laws on their face, their constitutionality as applied by law-enforcement officials, and the sufficiency of the evidence in the case record. These issues were also present in *Walker*. *Cox*, therefore, did not provide settled case precedent for handling *Walker*.

Another split decision involving a protest stand-in was handed down by the Court during its 1966 term. *Brown* v. *Louisiana*, 383 U.S. 131 (1966), arose out of the refusal of five young black men to leave the reading room of the all-white library after the librarian had explained that she did not have the book they requested. Although there was no noise or boisterous talking, the sheriff was called in and he arrested these demonstrators for breach of the peace. The Court again could not agree. Justice Fortas (who had replaced Justice Goldberg on the Court) wrote a plurality opinion, which was joined only by Chief Justice Warren and Justice Douglas. Justices Brennan and White each concurred separately, but each asserted a different rationale. Justices Black, Clark, Harlan, and Stewart dissented. Thus, although Brown's conviction was reversed, no real precedent was set. The five-man majority could not agree and Justice Black led a strong dissent. Justice Fortas, joined by Chief Justice Warren and Justice Douglas, expressed the belief that the state had violated the First and Fourteenth Amendments' guarantees of freedom of speech, assembly, and petition. Justice Brennan, however, confined his opinion to an analysis of the Louisiana statute, which was void in his view because it was overly broad and general. Justice White focused on the Fourteenth Amendment's equal-protection clause, which he believed, on the basis of the case record, had been violated by the demand that the young blacks leave the library. The four dissenters stressed the point that libraries were not the same as streets, and thus different standards should apply. Black's opinion also emphasized the power of the state to protect its own property. The Court's inability to formulate a clear policy was also demonstrated by its refusal of jurisdiction of two New York demonstration and stand-in cases: *Penn* v. *New York*, 383 U.S. 969 (1966), and *Baer* v. *New York*, 384 U.S. 154 (1966).

However, following quickly upon the heels of these two cases, *Greenwood* v. *Peacock*, 384 U.S. 808 (1966), demonstrated that two judicial blocs had definitely formed on the Court. The Court split five to four in an alignment later identical to that of *Walker*. Civil-rights workers in Greenwood, Mississippi, sought to have their case, which had resulted in a conviction for obstructing public streets, removed from state court to federal court. Writing for a five-man majority including Justices Black, Clark, Harlan, and White, Justice Stewart focused upon the narrowest issues possible for decision. This allowed the case to be decided on an issue of statutory construction of the Civil Rights Act of 1964 and the Voting Rights Act of 1965. Justice Stewart found that the defendants had not pursued the proper course of procedure. They had assumed that they could demand removal of their case in advance of the trial. However, they had no evidence to prove that the Mississippi law clearly and explicitly operated to deny them their federal rights "by the very act of bringing them to trial in the state court." Stewart stressed the need to go up the ladder of appropriate judicial procedures, allowing the law to take its course and the case to become fully ripe or developed. In addition there were other remedies that these defendants could have used, including a *habeas corpus* proceeding *after* the trial. Stewart's opinion clearly showed his dislike for jumping channels and for an infringing of the federal division of power as he interpreted it. For Stewart, it was essential to maintain the proper division of powers and to preserve the historical rights of the states. He believed in a limited role for the Supreme Court. Stewart also gave a very narrow construction to the Civil Rights Act of 1964 and concluded that the law did not "operate to work a wholesale dislocation of the historic relationship between state and federal courts in the administration of criminal law." Justice Douglas, writing for the dissenting bloc (Warren, Brennan, Fortas) in a twenty-page opinion, emphasized the chilling effect that the majority opinion would have. He believed that the Civil Rights Act of 1964 had intended for federal courts to step into areas where there had been a tradition of denial of equal protection and where state law not only was vague on its face but also had been applied in the past in a racially discriminatory fashion. If federal courts refused, then individuals would hesitate to challenge discriminatory policies, knowing that they would have to build in state courts a case record documenting these policies.

The final chapter in the series of demonstration cases immediately preceding *Walker* was written in the decision of *Adderley* v. *Florida*, 385 U.S. 39 (1966). Once again the Court was divided five to four in an alignment identical to that in *Walker*. Some of the elements in *Edwards* and in *Cox* were present in *Adderley*. Yet the Court distinguished both of these earlier cases. In *Adderley* thirty-two black students at Florida A & M University were arrested for demonstrating at the jail to protest segregation. Justice Black, speaking for a majority that included Justices Clark, Harlan, Stewart, and White, upheld the conviction for trespass on three grounds. First, jails were not the appropriate place for demonstrations; second, the Florida trespass law was a narrowly drawn statute, not vague or overbroad as the Louisiana laws had been; third, there was no violation of First Amendment rights. The majority opinion concluded with Black's forceful statement that "the state, no less than a private owner of property, has power to preserve the property under its control." Justice Douglas wrote for the dissenting bloc, which included Chief Justice Warren and Justices Brennan and Fortas. Douglas found no breach of the peace. He likened the jail to the Bastille and found it to be an obvious center for protest. Douglas believed that the political process had not been sensitive to the needs of blacks and thus they had had to move beyond conventional methods of petitioning. Although there had been no speeches or signs, the group had sung songs, and this brought them under the protection of the First Amendment, according to Douglas's views. The dissenters also attacked Justice Black's theory that the sheriff had the same rights over the jailhouse that a private-property owner had over his home.

These case decisions were the specific precedents dealing with rights and limitations of demonstrators. The Supreme Court would decide *Walker* against this backdrop, and the rule of *stare decisis* ("let the decision stand") would have to be dealt with. However, most of these earlier decisions did not firmly commit the Court to any definitive position. Each side in *Walker*, therefore, believed that they had a reasonable chance of winning. The attorneys for the opposing sides, after analyzing the past voting alignments, also needed to take into account as many facets of each Justice's value structure as possible and to present the issues so as to trigger an attitudinal variable that would secure the vote desired by that side.[22]

The Backgrounds and Pre-Court Careers of the Supreme Court Justices in *Walker*

In order to accomplish this goal it would be necessary to answer specific questions concerning the Justices who would decide *Walker*. According to the composite pictures drawn by political scientists like John R. Schmidhauser and Cortez A. M. Ewing, the typical Supreme Court Justice could be described in the following manner:

> [He] has generally been white, Protestant (with a penchant for a high social status denomination), usually of ethnic stock originating in the British Isles, and born in comfortable circumstances. . . . [He] tended to come from the professionalized upper middle class . . . [which was] politically active, and . . . [had] a tradition of judicial service. In college and legal education, the average justice was afforded very advantageous opportunities for training and association.[23]

Of the nine Justices who decided *Walker* this portrait would generally fit Justices Harlan, Stewart, and Clark but not Chief Justice Warren and Justices Black, Douglas, Brennan, White, and Fortas. A brief biographical analysis of each of these Justices is essential for documenting how their different life experiences influenced their judicial attitudes and votes.

CHIEF JUSTICE EARL WARREN

Earl Warren had been Chief Justice for fourteen years when the *Walker* case was decided in 1967. Appointed by President Eisenhower in 1953 Warren had become a powerful Chief Justice during his tenure. While one might not have predicted this particular career on the basis of an analysis of his background attributes, such an analysis does reveal a great deal about the development of his personality and attitude.[24]

A first-generation American, Warren came from a working-class family. His father was a railroad-car repairman for the Southern Pacific Railroad. He later became a building contractor and a real-estate broker, but during Warren's earliest years the family depended upon the railroad to provide the wages necessary for economic security.

Warren spent his formative years in Bakersfield, California, which at that time was very much a frontier town. Existing alongside each other were churches and gambling halls; Sunday School picnics and saloons; law-abiding, hard-working, honest citizens and thieves, prostitutes, and gun slingers. As a young man Warren observed and came into contact with all of these elements. Although his family's style of life in Bakersfield provided him with a sense of security, he was aware of the vicious labor-management feuds that had erupted into violence and strikes against the railroad from time to time.

Warren's father was convinced that education was the key to success; his savings were to be used to provide a college education for his son at the University of California at Berkeley. Warren himself was expected to work and to save his money. He had a paper route and also drove a mule-drawn grocery wagon. He later worked in the railroad yards during summer vacations. Although his parents constantly voiced their high expectations of their children (Warren had one sister), Warren himself never seemed to feel pressured to succeed. He was content to be a mediocre student. Law school became his goal because it dealt with the social sciences rather than the natural sciences, and he combined his last year as an undergraduate with his first year in law school at Berkeley's Boalt Hall.

Warren disliked several things about the law school's curriculum. He wanted greater emphasis on both "real" law and practical experience. Theory was of secondary importance to him, and he found himself drawn to the role of a trial lawyer. Thus, after serving in World War I, he began his career in public service working first in the City Attorney's office and then in the office of the District Attorney in Alameda County, California. These eighteen years were significant for Warren. During this period he developed his distaste for coerced confessions, biased juries, and overzealous police officials; his determination to get rid of corrupt, immoral, dishonest municipal officials; and his strong sense of right and wrong as the basis for decision and action by public servants. Warren never lost his sense of indignation toward unscrupulous sheriffs, legislators, judges, prosecutors, and policemen. His personal experiences in Alameda County insured that he would never accept official reports without some form of corroboration. He had encountered corruption and graft among law-enforcement officials and had conducted long and bitter fights to eliminate them.

Political-party affiliation was important in Warren's background from the beginning of his career. He considered himself a Republican, but due to an unusual provision in California law he was able to seek elected office by filing in the primary of the Democratic Party as well as the Republican Party. He always stressed non-partisanship in his campaigns for District Attorney of Alameda County, Attorney General of California, and finally Governor. His platforms and programs were generally more in line with the philosophy of the Democratic Party rather than that of the Republican Party.

During his long period of public service in California (1919–1953) Warren's ideas, beliefs, and attitudes emerged and were molded and shaped by his personal experiences. He "grew with each job" because he approached it with the determination to learn; in the process he "changed continually." "As his experiences increased, his mind absorbed new concepts."[25] During his terms as District Attorney and Attorney General he expanded and clarified his perception of these offices. Although he was a tough law enforcer, he wanted to win his public prosecutions fairly. However, there was a shadow on two cases that Warren prosecuted and won. It appeared later that a juror had been bought on one occasion and that a critical witness had committed perjury on another. Warren himself denied that the trials were anything but fair; nevertheless, he became even more diligent in setting high standards for public prosecutors. His insistence upon protection of the rights of the accused ultimately made it impossible for the police legally to convict the murderer of Warren's own father, and that case never came to trial. Warren also grew intellectually and morally as he worked to put an end to graft and corruption in law-enforcement agencies. He came to realize that great injustices could hide behind a sheriff's badge, and he carefully investigated to build cases that would bring these public-servant offenders to the bar of justice.

During Warren's three terms as Governor (1942–1954) he continued to grow as he met new demands. As Attorney General (1938–1942) during World War II he had been violently anti-Japanese and had led the movement for relocation of all Japanese from the West Coast. However, during his second (1946–1950) and third (1950–1953) terms as Governor, he worked to prevent demonstrations of racial prejudice and to aid peaceful resettlement of the returnees. His concept of the role of government also expanded, and he pressed for a health-insurance program that alienated many conservatives and brought charges of socialism. His role as the Vice-Presidential nominee of the Republican Party in 1948 and his subsequent increased involvement in national politics caused him to undertake intensive studies of the major domestic and international issues. Thus, once again, he demonstrated his ability to grow and develop as he met new expectations.

It should not have been surprising that Warren would take this same approach to his role as Chief Justice. While other men's attitudes jell or petrify by the time they reach their mid-fifties, Warren at sixty-two was still learning.[26] This was true in 1967 when Warren, now seventy-six, considered the issues raised by the demonstration case of *Walker* v. *Birmingham*.

JUSTICE HUGO L. BLACK

Hugo La Fayette Black spent his formative years in a small, rural county in east central Alabama. Clay County was synonymous with hard times, humble origins, and poverty. His father, a veteran of the Confederate Army, ran a small country store and was known to be a "usurious money lender."[27] However, he understood the value of education and moved his family to Ashland, the county seat of Clay County, so that his children might attend a good school. Black's mother came from a higher social, economic, and intellectual class than his father. She had been a postmistress and was later to serve as Black's first teacher. Her influence over the future Justice far exceeded that of his father. Religion was also an important factor during Black's formative years. The Protestant work ethic governed his home life, and regular church attendance at the local Baptist church was expected. Liquor was forbidden, although his father was a secret drinker.

As a teenager Black had watched with interest the trials at Ashland's courthouse. By the summer of 1904 he had made a clear decision concerning law as his future career. At the age of eighteen he moved to Tuscaloosa, Alabama, entering the University of Alabama School of Law. Although the school had only two professors and was limited in resources, it provided Black with basic skills and granted him an LL.B. degree when he completed the two-year curriculum.

Black began his legal career in Birmingham, a city quite different from Tuscaloosa as well as rural Clay County. The importance of these three geographic entities on the development of Black's personality, values, and attitude should not be underestimated. Clay County instilled in Black a protectiveness of the property rights of shopkeepers and merchants such as his father; Tuscaloosa produced in him a nostalgia for the beauty and romanticized traditions of the Old South; Birmingham brought him face-to-face with economic and political injustice.

Black's pre-court career included a number of jobs, each of which would later affect his "world view and style."[28] His professional career began as a specialist in damage suits, exposing him to the problems of labor-management conflicts as well as problems in criminal justice. He was appointed judge of the Birmingham Police Court and later elected public prosecutor. These positions brought him into contact with brutal law-enforcement officials and torture-chamber-type jails, for both of which he developed a lasting abhorrence.

Black was unusually talented as a trial lawyer; he also had a minor but successful criminal practice. He possessed the ability to sway juries and used dramatic techniques effectively. Although he made a point of not representing big corporations, this did not have an adverse effect on his personal income, which by 1925 approached $80,000 annually. He had an elegant home; an educated, attractive, and socially prominent wife[29]; and a growing family. He was a member of many groups including both the American Legion and the Ku Klux Klan. He was also a highly respected Baptist Sunday School teacher.[30]

Black's activities as special prosecutor investigating violations of Prohibition brought him to both state and national attention. Black's religious heritage and personal experiences combined to make him an ardent Prohibitionist. In the spring of 1924, working with the United States Assistant Attorney General he successfully prosecuted a number of violators in Mobile, Alabama. Anti-liquor feeling was high in Alabama, and Black's success as an investigator provided the basis for his decision to run for the office of United States Senator from Alabama. Alabama was a one-party (Democratic) state, but factions abounded and charismatic leaders fought for control. In order to win Black had to become a politician *par excellence:* dramatic yet cautious; cooperative yet independent; seemingly forthright yet devious. He was eminently successful in adjusting to this role.

As a freshman Senator in 1927 Black played the role of apprentice[31] and was relatively inconspicuous as he sought to master the procedures and traditions of the Senate. His first term was characterized primarily by opportunistic maneuvering to handle issues so as to secure re-election. With the advent of Franklin D. Roosevelt and his New Deal programs Black emerged as an independent force to be reckoned with. Originally Black was not part of the inner New Deal circle and was regarded by Roosevelt's advisors as an outside upstart. Ultimately, Black's success as head of a Senate Investigating Committee made his name a household word. He "brought a new dimension to one of the classic instruments of congressional power—the investigation."[32] Not until 1936 did Black become an active part of the FDR coalition. On at least two earlier occasions he had crossed swords with Roosevelt; however, the agreement of the two men concerning the "Nine Old Men"[33] who ruled the Supreme Court provided a solid basis for cooperation. Thus by 1936 Black had changed from a Democratic Party maverick to a party establishmentarian.[34] FDR wanted Black as a part of his new liberal Democratic Party, which was to include a new liberalized South of which Black was a good representative.

Yet Black had been a KKK member; he had joined the 1935 Senate filibuster against FDR's anti-lynching legislation and had refused to condemn the actions of Alabama officials in the infamous *Scottsboro* cases.[35] Even with these strikes against him, however, he still appeared more liberal than his colleagues from the South. His successful management of Presidential bills in the Senate gave rise to the speculation that FDR might encourage him to seek the Vice-Presidential nomination in 1940.

However, the Presidential offer to become the first New Deal appointee to the Supreme Court and the chance to use such a position to "change both the structure and function of the federal judiciary"[36] was extremely tempting to an acknowledged court critic, anxious to stop the "judicial overreaching of Congress."[37] Black succumbed and took his seat on the Supreme Court in 1937. He had been on the Court for thirty years when *Walker* was decided in 1967.

JUSTICE WILLIAM O. DOUGLAS

When the *Walker* case was argued before the Supreme Court in 1967 there was no doubt in anyone's mind that Justice William O. Douglas would support the civil-rights leaders. Appointed to the Court in 1939 Douglas at age sixty-nine had established a long history—some twenty-eight years—of support for the disadvantaged. The source of his judicial attitude can be found in part through an analysis of his background.

Douglas was raised in an atmosphere of economic insecurity. His father, a Presbyterian minister, had emigrated to the United States. His first major pastorate had been in Minnesota, where he met his future wife, a church organist. The Douglases had three children—two boys and a girl. William's early childhood was marred by severe infantile paralysis and anxiety over his father, whose health had never been good. When Rev. Douglas died in 1904, William was only five years old.

The Douglas family moved to Yakima, Washington, following the death of the father. There was very little money and both boys were expected to work from an early age. Douglas's mother took in washing while he chopped wood, delivered newspapers, washed store windows, swept floors, and mowed lawns. However, poverty was never an excuse for poor performance in school, and the three Douglas children excelled academically. Maternal demands for high grades, religious dedication, and hard work dominated Douglas's early life: he was described as pious, hard-working, and brilliant.[38]

The economic status of the family created a deep sense of class consciousness in the mind of William O. Douglas. He knew that he lived on the wrong side of the tracks: the beautiful homes of prosperous businessmen were on the other side. The Douglas children were not invited to the parties of the establishment, and Douglas felt that he was an outsider. He also resented being hired by fathers of his wealthy classmates to do jobs unsuitable for their sons. Only in the school classroom could Douglas compete as an equal, and he was valedictorian of his graduating class.

Although Douglas was not a political activist during his early years, he developed an intense dislike of Republicans. His mother had always voted Republican because her job security depended on wealthy Republicans. Douglas resented the control of wealthy Republicans, who, in his eyes, were pious hypocrites. It was true that they were the pillars of the Presbyterian Church, which the Douglases attended three times a week. However, according to Douglas, their handling of social problems and their attitude toward labor did not square with Christian doctrine. He resented their power. It would be very easy for Douglas later to identify with the Democratic Party as represented by FDR.

Douglas received a scholarship to Whitman College, where he majored in economics. During his four years as an undergraduate he held down three part-time jobs in order to send twenty dollars per month home to his mother. Yet he excelled academically. Douglas did not decide upon a legal career while at Whitman; his goal was to pursue graduate studies in English, and he firmly believed that he could secure a Rhodes scholarship that would allow him to study English literature at Oxford. He failed to get the scholarship. The impact of this failure was highly significant in that it reinforced Douglas's belief that the establishment controlled decision making and that the selection committee had sought a recipient from their own elite class of wealthy conservatives.

Having failed in his ambition to become a professor of English, Douglas became a man in search of a role. At this time two things occurred that persuaded him to pursue a legal career. First, he became good friends with an insurance salesman who never tired of extolling the power of the law as a source for righting society's wrongs. Second, in observing courtroom activity Douglas was impressed by a judge who reminded him of an Old Testament prophet and who seemed to personify order and righteousness. Thus Douglas found his calling. The question was first, where to go to law school, and second, how to pay for it.

Douglas decided almost immediately on an Ivy League law school and ultimately selected Columbia because of opportunities available for work in New York City. During his three years there he excelled both academically and financially. A job tutoring high-school seniors who were preparing applications for Ivy League schools paid quite well; moreover, Douglas was proving that he was not only equal but superior intellectually to those he perceived to be the establishment of wealthy Eastern bankers, financiers, and industrialists. These people wanted the best education for their sons and were willing to pay a poor boy from Washington state to guarantee it. For Douglas it was a sweet satisfaction.

Douglas was an outstanding student at Columbia Law School. He sat on the editorial board of the *Columbia Law Review* and was a research assistant for Professor Underhill Moore, an expert in commercial law. Graduation should have brought happiness and joy, but it was overshadowed by Douglas's disappointment at not being selected to clerk for Justice Harlan F. Stone. Stone had been dean of the law school as well as Douglas's professor. When Stone left Columbia and ultimately was appointed to the Supreme Court (1925), he followed the practice of many Justices in selecting as his clerk the top student from his alma mater. Douglas stood second in the Columbia Law School class of 1925; Albert McCormack ranked first and received the clerkship. For Douglas the world seemed bleak. In addition, he did not believe that his second place in the graduating class was the only criteria Stone used. Was the establishment again responsible?

However, Douglas was hired by the prestigious Wall Street firm of Cravath, Henderson, *et al.*[39] He was also invited to join the faculty at Columbia. Douglas profited from his experiences at

Cravath: he became an expert in commerical law and developed an excellent understanding of the maneuverings of Wall Street. At Columbia Douglas was not an outstanding teacher but received recognition for his legal articles and publications. His interest in an expanded legal curriculum, including courses in economics, history, and sociology, attracted the attention of the Dean of the Yale Law School. When the Columbia Law School faculty divided over curricular changes, Douglas was recruited by Yale and began his teaching duties there in 1928. By 1933 he had established a reputation as an expert in corporation law and had impressive publications and original field studies to his credit. Douglas, however, was contemptuous of many of his students at Yale. He believed that they were there simply because they were part of the establishment.

Ultimately even an endowed chair at Yale (Douglas had been appointed Sterling Professor of Law) seemed dull and mundane compared to the exciting world of Washington, D.C., in the 1930's. Douglas relished the idea of working in the New Deal programs, and in 1934 he agreed to direct an investigation for the Securities and Exchange Commission (SEC). It was then only a matter of time before he became chairman of the SEC itself in 1937 and Supreme Court Justice in 1939.

Douglas's rapid rise to the Court was due to a number of factors: his economic ideas were similar to FDR's, he had made friends among the top New Deal leadership, and he had established a solid record as an investigator of the Wall Street elite and the barons of the New York Stock Exchange. Douglas enjoyed exposing the rich and powerful who had misused their position, and he demanded accountability of this elite to the public. When Supreme Court Justice Louis D. Brandeis announced his retirement, Douglas began to lobby vigorously for the appointment. At first FDR was not inclined to appoint Douglas because he believed that the West needed geographic representation on the Court, and Douglas was perceived to be an Easterner. At this point Douglas began to emphasize his Washington state ties and his humble beginnings. He was successful, and on March 19, 1939, FDR nominated him to the Court.

Many believed that Douglas harbored political aspirations; he was suggested as a possible running mate for FDR in 1944. It was not until 1951 that Douglas publicly declared that he sought no career beyond that of Supreme Court Justice. By 1967, when *Walker* was decided, Douglas had already translated his belief that the law should be an instrument of social change into case votes and opinions for reversal of any and all types of discrimination against disadvantaged groups.[40]

JUSTICE TOM C. CLARK

Clark's rise to Associate Justice on the Supreme Court was primarily due to political ties. A Texas Democrat, Clark had been born into a politically active and prosperous family. They lived on the "best street in Dallas."[41] Scotch-Irish in descent, Clark's grandfather and father were both well-known as lawyers and politicians active in public affairs and Democratic politics. The family were strong Presbyterians, attending not only regular worship services but also the weekly Sunday School.[42]

Clark attended a public high school in Dallas. He was not a brilliant student but was popular and excelled in debate. After serving in World War I, Clark followed his family's tradition of legal careers. He enrolled in the University of Texas, where he secured his bachelor's degree and his law degree. He did not have to look for a job—the Dallas law firm headed by his father and brother received him as a matter of course.[43]

After five years of private law practice Clark entered the District Attorney's office as Civil District Attorney of Dallas County. His success during this period was remarkable. It was reported that he never lost a case; unless he was sure he had an ironclad prosecution he would not file a suit. Thus he developed the image of a winner. Clark also used this period to strengthen his ties to the Texas Democratic leadership in general and to Senator Tom Connally and Congressman Sam Rayburn in particular.

In 1932 Clark reentered private practice. He was still very active in politics, however, and promoted his law partner for Attorney General of Texas and later for Governor. Within five years his successful work in Democratic Party politics led to a federal appointment within the Department of Justice as special assistant to the Attorney General of the United States.[44]

Clark's work within the Department of Justice provided him with experiences upon which he would later draw as an Associate Justice of the Supreme Court. His work in the antitrust division brought him into contact with Senator Harry Truman, and a firm friendship developed between the two men. It also brought him into conflict with labor groups who, under the leadership of John L. Lewis, refused to obey an injunction to halt a coal strike. Clark successfully argued *United States* v. *United Mine Workers*, 330 U.S. 258 (1947), urging the Court to uphold a restraining order directed against labor. This case would be a significant precedent for *Walker*. Clark also worked with the relocation program for Japanese-Americans during World War II. In this capacity he dealt with two men who would later be his associates on the Court when *Walker* was decided—Earl Warren and Abe Fortas.[45]

Clark campaigned on behalf of Harry Truman's Vice-Presidential candidacy in 1944. With Truman's succession to the Presidency, it was only fifteen months before Clark received a Cabinet appointment as Attorney General.

The most significant issues during Clark's tenure as Attorney General dealt with civil liberties within the environment of the Cold War and with civil rights for blacks. Clark considered himself to be a champion of civil rights. He had insisted that the Federal Bar Association, which he had helped to organize and of which he was President, admit blacks to membership. He had recommended and secured an enlarged Civil Rights Division within the Department of Justice. Acting as *amicus curiae* in *Shelley* v. *Kraemer*, 334 U.S. 1 (1948), he wrote a persuasive brief against racially restrictive covenants.[46]

However, the NAACP was highly critical of Clark's performance as Attorney General. It insisted that he was not achieving enough, and some members even described him as being anti-civil-rights. When the Justice Department refused to take action against perpetrators of murders of black citizens in Monroe, Georgia, and Columbia, Tennessee, civil-rights leaders like Thurgood Marshall condemned Clark. Clark's defense was standard: the Federal Government had no constitutional power or authority to reach private acts of discrimination, only state acts. Clark argued that congressional legislation was necessary for the Justice Department to secure civil rights for blacks, and he began to push for such laws after 1947.[47]

The second significant area that Clark dealt with during the period when he was Attorney General was that of internal subversion. His experiences with this problem would have a major impact on his judicial attitude. Although publicly Clark insisted that his office would not become involved in Communist witch hunts, in practice it did. Clark developed three major approaches to deal with the "disloyal." He devised one program of deportation and repatriation for aliens (non-U.S. citizens) who made speeches derogatory to the American system. Clark also sought increased power for the Justice Department to investigate Communism and to use wiretaps to gather information. In particular, he wanted a loyalty program to monitor federal employees. Finally, Clark originated the notorious Attorney General's List of Subversive Organizations, which became one of his major tools to "combat communist propaganda."[48] His office published a list of all suspect organizations, and ultimately the loyalty of many innocent Americans came under attack as a result of guilt by association.[49] Thus it was not surprising that many people classified Attorney General Clark as an anti-civil-libertarian and deplored his appointment to the Supreme Court.

Truman, however, believed that Clark's activities had helped him to win his narrow victory in 1948. Clark seemed to have established a record as a good administrator while Attorney General, but it was no secret that he was ambitious for a Supreme Court appointment. He had expected to be appointed to Chief Justice Stone's position, but Truman had selected Fred Vinson to fill that vacancy. Clark had to wait two years until the death of Justice Frank Murphy created another vacancy. It seemed ironic that Clark should replace this left-liberal, Catholic Justice. No one contended that Clark was an intellectual or a brilliant lawyer who deserved the appointment on the basis of merit. It was his "great astuteness as a political technician" and his "amazing talent for making and using friends" that secured his appointment in the summer of 1949.[50]

When the *Walker* case was decided by the Court in 1967 Clark had been on the bench for eighteen years. He had rendered a number of pro-civil-rights opinions and had made some civil-libertarian decisions in this period. However, he had brought to the Court a "Cold War point of view" and had adhered to it tenaciously in every case in which protests against official governmental policy was present.[51] Of all the Justices who participated in *Walker* Clark was the one most likely to take judicial notice of the fact that one of the defendants in the case, Rev. Martin Luther King, Jr., was actively engaging in anti-Vietnam-War protests.[52] An Attorney General who had developed plans to stamp out internal subversion and who had worked closely with the FBI's J. Edgar Hoover[53] in information gathering would not likely bring an unbiased attitude to the *Walker* case.

JUSTICE JOHN MARSHALL HARLAN II

John Marshall Harlan fitted Professor John Schmidhauser's picture of the model Supreme Court Justice. He was a member of the establishment[54] socially, economically, politically, and religiously. Born in Chicago, he received an Ivy League education and later lived and worked in the East (New York City). A member of a high-status Protestant denomination (Presbyterian), Harlan also came from a family that revered the legal profession and was politically active, with deep roots in the Republican Party.[55]

Harlan's father, grandfather, and great-grandfather had all been attorneys. His father had been involved in civic affairs in Chicago and had served as Alderman. Harlan's grandfather, the first Justice John Marshall Harlan, was a political activist and lawyer as well as a distinguished member of the Supreme Court from 1877 to 1911. Harlan's great-grandfather was a Kentucky lawyer, Congressman, and state Attorney General.[56] Harlan's family heritage reached far back into American colonial history. The first Harlan to reach America came from Durham, England, in 1687. He was a Quaker, and religion played a part in his move from England to America. Once in America he, like his descendants, became involved in politics and in 1695 was elected Governor of Delaware.

Harlan was raised in an affluent family; economic security was never a worry. He was not lacking in role models to follow, and his pursuit of a legal career was no surprise. His early family environment provided him with love and affection but it was not permissive.[57] Harlan was expected to excel academically and did. Upon graduation from Princeton University he received a Rhodes Scholarship to attend Balliol College of Oxford University. Upon his return to the United States he pursued his legal studies at New York University and passed the bar exam in 1924.[58]

Harlan attracted the attention of a brilliant trial lawyer, Emory Buckner, who was impressed by Harlan's ability, his "sense of duty," and his "tireless capacity for hard work."[59] Buckner invited him to join the large and prestigious New York law firm of Root and Ballantine. The firm specialized in corporate law; most of its clients were large corporations such as du Pont.[60] Harlan later held a position as Assistant United States Attorney. He acquired a reputation as a brilliant trial lawyer, particularly in handling corporate suits.

During the thirty years that he spent as a Manhattan attorney, Harlan also acted as legal counsel for the New York State Crime Commission, which Governor Thomas E. Dewey had appointed to investigate gambling and racketeering. Harlan proved to be an incorruptible investigator and a successful prosecutor. He also became a very close friend of Governor Dewey, who, after retirement, joined Harlan's law firm as a senior partner.[61]

Harlan's ties to the Dewey faction of the Republican Party

made it politically expedient for President Eisenhower to reward him first with an appointment to the United States Second Circuit Court of Appeals for New York, Vermont, and Connecticut, and then, one year later, to promote him to the Supreme Court. Eisenhower was aware of the value of Dewey's support at the Republican Party convention in 1952.[62]

Harlan took his seat on the Court in 1955. When *Walker* reached the Court for decision in 1967 he had been there for twelve years and was sixty-seven years of age.

JUSTICE WILLIAM J. BRENNAN, JR.

William J. Brennan, Jr., was one of those paradoxical appointments that Presidents make from time to time. A Democrat and a Catholic, he was appointed by a Republican and Protestant President. An understanding of Brennan's appointment turns on an understanding of the man, his attitudes, and his qualities, which merged to raise him to presidential attention.

Brennan, like Warren and Fortas, was a first-generation American. His parents were Irish immigrants who had come to the United States in 1890 and settled in Newark, New Jersey. His father's first job was as an ordinary laborer heaving coal in a brewery. He was committed to the cause of organized labor and became a prominent labor leader and a union official for the American Federation of Labor (A. F. of L.). The world of New Jersey politics offered him economic and social advancement, and he was elected to four terms as City Commissioner. Democratic politics thus provided economic security for the Brennan family, which included eight children.[63]

William J. Brennan, Jr., was born on April 25, 1906, in Newark and attended public high school where, according to classmates, he took so many prizes and honors that there were "none left for the other students."[64] Although Brennan worked at such odd jobs as delivering milk and making change on Newark's Broad Street trolley, the money was merely pocket money,[65] *not* necessary to supplement the family income nor to provide for his college education, as was the case with Chief Justice Warren. His undergraduate career at the University of Pennsylvania was paid for by his father.

Brennan graduated *cum laude* from the Wharton School of Finance and then entered Harvard Law School in 1928 on a scholarship.[66] While a student at Harvard he came under the influence of Professor Felix Frankfurter, whose impact on his stu-

dents was profound. As an Associate Justice of the Supreme Court
his influence on junior Justices during their socialization period
on the Court was also of critical importance. The cornerstone of
Frankfurter's philosophy, which he taught at Harvard and demonstrated later on the Court, was that of judicial restraint—the
belief that the Court should not interfere with Congress. It was a
doctrine that Brennan had to deal with as a student and later as a
Justice.[67]

Brennan received his law degree in 1931, ranking near the top
of his class. His gregarious personality attracted many friends,
and one of particular importance was Bernard Shanley, who
would later be President Eisenhower's appointment secretary.
Following graduation from Harvard Brennan entered into private
law practice with a prestigious law firm in Newark, where he was
a trial lawyer specializing in labor law. He gained a high reputation for resolving difficult management-employee problems.

World War II interrupted his practice but did allow him to
work within the Army General Staff Corps on industrial and
labor-manpower cases. He served as a legal aide under James P.
Mitchell, then Director of the Civilian Personnel Division of the
Army Service Forces. One of his important assignments was to
maintain good relations between unions and companies working
on war contracts. Brennan ultimately became Labor Branch
Chief of the Civilian Personnel Division of Army Ordnance.[68]
These experiences helped to expand Brennan's knowledge of labor law and gave him practical experience in dealing with labor-
management disputes. In addition, he became close friends with
his army superior, James P. Mitchell, who would ultimately become Secretary of Labor under President Eisenhower.

Following the war Brennan returned to his law firm in New
Jersey, where he soon found himself deluged with more clients
and business than he could handle. While his father had seen
labor-management problems from the side of labor, Brennan
found himself representing large manufacturing enterprises in
their disputes with labor. As legal counsel in labor matters to
Western Electric Company in Kearney, New Jersey, Brennan
again had James Mitchell as his superior. World War II had set
off a wave of labor disputes and Brennan's experience was in
demand.[69] In fact, his practice had grown so large that by 1949 his
health was suffering. He needed a different type of job, and his
friends came to his aid. Most of these friends were Republicans
who willingly overlooked Brennan's father's political activity and

focused only on the fact that Brennan himself had never been actively involved in Democratic Party politics.

Acting on the suggestions of important leaders of the Republican Party in New Jersey, Republican Governor Alfred E. Driscoll offered Brennan an appointment to the state bench and in 1949 Brennan took his place on the New Jersey Superior Court. The following year he was assigned to the Appellate Division of the Superior Court. At this time his activities to modernize court procedure brought him to the attention of Arthur T. Vanderbilt, Chief Justice of the Supreme Court of New Jersey. Vanderbilt came to feel admiration and affection for the younger justice and thus became a sponsor for his protegé. Vanderbilt urged Governor Driscoll to promote Brennan to the New Jersey Supreme Court, and Driscoll obliged by appointing Brennan for the term of March 24, 1952–March 19, 1956.[70]

Brennan's activities on the state bench from 1949 to 1956 gave him invaluable experience and thrust him into positions of high visibility. His judicial opinions and his activities as a "crusader for speedier trials" brought favorable publicity.[71] His plans for ending congestion in the courts was seen as a model for other states. Thus, early in 1956 he was invited to address the U.S. Attorney General's Special Conference on Congestion in the Courts, and his discussion of the new procedures that he had helped formulate for New Jersey created a favorable impression in the mind of Eisenhower's Attorney General, Herbert Brownell.[72]

When Associate Justice Sherman Minton announced his retirement, Brennan's friends immediately suggested the young justice for the vacancy on the Supreme Court of the United States. President Eisenhower listened to recommendations from Secretary of Labor James Mitchell, from Bernard Shanley, his appointment secretary, and from Attorney General Herbert Brownell. Brennan satisfied two of Eisenhower's criteria: youth and judicial experience. His friends believed that his views were similar to those of the President and that he was a moderate in his judicial philosophy.

Brennan's judicial record on the New Jersey bench indicated that he held firm convictions against violations of Fourth and Fifth Amendment rights. He believed that evidence secured illegally should not be used to convict the accused and that no accused person should be subjected to intense police interrogation designed to secure a confession. However, Brennan was less dogmatic and more willing to overlook police infractions of the rules in cases involving gambling offenders in New Jersey than in those involving blacks, indigents, and juveniles accused of crimes.[73] He looked at the issues in each case, and his state-court opinions were classified as "clear, thoughtful, forceful, yet moderate."[74]

Eisenhower apparently found this record satisfactory and nominated Brennan to fill the vacancy on the Supreme Court. Brennan was confirmed by the Senate in the spring of 1957. By the time of the *Walker* decision in 1967 he had built a ten-year record as a liberal Justice who could be counted on to support individual rights.

JUSTICE POTTER STEWART

Potter Stewart's background was similar in many ways to that of John Marshall Harlan. Born into a politically active family, he was provided with a legal and political role model in the person of his father. As a child growing up in Cincinnati, Ohio, he would listen to his father rehearsing his courtroom arguments while shaving. James Garfield Stewart passed to his son a family tradition of civic and political involvement, a deep commitment to the Republican Party, and a record of legal achievements. The elder Stewart served as mayor of Cincinnati from 1938 to 1947 and at the time of his son's appointment to the Court was himself a judge on the Ohio Supreme Court.[75]

Stewart studied at the prestigious and exclusive Hotchkiss Preparatory School in Lakeville, Connecticut. Hotchkiss was *the* prep school for Yale, and Stewart, as expected, entered Yale College. He graduated *cum laude* and Phi Beta Kappa and was awarded a fellowship to Cambridge University to study international law.[76]

During his undergraduate years at Yale Stewart wavered between journalism and law as his future career. He was chairman of the Yale *Daily News* and during his summer vacations in Cincinnati gained practical experience by working as a cub reporter for the *Times-Star*, the Taft family newspaper.[77] However, upon returning from England he entered Yale Law School, where he made law review and graduated *cum laude*. During World War II he served with the Navy and then spent three years with a Wall Street law firm before returning to Cincinnati to immerse himself in politics.[78]

Following family tradition Stewart ran for city council and was elected for two terms, serving one year as Vice Mayor of the city. His commitment to the Republican Party and his belief in civic responsibility made him a serious and dedicated campaigner. Having decided to enter politics, he campaigned day and night;

he seemed to attend every meeting, small or large, near or far, early or late. Old-time professional Republicans in Ohio welcomed him to their ranks.[79]

Ohio Republican politics had long been dominated by the Taft family, and it was not surprising that Stewart backed Senator Robert A. Taft in his bid for the Republican Party's nomination to the Presidency in 1952. Eisenhower's victory in securing with Dewey's support the nomination over Taft could have created irreconcilable factions within the party, and to heal party wounds Eisenhower sought to use job appointments as a means for consoling Eastern (Dewey) and Midwestern (Taft) Republicans. Thus in 1954 Stewart was offered an appointment to the federal bench—the Sixth Circuit Court of Appeals.[80] Stewart at that point had to decide whether to continue in politics. He concluded that he wanted "to be part of the law" and accepted the appointment.[81]

Four years later, in 1958, Eisenhower faced the task of selecting his fifth appointment to the Supreme Court. During this period Stewart had gained the judicial experience and expertise that Eisenhower considered to be of singular importance. Moreover, Eisenhower had been assured that Stewart held the right ideological views, and Stewart was backed by the conservative Ohio Republican Senator John Bricker, who himself believed in limiting the power of the Court.[82]

Although Bricker lost his bid for re-election to the Senate, Stewart's nomination went forward unopposed by Democrats, who found his credentials acceptable. Stewart's judicial record on the Court of Appeals had revealed a few of his ideas about the role of the Court and the proper function of a Justice. At least four characteristics could be documented on the basis of this record. First, his opinions defied the label of liberal or conservative. Second, his main strength seemed to be his ability to write "solid, keenly reasoned opinions" in "clear and forceful" English: his particular "grace" was his writing.[83] Third, he had a clear perception of his judicial duty deciding only on the basis of specific case issues interpreted as narrowly as possible.[84] Fourth, his opinions also indicated his belief in fairness, which he once said "is really what justice is."[85] It was, perhaps, Stewart's record of deciding issues narrowly that made him acceptable to Democrats like Senator James O. Eastland, Chairman of the Senate Judiciary Committee.[86] Nominated to the Court in 1958 and confirmed in 1959,[87] Stewart had been serving on the high bench for eight and a half years when *Walker* was decided in June 1967.

JUSTICE BYRON R. WHITE

Byron R. White possessed one attribute that none of his judicial colleagues could claim: he had been a professional athlete. A top football player would seem to be out of character as a Supreme Court Justice. However, White combined a powerful physique with a brilliant intellect. His friendship with a President who came from a family that admired this precise combination helped to bring about his appointment in 1962 as Associate Justice of the Supreme Court.[88]

White did not come from a wealthy, well-educated, socially prominent family. He was born in Fort Collins, Colorado, and spent his formative years in a small farming community (Wellington) in northern Colorado. White's father had been orphaned at an early age, and neither he nor White's mother had completed high school. The couple had moved to Colorado from Iowa following their marriage, and White's father worked as branch manager for a lumber-supply company. The family was staunchly Republican in their politics and White's father was politically active, serving as Mayor of Wellington for a time.

White attended the local high school and worked in the sugar-beet fields and with a railroad section crew. The family was poor, but unlike that of William O. Douglas, it did not feel poor since everyone in the community lived in similar circumstances.[89]

White's parents were determined that their two sons should have both a high-school and a college education, since they believed that education was the ladder to success. They encouraged White to work hard so that he could receive an academic scholarship to the University of Colorado. He was successful.[90]

During his undergraduate years at the University of Colorado, White supplemented his scholarship by waiting tables in fraternity and sorority houses. He maintained a high scholastic standing, graduating Phi Beta Kappa and valedictorian.[91] Achievements bringing the greatest fame, however, occurred on the football field. His spectacular performances in his senior year earned him the title "triple threat halfback." The Pittsburgh Steelers, a professional football team, offered him $15,000 to play for them for one season; Oxford University was ready to receive him on a Rhodes Scholarship at the same time. White managed to accept both offers. After starring for the Steelers in 1938, White was in excellent condition to play rugby for Oxford during 1939.[92]

White apparently decided on a legal career in the same manner that he had decided to abandon the Republican Party for the

Democratic FDR New Deal coalition. White had compared the platforms, programs, and promises of the two parties and had reasoned that those of the Democratic Party were better. He applied this same kind of analysis to evaluate his personal skills in order to select a career, and law came out in first place.[93]

Using funds from his football earnings White entered Yale Law School in October 1939. He did not pursue an uninterrupted legal career, however. During 1940–41 he left Yale to play football with the Detroit Lions, primarily to make money. World War II interrupted his activities and he joined Naval Intelligence and was posted to the South Pacific. It was not until 1946 that White could complete his law degree from Yale. He graduated *magna cum laude* that year and was immediately accepted for the clerkship position with Chief Justice Fred Vinson.[94] During this year in Washington, White reestablished a previous friendship with John F. Kennedy. He had met Kennedy in England at a Rhodes Scholarship reception given by Kennedy's father, who was the American ambassador. The two men met a second time in the Solomon Islands during World War II. When White left Washington in 1947 he would not see Kennedy again except for one brief meeting when as Senator from Massachusetts Kennedy delivered an address at the University of Denver.[95]

White spent thirteen years in private practice in Denver, his specialty being corporation law. In 1959 he became extremely active in politics and headed a group of Colorado lawyers who were pushing the Kennedy presidential candidacy. Kennedy's victory in November 1960 resulted in White's appointment as Deputy Attorney General, a post he held from 1961 to 1962.[96] In this position White's most important task was dealing with the "Freedom Riders" in Montgomery, Alabama, in May 1961. White's experiences during this period were significant in light of his later participation as a Supreme Court Justice in the *Walker* case. The local violence that engulfed participants in the "Freedom Rides" when they reached Montgomery on May 19, 1961, had made it necessary for the Attorney General's office to take action. White helped to organize a special force of U.S. marshals and send them to Montgomery to protect the civil-rights demonstrators. In addition, he was involved in the decision to apply for an *ex parte* injunction directed against state and local Alabama groups forbidding them to interfere with the "Freedom Riders." The federal government based its power to do this on the commerce clause of the Constitution. Thus White had seen an *ex parte* injunction used to support and protect civil-rights demonstrators.[97]

When the *Walker* case came to the Supreme Court in 1967, White had been on that tribunal for five years, having been appointed by President Kennedy in 1962. White was the only member of the Court with recent personal experience dealing specifically with protest demonstrators in Alabama.

JUSTICE ABE FORTAS

Abe Fortas did not fit the model of the Anglo-Saxon, Protestant judicial figure postulated by many political scientists as the prototype of a Supreme Court Justice. He was born into an immigrant family and was a first-generation American. His family, who were Orthodox Jews, had emigrated from England and settled in Tennessee.[98] The family's socio-economic status was lower-middle-class, and their social contacts were limited to the small Jewish community (6,000 out of a total population of 160,000) in Memphis. Fortas's father held a number of jobs, including shopkeeper, jeweler, pawnbroker, and cabinet maker, and he drifted from one trade to another. His influence on his son seemed negligible.

Fortas inherited from his family a belief in the value of education as a means of rising within the American social and economic structure. He finished public high school in Memphis in three years and was second in his class. His academic diligence and success in debate won him a scholarship to a small liberal-arts school. When he entered he was only sixteen years old and in a definite religious minority: only six Jewish students. As a child Fortas had attended synagogue regularly; however, at college he dropped out of organized religious activities except for the daily Presbyterian chapel services that were mandatory.

Graduating at nineteen, Fortas calculated that his talents were appropriate for a legal career and applied to both Harvard and Yale law schools. He chose Yale because its scholarship offer exceeded Harvard's.

Fortas was influenced most profoundly at Yale by two professors: Thurman Arnold and William O. Douglas. The former would become his law partner and the latter his associate on the Supreme Court. Fortas excelled at Yale. He was editor-in-chief of the *Yale Law Journal*—an honor usually given to the student highest in academic rank. He was also invited to join the Yale Law School faculty upon graduation.

At this point in Fortas's career a number of variables can be considered in attempting to understand his personality and values. His had been a background of relative economic insecurity;

he lacked a successful role model in his father; religion had been put aside at an early age; education and academic honors were seen as the means to success. His personality has been described as moody and introspective. Yet he also understood the necessity of socialization and could be charming and gregarious when he chose.

Fortas's pre-court career placed him primarily within the federal bureaucracy and connected him closely to the Democratic Party. Although he taught part-time at Yale, he worked in such New Deal programs as the Agricultural Adjustment Administration and the Securities and Exchange Commission; he served as General Counsel to the Public Works Administration and was Undersecretary of the Interior Department. His friendship with Professors Thurman Arnold and William O. Douglas had brought him into the vanguard of the New Deal and diverse activities: negotiating marketing agreements, investigating public utilities, rewriting bankruptcy statutes, and dealing with the relocation problems of Japanese-Americans during World War II. In this last capacity he became acquainted with Tom Clark and Earl Warren.

Following the war, Fortas entered private practice in Washington, D.C., with his former professor and colleague, Thurman Arnold. They created a highly successful law firm; it was, however, marked by two entirely different emphases. On the one hand, the firm represented civil-liberties claimants—particularly governmental employees who had been dismissed from their jobs as loyalty-security risks during the McCarthy Communist witch hunts of the late 1940's and early 1950's. On the other hand, the firm was committed to the goal of financial success and as a result represented some of the largest and wealthiest corporations in America, including Coca-Cola, Lever Brothers, and Western Union.

By the 1960's the firm was one of the three largest and wealthiest in Washington, with Fortas making around $200,000 a year. The firm was admired and acclaimed by civil libertarians and financiers alike. Appointed by the Court to argue for the Sixth Amendment right to counsel in state trials for the indigent Clarence Earl Gideon, Fortas received no fee and poured his personal time, energy, and resources into the case. At the same time, Fortas was advising clients like Braniff Airlines on how to maneuver successfully within the gray areas of numerous federal rules and regulations.

Fortas's marriage in 1935 to Carolyn Agger (B.A. Barnard College; LL.B. Yale Law School) reinforced his dual role perception and value system. Mrs. Fortas later described her husband as a liberal, but not a doctrinaire liberal. She considered him a conservative in the sense of understanding the realities of the business world in which he lived and worked.

Fortas did not seek promotion to the Supreme Court; his was much more the case of the "role seeking the man."[99] As a personal friend and legal advisor to Vice President Lyndon B. Johnson, whom he had known from the earliest days of the New Deal, Fortas was one of the first people to whom President Johnson turned upon assuming office after the assassination of John F. Kennedy in November 1963. The resignation of Justice Arthur Goldberg to assume the position of United States Ambassador to the United Nations left vacant the so-called Jewish seat on the Court in 1965. President Johnson was determined that Fortas should take this position, and his insistence succeeded. Fortas was confirmed by the Senate and took his seat on the Court in 1965—two years before the *Walker* case would be decided.

Opinion Day: The Supreme Court Announces the *Walker* Decision

The decision in *Walker* was handed down on the last day (June 12) of the Supreme Court's 1966–1967 term. The Court at that time still followed the tradition of reserving Monday as the day for announcement of decisions. Later the tradition would be modified so that Court decisions might be announced on other days as well, although Monday still continued to be preferred.[100]

June is a busy month for the Court as it prepares for its recess. By tradition prior notice is not given concerning the date on which a Court decision is to be announced. Reporters, parties to the case, and lawyers simply have to guess. The press was correct in assuming, however, that the last Monday of the Court's 1966–1967 term would be significant, and the courtroom was therefore packed when the *Walker* decision was announced.

Following the usual practice, Chief Justice Earl Warren nodded to Justice Potter Stewart to announce the decision. As soon as Stewart stated the case name, the printed text of *Walker* was distributed by the Court Clerk's office to the assembled reporters.[101] They were then in a position to follow the unfolding of the Court's argument. Two major points were quickly recognized by the press: first, the civil-rights demonstators had lost; second, the Court had split five to four, with Chief Justice Warren in the minority. The arguments, reasoning, and rationales were there in the printed

Court record for all time and for all to read. Justice Potter Stewart had written the opinion for a five-man majority that included Justices Black, Clark, Harlan, and White. Since Chief Justice Warren was not with the majority, the opinion had been assigned to Justice Stewart by the senior Associate Justice voting with the majority—in this instance, Justice Black.[102] The four dissenters included Chief Justice Warren and Justices Douglas, Brennan, and Fortas. With three of the dissenting Justices writing separate dissents, the total Court record was approximately forty-three pages long.[103] It clearly indicated intense differences of judicial attitude, opposing perceptions of issues, and conflicting interpretations of precedent.

WALKER v. BIRMINGHAM
388 U.S. 307; 87 S.Ct. 1824; 18 L.Ed.2d 1210 (1967)

Mr. Justice Stewart delivered the opinion of the Court, saying in part:

On Wednesday, April 10, 1963 officials of Birmingham, Alabama, filed a bill of complaint in a state circuit court which asked for injunctive relief against 139 individuals and two organizations. The bill . . . stated that:

> Respondents [had] sponsored . . . 'sit-in' demonstrations, 'kneel-in' demonstrations, mass street parades, trespasses on private property . . . congregating in mobs, . . . [and] unlawfully picketing private places of business. . . .

It was alleged that this conduct was "calculated to provoke breaches of the peace, threaten[ed] the safety, peace and tranquility of the City," and placed "an undue burden and strain upon the manpower of the Police Department.". . .

The circuit judge granted a temporary injunction . . . enjoining the petitioners from . . . participating in or encouraging mass street parades. . . .

The petitioners announced that "injunction or no injunction we are going to march. . . ." The next afternoon . . . a large crowd gathered. . . . A group of about 50 or 60 proceeded to parade along the sidewalk while a crowd of 1,000 to 1,500 onlookers stood by, "clapping, and hollering, and [w]hooping." . . . On Easter Sunday, April 14, a crowd of between 1,500 and 2,000 people congregated in the midafternoon in the vicinity of Seventh Avenue and Eleventh Street North in Birmingham. One of the petitioners was seen organizing members of the crowd in formation. A group of about 50, headed by three other petitioners, started down the sidewalk two abreast. At least one other petitioner was among the marchers. Some 300 or 400 people from among the onlookers followed in a crowd that occupied the entire width of the street and overflowed onto the sidewalks. Violence occurred. Members of the crowd threw rocks that injured a newspaperman and damaged a police motorcycle.

The next day the city officials who had requested the injunction applied to the state circuit court for an order to show cause why the petitioners should not be held in contempt for violating it. At the ensuing hearing the petitioners sought to attack the constitutionality of the injunction on the ground that it was vague and overbroad, and restrained free speech. They also sought to attack the Birmingham parade ordinance upon similar grounds, and upon the further ground that the ordinance had previously been administered in an arbitrary and discriminatory manner.

The circuit judge refused to consider any of these contentions, pointing out that there had been neither a motion to dissolve the injunction, nor an effort to comply with it by applying for a permit from the city commission before engaging in the Good Friday and Easter Sunday parades. Consequently, the court held that the only issues before it were whether it had jurisdiction to issue the temporary injunction, and whether thereafter the petitioners had knowingly violated it. Upon these issues the court found against the petitioners, and imposed upon each of them a sentence of five days in jail and a $50 fine, in accord with an Alabama statute. The Supreme Court of Alabama affirmed. . . .

Howat v. *Kansas* [1922] was decided by this Court almost 50 years ago. That was a case in which people had been punished by a Kansas trial court for refusing to obey an antistrike injunction. . . .

This Court . . . fully approved the validity of the rule of state law upon which the judgment of the Kansas court was grounded: "An injunction duly issuing out of a court of general jurisdiction with equity powers upon pleadings properly invoking its action, and served upon persons made parties therein and within the jurisdiction, must be obeyed by them however erroneous the action of the court may be, even if the error be in the assumption of the validity of a seeming but void law going to the merits of the case. It is for the court of first instance to determine the question of the validity of the law, and until its decision is reversed for error by orderly review, either by itself or by a higher court, its orders based on its decision are to be respected, and disobedience of them is contempt of its lawful authority, to be punished."

In the present case, however, we are asked to hold that this rule of law, upon which the Alabama courts relied, was constitutionally impermissible. We are asked to say that the Constitution compelled Alabama to allow the petitioners to violate this injunction, to organize and engage in these mass street parades and demonstrations, without any previous effort on their part to have the injunction dissolved or modified, or any attempt to secure a parade permit in accordance with its terms. Whatever the limits of *Howat* v. *Kansas*,* we cannot accept the petitioners' contentions in the circumstances of this case. . . . This is not a case where the injunction was transparently invalid or had only a frivolous pretense to validity. We have consistently recognized the strong interest of state and local governments in regulating the use of their streets and other public places. . . . When protest takes the form of mass demonstrations, parades, or picketing on public streets and sidewalks, the free passage of traffic and the prevention of public disorder and violence become important objects of legitimate state concern. As the Court stated, in *Cox* v. *Louisiana*, "We emphatically reject the notion . . . that the First and Fourteenth Amendments afford the same kind of freedom to those who would communicate ideas by conduct such as patrolling, marching, and picketing on streets and highways, as these amendments afford to those who communicate ideas by pure speech." . . .

The generality of the language contained in the Birmingham parade ordinance upon which the injunction was based would unquestionably raise substantial constitutional issues concerning some of its provisions. . . . The petitioners, however, did not even attempt to apply to the Alabama courts for an authoritative construction of the ordinance. Had they done so, those courts might have given the licensing authority granted in the ordinance a narrow and precise scope. . . . It could not be assumed that this ordinance was void on its face. The breadth and vagueness of the injunction itself would also unquestionably be subject to substantial constitutional question. But the way to raise that question was to apply to the Alabama courts to have the injunction modi-

---

*In *In re Green*, 369 U.S. 689, the petitioner was convicted of criminal contempt for violating a labor injunction issued by an Ohio court. Relying on the pre-emptive command of the federal labor law, the Court held that the state courts were required to hear Green's claim that the state court was *without jurisdiction* to issue the injunction. The petitioner in *Green*, unlike the petitioners here, had attempted to challenge the validity of the injunction *before* violating it by promptly applying to the issuing court for an order vacating the injunction. The petitioner in *Green* had further offered to prove that the court issuing the injunction had agreed to its violation as an appropriate means of testing its validity.

fied or dissolved. The injunction in all events clearly prohibited mass parading without a permit, and the evidence shows that the petitioners fully understood that prohibition when they violated it.

The petitioners also claim that they were free to disobey the injunction because the parade ordinance on which it was based had been administered in the past in an arbitrary and discriminatory fashion. In support of this claim they sought to introduce evidence that, a few days before the injunction issued, requests for permits to picket had been made to a member of the city commission. One request had been rudely rebuffed and this same official had later made clear that he was without power to grant the permit alone, since the issuance of such permits was the responsibility of the entire city commission. Assuming the truth of this proffered evidence, it does not follow that the parade ordinance was void on its face. The petitioners, moreover, did not apply for a permit either to the commission itself or to any commissioner after the injunction issued. Had they done so, and had the permit been refused, it is clear that their claim of arbitrary or discriminatory administration of the ordinance would have been considered by the state circuit court upon a motion to dissolve the injunction.

This case would arise in quite a different constitutional posture if the petitioners, before disobeying the injunction, had challenged it in the Alabama courts, and had been met with delay or frustration of their constitutional claims. But there is no showing that such would have been the fate of a timely motion to modify or dissolve the injunction. There was an interim of two days between the issuance of the injunction and the Good Friday march. The petitioners give absolutely no explanation of why they did not make some application to the state court during that period. The injunction had issued *ex parte;* if the court had been presented with the petitioners' contentions, it might well have dissolved or at least modified its order in some respects. If it had not done so, Alabama procedure would have provided for an expedited process of appellate review. It cannot be presumed that the Alabama courts would have ignored the petitioners' constitutional claims. . . .

The rule of law that Alabama followed in this case reflects a belief that in the fair administration of justice no man can be judge in his own case, however exalted his station, however righteous his motive, and irrespective of his race, color, politics, or religion. This Court cannot hold that the petitioners were constitutionally free to ignore all the procedures of the law and carry their battle to the streets. One may sympathize with the petitioners' impatient commitment to their cause. But respect for judicial process is a small price to pay for the civilizing hand of law, which alone can give abiding meaning to constitutional freedom.

Affirmed.

Mr. Chief Justice Warren, whom Mr. Justice Brennan and Mr. Justice Fortas join, dissenting.

Petitioners in this case contend that they were convicted under an ordinance that is unconstitutional on its face because it submits their First and Fourteenth Amendment rights to free speech and peaceful assembly to the unfettered discretion of local officials. They further contend that the ordinance was unconstitutionally applied to them because the local officials used their discretion to prohibit peaceful demonstrations by a group whose political viewpoint the officials opposed. The Court does not dispute these contentions, but holds that petitioners may nonetheless be convicted and sent to jail because the patently unconstitutional ordinance was copied into an injunction—issued *ex parte* without prior notice or hearing on the request of the Commissioner of Public Safety—forbidding all persons having notice of the injunction to violate the ordinance without any limitation of time. . . .

The salient facts can be stated very briefly. Petitioners are Negro ministers who sought to express their concern about racial discrimination in Birmingham, Alabama by holding peaceful protest demonstrations in that city on Good Friday and Easter Sunday 1963. For obvious reasons, it was important for the significance of the demonstrations that they be held on those particular dates. A representative of petitioners' organization went to the City Hall and asked "to see the person or persons in charge to issue permits, permits for parading, picketing, and demonstrating." She was directed to Public Safety Commissioner Connor, who denied her request for a permit in terms that left no doubt that petitioners were not going to be issued a permit under any circumstances. "He said, 'No, you will not get a permit in Birmingham, Alabama to picket. I will picket you over to the City Jail,' and he repeated that twice." A second, telegraphic request was also summarily denied, in a telegram signed by "Eugene 'Bull' Connor," with the added information that permits could be issued only by the full City Commission, a three-man body consisting of Commissioner Connor and two others. According to petitioners' offer of proof, the truth of which is assumed for purposes of this case, parade permits had uniformly been issued for all other groups by the city clerk on the request of the traffic bureau of the police department, which was under Commissioner Connor's direction. The requirement that the approval of the full Commission be obtained was applied only to this one group.

Understandably convinced that the City of Birmingham was not going to authorize their demonstrations under any circumstances, petitioners proceeded with their plans despite Commissioner Connor's orders. On Wednesday, April 10, at 9 in the evening, the city filed in a state circuit court a bill of complaint seeking an *ex parte* injunction. . . . The Circuit Court issued the injunction in the form requested, and in effect ordered petitioners and all other persons having notice of the order to refrain for an unlimited time from carrying on any demonstrations without a permit. A permit, of course, was clearly unobtainable; the city would not have sought this injunction if it had any intention of issuing one.

Petitioners were served with copies of the injunction at various times on Thursday and on Good Friday. Unable to believe that such a blatant and broadly drawn prior restraint on their First Amendment rights could be valid, they announced their intention to defy it and went ahead with the planned peaceful demonstrations on Easter weekend. On the following Monday, when they promptly filed a motion to dissolve the injunction, the court found them in contempt, holding that they had waived all their First Amendment rights by disobeying the court order.

These facts lend no support to the court's charges that petitioners were presuming to act as judges in their own case, or that they had a disregard for the judicial process. They did not flee the jurisdiction or refuse to appear in the Alabama courts. Having violated the injunction, they promptly submitted themselves to the courts to test the constitutionality of the injunction and the ordinance it parroted. They were in essentially the same position as persons who challenge the constitutionality of a statute by violating it, and then defend the ensuing criminal prosecution on constitutional grounds. It has never been thought that violation of a statute indicated such a disrespect for the legislature that the violator always must be punished even if the statute was unconstitutional. On the contrary, some cases have required that persons seeking to challenge the constitutionality of a statute first violate it to establish their standing to sue. . . . I believe [the Birmingham parade ordinance] is patently unconstitutional on its face. Our decisions have consistently held that picketing and parading are means of expression protected by the First Amendment, and that the right to picket or parade may not be subjected to the unfettered discretion of local officials.

The unconstitutionality of the ordinance is compounded, of course, when there is convincing evidence that the officials have in fact used their power to deny permits to organizations whose views they dislike. The record in this case hardly suggests that Commissioner Connor and the other city officials were motivated in prohibiting civil rights picketing only by their overwhelming concern for particular traffic problems.... The only circumstance that the court can find to justify ... [its decision] is that Commissioner Connor had the foresight to have the unconstitutional ordinance included in an *ex parte* injunction, issued without notice or hearing or any showing that it was impossible to have notice or a hearing, forbidding the world at large (insofar as it knew of the order) to conduct demonstrations in Birmingham without the consent of the city officials. This injunction was such potent magic that it transformed the command of an unconstitutional statute into an impregnable barrier....

I do not believe that giving this Court's seal of approval to such a gross misuse of the judicial process is likely to lead to greater respect for the law any more than it is likely to lead to greater protection for First Amendment freedoms. The *ex parte* temporary injunction has a long and odious history in this country, and its susceptibility to misuse is all too apparent from the facts of the case. As a weapon against strikes, it proved so effective in the hands of judges friendly to employers that Congress was forced to take the drastic step of removing from federal district courts the jurisdiction to issue injunctions in labor disputes. The labor injunction fell into disrepute largely because it was abused in precisely the same way that the injunctive power was abused in this case. Judges who were not sympathetic to the union cause commonly issued, without notice or hearing, broad restraining orders addressed to large numbers of persons and forbidding them to engage in acts that were either legally permissible or, if illegal, that could better have been left to the regular course of criminal prosecution.... Such injunctions, so long discredited as weapons against concerted labor activities, have now been given new life by this Court as weapons against the exercise of First Amendment freedoms.

... The majority opinion in this case rests essentially on a single precedent, and that a case the authority of which has clearly been undermined by subsequent decisions. *Howat* v. *Kansas*, 258 U.S. 181 (1922), was decided in the days when the labor injunction was in fashion.

. . . Insofar as *Howat* v. *Kansas* might be interpreted to approve an absolute rule that any violation of a void court order is punishable as contempt, it has been greatly modified by later decisions. In *In re Green*, 369 U.S. 689 (1962), we reversed a conviction for contempt for a state injunction forbidding labor picketing because the petitioner was not allowed to present evidence that the labor dispute was arguably subject to the jurisdiction of the National Labor Relations Board and hence not subject to state regulation.

. . . It is not necessary to question the continuing validity of the holding in *Howat* v. *Kansas*, however, to demonstrate that neither it nor the *Mine Workers* case supports the holding of the majority in this case. . . . This case involves an entirely different situation. The Alabama Circuit Court did not issue this temporary injunction to preserve existing conditions while it proceeded to decide some underlying dispute before it, and the court in practical effect merely added a judicial signature to a pre-existing criminal ordinance. Just as the court had no need to issue the injunction to preserve its ability to decide some underlying dispute, the city had no need of an injunction to impose a criminal penalty for demonstrating on the streets without a permit. The ordinance already accomplished that. In point of fact, there is only one apparent reason why the city sought this injunction and why the court issued it: to make it possible to punish petitioners for contempt rather than for violating the ordinance, and thus to immunize the unconstitutional statute and its unconstitutional application from any attack.

Mr. Justice Douglas, with whom The Chief Justice, Mr. Justice Brennan, and Mr. Justice Fortas concur, dissenting.

We sit as a court of law functioning primarily as a referee in the federal system. Our function in cases coming to us from state courts is to make sure that state tribunals and agencies work within the limits of the Constitution. Since the Alabama courts have flouted the First Amendment, I would reverse the judgment.

Picketing and parading are methods of expression protected by the First Amendment against both state and federal abridgment. . . . Since they involve more than speech itself and implicate street traffic, the accommodation of the public and the like, they may be regulated as to the times and places of the demonstrations. . . . But a state cannot deny the right to use streets or parks or other public grounds for the purpose of petitioning for the redress of grievances. . . .

The rich can buy advertisements in newspapers, purchase radio or television time, and rent billboard space. Those less affluent are restricted to the use of handbills . . . or petitions, or parades, or mass meetings. This "right of the people peaceably to assemble, and to petition the Government for a redress of grievances," guaranteed by the First Amendment, applicable to the States by reason of the Fourteenth . . . was flouted here. . . .

The record shows that petitioners did not deliberately attempt to circumvent the permit requirement. Rather they diligently attempted to obtain a permit and were rudely rebuffed and then reasonably concluded that any further attempts would be fruitless.

The right to defy an unconstitutional statute is basic in our scheme. Even when an ordinance requires a permit to make a speech, to deliver a sermon, to picket, to parade, or to assemble, it need not be honored when it is invalid on its face. . . .

By like reason, where a permit has been arbitrarily denied, one need not pursue the long and expensive route to this Court to obtain a remedy. The reason is the same in both cases. For if a person must pursue his judicial remedy before he may speak, parade, or assemble, the occasion when protest is desired or needed will have become history and any later speech, parade or assembly will be futile or pointless.

Howat v. *Kansas*, 258 U.S. 181, states the general rule that court injunctions are to be obeyed until error is found by normal and orderly review procedures. See *United States* v. *Mine Workers*, 330 U.S. 258, 293–294. But there is an exception where "the question of jurisdiction" is "frivolous and not substantial." . . .

Moreover, a state court injunction is not *per se* sacred where federal constitutional questions are involved. *In re Green,* 369 U.S. 689 held that contempt could not be imposed without a hearing where the state decree bordered the federal domain in labor relations and only a hearing could determine whether there was federal preemption. In the present case the collision between this state court decree and the First Amendment is so obvious that no hearing is needed to determine the issue. . . . An ordinance—unconstitutional on its face or patently unconstitutional as applied—is not made sacred by an unconstitutional injunction that enforces it. It can and should be flouted in the manner of the ordinance itself. Courts as well as citizens are not free "to ignore all the procedures of the law," to use the Court's language. The "constitutional freedom" of which the Court speaks can be won only if judges honor the Constitution.

Mr. Justice Brennan, with whom The Chief Justice, Mr. Justice Douglas, and Mr. Justice Fortas join, dissenting.

Under cover of exhortation that the Negro exercise "respect for judicial process," the Court empties the Supremacy Clause of its primacy by elevating a state rule of judicial administration above the right of free expression guaranteed by the Federal Constitution. And the Court does so by letting loose a devastatingly destructive weapon for suppression of cherished freedoms heretofore believed indispensable to maintenance of our free society. . . .

Like the Court, I start with the premise that States are free to adopt rules of judicial administration . . . to require respect for their courts' orders. . . . But this does not mean that this valid state interest does not admit of collision with other and more vital interests. Surely the proposition requires no citation that a valid state interest must give way when it infringes on rights guaranteed by the Federal Constitution. The plain meaning of the Supremacy Clause requires no less.

In the present case we are confronted with a collision between Alabama's interest in requiring adherence to orders of its courts and the constitutional prohibition against abridgment of freedom of speech, more particularly "the right of the people peaceably to assemble," and the right "to petition the Government for a redress of grievances." . . .

The vitality of First Amendment protections has, as a result, been deemed to rest in large measure upon the ability of the individual to take his chances and express himself in the face of such restraints, armed with the ability to challenge those restraints if the State seeks to penalize that expression. . . . Were it not for the *ex parte* injunction, petitioners could have paraded first and challenged the permit ordinance later. But because of the *ex parte* stamp of a judicial officer on a copy of the invalid ordinance they are barred not only from challenging the permit ordinance, but also the potentially more stifling yet unconsidered restraints embodied in the injunction itself. . . .

Yet by some inscrutable legerdemain these constitutionally secured rights to challenge prior restraints invalid on their face are lost if the State takes the precaution to have some judge append his signature to an *ex parte* order which recites the words of the invalid statute. . . . I would expect this tribunal, charged as it is with the ultimate responsibility to safeguard our constitutional freedoms, to regard the *ex parte* injunction tool to be far more dangerous than statutes to First Amendment freedoms. One would expect this Court particularly to remember the stern lesson history taught courts, . . . that the *ex parte* injunction represents the most devastating of restraints on constitutionally protected activities. . . .

It is said that petitioners should have sought to dissolve the injunction before conducting their processions. That argument is plainly repugnant to the principle that First Amendment freedoms may be exercised in the face of legislative prior restraints, and *a fortiori* of *ex parte* restraints broader than such legislative restraints, which may be challenged in any subsequent proceeding for their violation. . . .

The suggestion that petitioners be muffled pending outcome of dissolution proceedings without any measurable time limits is particularly inappropriate in the setting of this case. Critical to the plain exercise of the right of protest was the timing of that exercise. First, the marches were part of a program to arouse community support for petitioners' assault on segregation there. A cessation of these activities, even for a short period, might deal a crippling blow to petitioners' efforts. Second, in dramatization of their cause, petitioners, all ministers, chose April 12, Good Friday, and April 14, Easter Sunday, for their protests hoping to gain the attention to their cause which such timing might attract. Petitioners received notice of the order April 11. The ability to exercise protected protest at a time when such exercise would be effective must be as protected as the beliefs themselves. . . .

The Court today lets loose a devastatingly destructive weapon for infringement of [First Amendment] freedoms . . . . We cannot permit fears of "riots" and "civil disobedience" generated by slogans like "Black Power" to divert our attention from what is here at stake—not violence or the right of the State to control its streets and sidewalks, but the insulation from attack of *ex parte* orders and legislation upon which they are based even when patently impermissible prior restraints on the exercise of First Amendment rights, thus arming the state courts with the power to punish as a "contempt" what they otherwise could not punish at all. Constitutional restrictions against abridgments of First Amendment freedoms limit judicial equally with legislative and executive power. . . .

Walker: Analysis of a Judicial Output (Decision)

Written judicial opinions such as these are a beginning point for analysis and understanding of judicial decision making. Supplementing the opinion with the voting records of Justices as well as their background experiences creates a better understanding of a case decision—the output of the judicial system.

In *Walker* four separate written opinions are available for analysis. The majority opinion written by Justice Stewart offers insight into his perception of the total case; in addition, it contains statements and theories held by the other four Justices who voted with him. By necessity majority opinions are compromises in which the writer seeks agreement among the members of his bloc. Stewart's opinion in *Walker* therefore contains some of the specific ideas and values of Justices Black, Clark, Harlan, and White.

The Five-Man Majority in *Walker*

Analysis of Stewart's written opinion reveals at least four key issues underlying the thinking of the majority. First, Stewart had a very narrow focus on the facts in the case. This was Stewart's usual approach to decision making.[104] His earlier judicial experiences before coming to the Supreme Court had indicated that he believed in a limited role for the Court and in judicial self-restraint. Part of this philosophy was his conviction that the Court should decide only the issue that was dispositive of the case, hence his support for a narrow focus on the issue, a narrow decision, and a narrow remedy.[105] The Ashwander Rules (particularly numbers two, three, and four) had been set out by Justice Brandeis in *Ashwander* v. *T.V.A.*, 297 U.S. 288 (1936), and they were central to Stewart's approach to decision making. He believed that the Court should not "anticipate questions of constitutional law in advance of the necessity of deciding it." Nor should the Court "formulate a rule of constitutional law broader than is required by the precise facts to which it is to be applied." Finally, the Court would not "pass upon a constitutional question . . . if there is also present some other ground upon which the case may be disposed of."[106]

Stewart used this narrow framework as he wrote the majority opinion in *Walker*. Adopting this method was satisfying and appropriate for him personally, since he perceived it to be the approach of a legal expert and closest to his perception of himself as a lawyer.[107] Moreover, such an approach had traditional standing and had evoked respect for a long time. It was a safe judicial method or strategy of decision making that could be justified and defended on the basis of historical and traditional usage.

Stewart's approach in *Walker* allowed him to take such a narrow view of the multitude of available facts clamoring for his attention. Stewart and the other Justices in the majority accepted the facts that the city of Birmingham presented. A picture of a huge, disorderly, and hostile mob emerged, and the picture's title was "Violence."

For example, the city of Birmingham stated that the demonstrations had included sit-ins, which constituted trespass on private property; they had involved mass parades in which mobs had congregated upon the public street; private businesses had been subjected to the harassment of unlawful picketing. According to the official Birmingham view, the Good Friday demonstration had involved a crowd of 1,000 to 1,500 plus a vanguard of some 50 to 60 militants. The behavior of all these people was alleged to have been disruptive as they marched, "clapping and hollering and [w]hooping." The crowd spilled over from the sidewalks into the streets. The Easter Sunday demonstrations were pictured in equally frightening terms. The crowd had now grown to some 2,000 people plus its 50-member vanguard. They had congregated on, and occupied the entire width of, the streets and sidewalks. Moreover, violence occurred: black demonstrators threw rocks, injuring a newspaperman and damaging a police motorcycle. In addition they disrupted church services by conducting kneel-ins "in violation of the wishes and desires of said churches."[108]

Among the five majority Justices, this picture would have had a special degree of creditability for Justices Black and White. They were both predisposed to see the scenes in Birmingham through the eyes of the police and city officials and thus to be easily convinced that the community was on the brink of a potentially devastating riot.

Justice Black had emotional mental pictures of mob violence and riots that dated back to his early days in Alabama. He had known the old city of Birmingham with all its race problems, and his mental picture agreed with the scene painted by Birmingham officialdom in 1963.[109] Justice White did not have such an impression of Birmingham, but he had equally vivid and more recent ones of Montgomery, Alabama. Violence had accompanied the "Freedom Rides" to Montgomery in 1961, and White as Deputy Attorney General had listened to telephone descriptions of the riots as the events were taking place.[110] Certainly Justices Black and White undergirded the majority's focus on the violence and disorder created by the civil-rights demonstrators in Birmingham.

A second critical issue that influenced the five Justices in the majority to decide against the civil-rights demonstrators involved the legal procedural rules. Stewart's majority opinion indicated that these Justices were negatively influenced by the failure of the demonstrators to exhaust all of their appropriate and available legal remedies before resorting to questionable acts. Stewart, speaking for the majority, declared that the civil-rights leaders should themselves have applied to the entire commission for a parade or demonstration permit. The inquiries of Mrs. Hendricks and Rev. Shuttlesworth to Commissioner Connor were insufficient. Stewart refused at this point to consider historical Birmingham practices for granting permits; he looked at the law on its face and not as applied. Another procedural irregularity that Stewart condemned was the failure of the demonstrators to file a motion asking the Alabama court to vacate the *ex parte* injunction. He pointed out that there was time (two days) to apply for this dissolution, and the petitioners in *Walker* never explained to his satisfaction why they did not do this. Because Stewart began with the premise that there had not been a good-faith attempt to secure the permit, it was logical for him to reach this second conclusion, and as a result his legal mind was vexed by the failure of the civil-rights demonstrators to seek a court remedy before they marched.[111] Since they had not, Stewart believed that it would be improper for the Supreme Court to consider the unconstitutionality of either the Birmingham parade ordinance or the *ex parte* injunction. Both questions, he believed, should have been raised in Alabama courts and been ruled on by those courts before the demonstrators proceeded to march.[112]

Justice White would have supported this approach, since he had observed an impartial use of an *ex parte* injunction that had actually worked to help civil-rights demonstrators. This had occurred during his pre-court career when he was Deputy Attorney General and involved in the Montgomery "Freedom Rides."[113]

At any rate, the majority Justices were unwilling to concede that the demonstrators in *Walker* could not have secured justice from Alabama courts. Moreover, as Stewart explained at length, if the Alabama courts had not construed the ordinance and injunction properly, the demonstrators could then have raised these issues before the Supreme Court. Although Stewart conceded that the ordinance was *probably* unconstitutional as applied and also void due to overbreadth and vagueness, he stated this as dicta only, and it did not affect the holding of the Court.[114]

Finally, the fact that the demonstrators had knowingly and deliberately violated a court order (the *ex parte* injunction) placed them outside of the protection of the legal processes. The Supreme Court majority refused to see any mitigating circumstances in the environment of Birmingham that were sufficient to excuse intentional violation of a court order.

Stewart apparently had total support for these arguments from the members of his bloc. There were no separate concurrences. He would certainly have had the support of Justice Harlan, who, like Stewart, was intensely committed to the doctrine of working within the orderly judicial and political processes to secure change in the system. The similarity of Stewart's and Harlan's attitudes toward the particular issue of appropriate legal procedures emerged from their similar backgrounds and pre-court experiences.

Both Justices were Midwesterners, Harlan coming originally from Illinois and Stewart from Ohio. Both had been educated at prestigious Ivy League schools, Harlan at Princeton and Stewart at Yale. Both had studied abroad in England, Harlan on a Rhodes Scholarship to Oxford University, Stewart on a Henry Award to Cambridge University. Both had come from wealthy families that had traditions of legal and judicial careers and active political involvement. Both men had prior judicial experience, Harlan on the Second Circuit Court of Appeals and Stewart on the Sixth Circuit Court of Appeals. Both men were nominated for their Supreme Court position by President Eisenhower and probably for similar reasons. Harlan belonged to the Dewey faction of the Republican Party in the 1940's and early 1950's; Stewart supported the Ohio-based Taft group within the Republican Party.

Finally, both men wanted to be perceived as meticulous legal craftsmen. Harlan sought the role of a justice *par excellence*, while Stewart saw himself as a lawyer *par excellence*. They had similar perceptions of the role of the Court and believed in a case-by-case method of decision making that would avoid sweeping changes. They gave priority to methods of judicial analysis. Looking at each case under a judicial microscope, these Justices magnified legal issues so as to block out economic, social, or political data. Mechanical jurisprudence was their preferred strategy for decision making.[115]

It was not surprising, therefore, that in the *Walker* case both Justices chose to look only at the official Court record, to concen-

trate on the narrowest constitutional issues, to refuse to take judicial notice of reality as opposed to theory, and to insist upon
procedural regularity. Questions of federalism (Article VI versus
the Tenth Amendment) and questions relating to the power of the
Supreme Court as a referee in this system preoccupied the minds
of legal craftsmen like Stewart and Harlan. The legal-craftsman
approach also included a reliance upon precedents and adherence
to the rule of *stare decisis*. In the *Walker* decision Justices Clark
and White would have strongly supported this approach.

One significant precedent raised in the *Walker* case was that of
United States v. *United Mine Workers*, 330 U.S. 258 (1946). Justice
Clark, as Attorney General, had argued this case before the Supreme Court. He would, therefore, be extremely sensitive to its
usage in *Walker*. Justice White was also concerned about *Mine
Workers* as precedent, since he was clerking for Chief Justice
Fred Vinson when the case was decided. Moreover, Vinson had
written the opinion and, as his clerk, White had personally been
involved in the writing. Vinson generally indicated to his clerks
what his attitude in a particular case was, gave them some of
his reasons, and then had them complete the opinion. This
meant that White would have had an extended input into the
Mine Workers opinion.[116] The intense feelings and attitudes of
Justices Clark and White with regard to judicial precedent were
reflected in *Walker* in Stewart's explanation of the Court's decision in *Mine Workers* and his footnote limiting the later decision
of *In re Green*, 369 U.S. 689 (1962).

A third major concern that Stewart articulated for the majority
in *Walker* dealt with the issue of federalism—a proper division of
power between the national government and the state governments. Stewart himself had early demonstrated his concern for
protecting states' rights as guaranteed by the Tenth Amendment.
In any case involving the use of the Fourteenth Amendment by
the national government to make the Bill of Rights apply to the
states, Stewart generally began his own analysis with a "pre-
sumption of state sovereignty."[117] On this issue he reflected the
views of President Eisenhower, who had appointed him. Even
when First Amendment rights were asserted as being violated by
the state (as in *Walker*), Stewart still insisted that states could
consider the exact nature of the First Amendment right involved.
If the right were one of "pure" speech, then states would be rigidly bound by the prohibitions incorporated through the Fourteenth Amendment.[118]

Justice Black was in complete harmony with this view. Black

believed that "pure" speech was protected against any state or national action; however, picketing on public streets and sidewalks as well as other forms of demonstrations were not the same as "pure" speech and therefore not entitled to the same degree of protection. Justice Black's narrow view of civil liberties that were "totally incorporated" by the Fourteenth Amendment and thus off limits to state as well as federal encroachment had not been thoroughly understood during the late 1940's and the 1950's. During that period Justice Black had been classified as a liberal, along with Justice Douglas, who could be counted on to support individual civil liberties against governmental encroachment.[119]

However, the demonstration cases of the 1960's revealed a different dimension on Black's scale of values. Many judicial analysts had forgotten Black's early environment when, as the son of a storekeeper, he saw the problems of small businessmen and private-property owners. Property was something personal, gained by toil and hard work and protected by the Lockean theory of rights of control and possession. When demonstrators engaged in sit-ins on the property of a businessman or even of government, they ran the danger of triggering Black's almost forgotten bias toward the sanctity of property.

Justice Black did believe that *speech* was protected. However, he was talking about verbal persuasion. When speech led to action that might be destructive of either private or governmental property, it lost its protected position. Justice Black's decision in *Adderly v. Florida*, 385 U.S. 39 (1966), suggested that he remembered the Confederate classic "The Bonnie Blue Flag" and its demand for protection of "rights of property . . . gained by honest toil." The halls of the University of Alabama had rung with the sounds of this refrain long before Black's nostalgia for the past had tempted him to vocalize many old Southern songs for the edification of his law clerks.[120]

Thus when civil-rights demonstrators endangered rights of property they could not count on Justice Black's support. Instead, Black's attitude and voting behavior indicated that he was now inclined to stress the power of the state to protect itself—its streets, parks, jails, and courthouses.[121]

A final issue to be considered in an assessment of the majority opinion and voting alignment in *Walker* is that of the time lag.[122] The events of the Birmingham demonstrations had occurred in 1963, but, due to foot dragging and pen paralysis on the part of the Alabama court *Walker* had not reached the Supreme Court until 1967. Thus, it is appropriate to inquire whether the majority opinion offered any evidence indicating that events occurring within this time frame had influenced the judicial decision in *Walker*.

The environment surrounding the decision-making process in 1967 was quite different from that in 1963. There were two major reasons for this change. First, racial violence had erupted in Northern urban areas; second, the respected civil rights' leader, Rev. Martin Luther King, Jr. (a principal defendant in *Walker*), identified himself with Vietnam War protestors. Although the system had responded to the demands of civil-rights advocates, and Congress and President Lyndon Johnson had cooperated to pass the Civil Rights Act of 1964 and the Voting Rights Act of 1965, racial violence had increased. Chicago, Los Angeles, and San Francisco had experienced devastating riots in 1965 and 1966.

The decision in *Walker* indicated that both majority and minority Justices were aware of these events. An examination of Stewart's hypotheses concerning the possible actions of the Alabama courts had the demonstrations complied with the laws indicated the belief of the majority that the Alabama legal process was open and responsive to racial demands. Thus the civil-rights demonstrators did not have to "carry their battle to the streets." Stressing "respect for judicial process," Stewart reflected the view of the late 1960's that held that riots and destructive demonstrations had no place in a society ruled by "the civilizing hand of law."[123] In the early 1960's the Court had demonstrated a greater sympathy for minority rights, but that was before the riots of 1965 and 1966 and at a time when Congress and President seemed unresponsive. The sharp dissent of Justice Brennan charged the majority with bias due to the events of 1965–67. The Court, Brennan claimed, had permitted "fears of 'riots' and 'civil disobedience,' generated by slogans like 'Black Power' to divert our attention from what is here at stake."[124]

Did King's anti-Vietnam policy affect the Justices? The majority opinion contains little to document this theory. Stewart did conclude his opinion however by reminding the civil-rights workers that "no man can be judge in his own case, however exalted his station, however righteous his motives." This could be read as an indictment of King, who as holder of the Nobel Peace Prize had gained international attention. Of all of the majority Justices, however, the one most likely to be affected by King's criticism of American involvement in Vietnam was Justice Clark. He had carried his Cold War fears from his pre-Court position as Attorney General to his position as Associate Justice. As Attorney

General he had supported FBI investigations that violated First Amendment freedoms, thus revealing the intensity of his attitude when confronted with threats of Communist subversion. Clark's voting record in cases involving issues of internal security revealed clearly that he supported the right of the state to protect itself from those whose criticism might cause loss of respect for the United States.[125] King's action in opposing the Vietnam War could easily be interpreted as doing exactly that.

The Dissenters in *Walker*

The Court division in *Walker* had resulted in a five-to-four alignment, with Chief Justice Warren and Justices Douglas, Brennan, and Fortas in dissent. Three of these four felt it necessary to write separate—and strongly worded—opinions. Dissent in general plays an important role in the American judicial process. It has been described as an "appeal to the bar of history" as well as to "sober second thought."[126] To insure precisely this, Warren, Douglas, and Brennan stated in detail their own perceptions and analyses of the *Walker* case.

The views of the dissenters differed from the majority on the questions of facts and events, the motives of the groups involved, the actual availability of legal precedents, and, finally, the central question that the Court should ask. As a result the three written dissents (Justice Fortas joined all three, but did not write a separate opinion) attempted to take apart the arguments advanced by the majority and to do this by using accepted legal theories as well as factual data. The perception of the facts in *Walker* was the beginning point of division between the five Justices in the majority and the four in the minority.

Warren characterized the demonstrations as peaceful protests. His set of facts included the two attempts made early in the week to secure a permit, and he refused to differentiate between those who made these requests (Mrs. Lola Hendricks and Rev. Fred Shuttlesworth) and the major petitioners involved in the *Walker* case, who had not attempted to secure a permit. Warren did not perceive any massive offensive engaged in by the demonstrators. He did not accept the city's protestation that their department was strained to the breaking point in order to cope with the disorders. Neither did Warren believe that kneel-in demonstrations in churches were menacing in nature. He did not accept the city's claim that its action was generated by its overwhelming concern for traffic problems.[127]

Douglas's dissent, like Warren's, began with a restatement of the facts to concentrate upon the attempts of Mrs. Hendricks and Rev. Shuttlesworth to secure a permit. Douglas used this to counteract the majority's contention that the petitioners in *Walker* had tried to get around the permit requirement. For Douglas and Warren, the attempts made by the two members of the ACMHR should be considered as action taken by Walker *et al.* Douglas also stressed the fact that evidence proving that the Birmingham ordinance had never been administered through action of the entire commission had been deliberately ignored by the Alabama courts and now by the Supreme Court majority.[128]

Brennan used his separate dissent to focus on still more issues that the majority had not used. One of these was the environment in Birmingham in 1963. Brennan categorized Birmingham as "a world symbol of implacable official hostility to Negro efforts to gain civil rights."[129] While Stewart and the majority insisted that the civil-rights leaders should not have assumed that they could not receive justice from an Alabama court, Brennan and the other three dissenters believed otherwise. Brennan, like Douglas and Warren, wrote into his dissent the description of the ACMHR members' attempt to secure a parade or demonstation permit and equated their action with that of the petitioners in *Walker*. Brennan also described in detail the events of Good Friday and Easter Sunday, thus making certain that this account would become a permanent part of the official court record in the *Walker* decision. His description, like Warren's, stressed the orderly nature of both parades. There was, according to Brennan, only one episode of violence.[130]

These three descriptions of the facts and events in *Walker*, so different from that of the majority, owed much to the differing background experiences that the dissenters brought to the case. Chief Justice Warren's personal experiences guided his approach to *Walker*, and he refused to accept the city of Birmingham's picture of events without extensive corroboration. His early life in Bakersfield, California, had given him an awareness of the viciousness of labor-management feuds. He had seen some of the ugliness of the railroad strikes. As a young man Warren had observed the misuse of injunctive power against labor. His later experiences as District Attorney in Alameda County made him aware that many governmental officials misused power. As a prosecuting attorney in Alameda County Warren had fought vigorously against graft and corruption within the local law-enforcement agencies. His firsthand experiences had revealed that sheriffs, policemen, prosecutors, and judges often acted unethically.[131]

These experiences would make Warren suspicious of powerful local city officials such as the Birmingham City Commissioners in general and Public Safety Commissioner Connor in particular. Warren scrutinized court records and all other possible sources for information about the actual practices for granting parade or demonstration permits in Birmingham. He found a record of "continuing abuse of civil rights protestors" by officials of the city of Birmingham and by Connor, a self-proclaimed "white supremacist."[132]

Douglas was inherently suspicious of holders of power. His early experiences with the establishment in Yakima, Washington, reinforced by those in New York City at Columbia Law School as well as his teaching at Yale, had convinced him that family connections and wealth worked to hold down the poor and the disadvantaged. The vigor with which he attacked the Wall Street establishment from his position on the SEC demonstrated the intensity of his belief.[133] Thus in *Walker* it was not surprising to find him saying, "The rich can buy advertisements in newspapers, purchase radio or television time, and rent billboard space. Those less affluent are restricted to the use of handbills or petitions, or parades, or mass meetings."[134] In addition, Douglas's experiences as an investigator had created in him a passion for facts, and, like Warren, he subjected the record in *Walker* to an analysis leading to conclusions diametrically opposed to those of the majority.

Of all the Justices who participated in the *Walker* decision, Justice Brennan was better informed on the history and the application of the *ex parte* injunction, which was a key issue. In the second paragraph of his lengthy dissent Brennan asserted that the *ex parte* injunction was the central problem in the case, and he proceeded to discuss the origin of this "dangerous tool."[135] Brennan's experiences in labor-management disputes during his army career and during his years in private practice had made him an expert in labor law. His father's activities as a union leader in the A. F. of L. had also contributed to Brennan's knowledge of labor history and activity.[136]

Brennan's dissent urged the Court to remember "the stern lesson history taught courts in the context of the labor injunction, that the *ex parte* injunction represents the most devastating of restraints on constitutionally protected activities." Brennan also condemned the *ex parte* injunction because it had been used to change the entire nature of the *Walker* case. "Were it not for the *ex parte* injunction," he said, "petitioners could have paraded first and challenged the permit ordinance later."[137] Yet the *ex parte* "stamp of a judicial officer"[138] had so changed the "invalid ordinance"[139] that courts, admitting that the ordinance itself was probably invalid, ignored that issue and convicted the civil-rights workers for *violation* of the *ex parte* injunction.

Brennan also used his expertise in labor law to distinguish *Walker* from the precedents of *Howat* v. *Kansas*, 258 U.S. 181 (1922), and *United States* v. *United Mine Workers*, 330 U.S. 258 (1947). He reinterpreted and explained the limits placed on these early cases by *In re Green*, 369 U.S. 689 (1962). Since all of these had involved labor problems—Brennan's acknowledged area of specialization —his dissent struck a blow at the majority opinion on this point.[140]

Brennan's assessment of these three case precedents was accepted as correct by Chief Justice Warren, who characterized the *ex parte* injunction as having a "long and odious history."[141] Warren also emphasized the fact that *ex parte* injunctions had often been misused, and he believed that this had occurred in *Walker*. Here the Court had applied it so as to discriminate on the basis of race; in earlier cases judges had used it to discriminate against labor. Warren contended that "respect for the courts and for judicial process was not increased by the history of the labor injunction."[142] Therefore, he could not believe that civil-rights demonstrators would show greater respect and deference to the courts when the injunction was applied against them. Warren buttressed these arguments with extensive quotes from authoritative books in labor law and labor history that demonstrated the effect of the misuse of *ex parte* injunctions.[143]

Warren and Brennan also agreed that the *ex parte* injunction in *Walker* had been used as an ingenious device deliberately designed to allow the city of Birmingham to punish the demonstrators for contempt rather than trespass. This "immuniz[ed] the unconstitutional statute and its unconstitutional application from any attack."[144]

Justice Fortas was the junior Associate Justice on the Court in 1967. Although he did not write a separate dissent, he personally joined each of the three dissenting opinions written by his colleagues. Fortas's pre-court record had demonstrated his concern for fair and unbiased legal procedures, including all of the guarantees of the Fifth Amendment and Sixth Amendment in particular. Many of the cases handled by his law firm had involved political casualties of the Cold War period—men and women who had been dismissed from their jobs because they were suspected of being Communist sympathizers. Fortas had defended many of these, often without a fee. His attitude toward loyalty-security issues versus First Amendment rights had placed him at odds with Justice Clark in particular. His attitude toward the opinion writer in *Walker*, Justice Stewart, was one of indifference and therefore Stewart's arguments focusing on legal procedure would leave Fortas unmoved and highly skeptical. Instead, his deep professional respect for his former professor, employer, and longtime friend—Justice Douglas—would predispose him to agree with the minority.[145]

Finally, it should be noted that the majority and the minority in *Walker* had approached the case asking different constitutional questions. The precise question a court asks often determines the answer it gets. For Stewart and the majority the question was, "[Does the] Constitution compel Alabama to allow petitioners to violate this injunction . . . without any attempt to secure a parade permit . . . ?"[146] For the dissenters, however, the question could be stated, "Does the Supremacy Clause of the Constitution require that state procedure violating First Amendment guarantees be struck down as unconstitutional?" Given the facts obviously assumed by each question it is easy to see why the Court would be divided in its decision.

Nevertheless, a majority of five was sufficient for deciding that the civil-rights demonstrators in *Walker* were in contempt of court for violating an *ex parte* injunction and therefore must pay for their crime. Throughout the written decision the Supreme Court majority had pointedly avoided referring by name to the individuals involved. Yet the decision affected the lives of real men, and, as a result, at the end of October 1967 and in compliance with the Court's decision, Rev. Martin Luther King, Jr., Rev. Ralph Abernathy, Rev. A. D. King, and Rev. Wyatt T. Walker returned to Birmingham, Alabama, to serve their five-day jail sentence. Each man had lost equally in *Walker* v. *Birmingham*.

Despair and depression, however, should not have gripped the losers in *Walker*. Those who understood the workings of the judicial process knew that the openness of the system permits constitutional issues to be re-examined in the context of new cases. In fact, the feedback stage had already generated a number of new cases presenting the same questions as those raised by *Walker*. In a very short time the losers in *Walker* would find that the judicial process would move forward to protect individuals from *ex parte* injunctions and to reassess the constitutional protections for those claiming the right to protest.

NOTES

1. Stephen L. Wasby, *The Supreme Court in the Federal Judicial System* (New York: Holt, Rinehart and Winston, 1978), p. 167.

2. Harold Spaeth and David Rohde, *Supreme Court Decision Making* (San Francisco: Freeman, 1976), p. 155.

3. Glendon Schubert, *The Judicial Mind Revisited* (New York: Oxford University Press, 1974), pp. 18–19.

4. Charles H. Sheldon, *The American Judicial Process:* Models and Approaches (New York: Dodd, Mead, 1974), pp. 24–49.

5. Alan F. Westin, *The Trial of Martin Luther King* (New York: Crowell, 1974).

6. *Ibid.*

7. *NAACP* v. *Alabama*, 377 U.S. 288 (1964), *NAACP* v. *Button*, 371 U.S. 415 (1963).

8. David L. Lewis, *King: A Biography*, 2nd ed. (Urbana, Ill.: University of Illinois Press, 1978), pp. 171–209.

9. Martin Luther King, Jr., *Why We Can't Wait* (New York: Harper and Row, 1963), pp. 44–49, 55–75.

10. *Walker* v. *City of Birmingham*, 388 U.S. 307 (1967).

11. Alan F. Westin, *The Trial of Martin Luther King*, pp. 83–88.

12. Merlo J. Pusey, *Charles Evans Hughes*, vol. 2 (New York: Macmillan, 1951), pp. 667–68. Chief Justice Hughes described Justice Van Devanter using this term.

13. *Walker* v. *Birmingham*, 279 Ala. 53, 181 So. 2d 493 (1965).

14. Alan F. Westin, *The Trial of Martin Luther King*, pp. 180–82.

15. Glendon Schubert, *Constitutional Politics: The Political Behavior of Supreme Court Justices and the Constitutional Policies That They Make* (New York: Holt, Rinehart and Winston, 1964), pp. 89–100.

16. Alan F. Westin, *The Trial of Martin Luther King*, pp. 187, 213, 220, and 225.

17. Alan F. Westin, *The Anatomy of a Constitutional Law Case* (New York: Macmillan, 1958), pp. 110–11.

18. John P. Frank, *Marble Palace: The Supreme Court in American Life* (New York: Knopf, 1968).

19. Walter F. Murphy, *Elements of Judicial Strategy* (Chicago: The University of Chicago Press, 1964), pp. 78–84.

20. Glendon Schubert, *The Constitutional Polity* (Boston: Boston University Press, 1970), pp. 79–125.

21. Joel B. Grossman and Joseph Tanenhaus, eds., *Frontiers of Judicial Research* (New York: Wiley, 1969).

22. Harold J. Spaeth, *Supreme Court Policy Making: Explanation and Prediction* (San Francisco: Freeman, 1979), pp. 128–37.

23. John R. Schmidhauser, *Judges and Justices: The Federal Appellate Judiciary* (Boston: Little, Brown, 1979), p. 96.

24. Leo Katcher, *Earl Warren: A Political Biography* (New York: McGraw-Hill, 1967).

25. *Ibid.*

26. *Ibid.*, p. 189.

27. Gerald T. Dunne, *Hugo Black and the Judicial Revolution* (New York: Simon and Schuster, 1977), p. 88.

28. James David Barber, "The Presidential Character," in Peter Woll, ed., *American Government: Readings and Cases*, 7th ed. (Boston: Little, Brown, 1981) p. 364.

29. Gerald T. Dunne, *Hugo Black and the Judicial Revolution*, p. 100. Black married Josephine Foster, a minister's daughter and a socially prominent member of Birmingham's elite. However, she was a nonconformist in her own way. Refusing a Southern education, she went to New York City to attend Barnard College of Columbia University.

30. *Ibid.*

31. Richard F. Fenno, Jr., "The Internal Distribution of Influence: The House," in David B. Truman, ed., *Congress and America's Future*, 2nd ed. (Englewood Cliffs, N.J.: Prentice-Hall, 1973), p. 84. Fenno defines and describes the "apprentice" and the "protégé" in the congressional system.

32. Gerald T. Dunne, *Hugo Black and the Judicial Revolution*, pp. 149–51.

33. Fred Rodell, *Nine Men: A Political History of the Supreme Court from 1790 to 1955* (New York: Random House, 1955). See page 217 for a discussion of "the Nine Old Men."

34. Gerald T. Dunne, *Hugo Black and the Judicial Revolution*, p. 166.

35. *Ibid.*, p. 167.

36. *Ibid.*, p. 165.

37. *Ibid.*, pp. 163, 165.

38. James F. Simon, *Independent Journey: The Life of William O. Douglas* (New York: Harper and Row, 1980).

39. The Cravath firm was one of the largest and most prestigious corporate law firms in New York. Paul D. Cravath began his career as a partner in the firm of Carter, Hughes, and Cravath in the fall of 1887. Both Charles Evans Hughes and Paul D. Cravath were Columbia Law School graduates. Cravath was a prize fellow of the Class of 1886. For a history of the firm see, Robert T. Swain, *The Cravath Firm and Its Predecessors 1819–1947* (New York: Ad Lib, 1946).

40. James F. Simon, *Independent Journey: The Life of William O. Douglas,* p. 354.

41. *Time,* 8 August 1949.

42. Anna Rothe, ed., *Current Biography* (New York: Wilson, 1945), pp. 107–11.

43. *Ibid.,* p. 108.

44. *Ibid.*

45. *Ibid.*

46. Richard Kirkendall, "Tom C. Clark," in Leon Friedman and Fred L. Israel, eds., *The Justices of the United States Supreme Court 1789–1969: Their Lives and Major Opinions* (New York and London: Chelsea House, 1969), pp. 2665–67.

47. *Ibid.*

48. *Ibid.,* p. 2666.

49. C. Herman Pritchett, *The American Constitution,* 2nd ed. (New York: McGraw-Hill, 1968), pp. 521–50.

50. *Holiday,* February 1950.

51. Richard Kirkendall, "Tom C. Clark," p. 2671.

52. Alan F. Westin, *The Trial of Martin Luther King,* p. 242.

53. See William C. Sullivan, *The Bureau: My Thirty Years in Hoover's F.B.I.* (New York: Norton, 1979), pp. 135–45. FBI Director J. Edgar Hoover's suspicions concerning the loyalty of Rev. Martin Luther King, Jr., led to in-depth investigations and monitoring of the civil-rights leader's activities. Hoover was certain that King was a Communist, and Justice Tom Clark and his son Ramsey Clark (later Attorney General) were aware of Hoover's criticism of King.

54. *National Review,* 22 October 1971.

55. *New Yorker,* 4 December 1954.

56. *Ibid.*

57. *Ibid.*

58. *Time*, 22 November 1954.

59. *National Review*, 22 October 1971.

60. *New Yorker*, 4 December 1954.

61. *U.S. News and World Report*, 18 March 1955.

62. *Ibid.*

63. *Time*, 8 October 1956.

64. *U.S. News and World Report*, 12 October 1956.

65. M. D. Candee, ed., *Current Biography* (New York: Wilson, 1957), pp. 72–74.

66. *Ibid.*

67. *Nation*, 13 October 1956.

68. M. D. Candee, ed., *Current Biography* (New York: Wilson, 1957), pp. 72–74.

69. *Ibid.*

70. *Ibid.*

71. *Life*, 29 October 1956.

72. *Time*, 8 October 1956.

73. *U.S. News and World Report*, 12 October 1956. See also *Nation*, 13 October 1956.

74. *Nation*, 13 October 1956. See also *New Republic*, 8 October 1956.

75. *Time*, 20 October 1958.

76. *Ibid.*

77. *Ibid.*

78. *Ibid.*

79. *Newsweek*, 20 October 1958.

80. *U.S. News and World Report*, 17 October 1958.

81. *Life*, 20 October 1958.

82. *Reporter*, 5 February 1959.

83. *Newsweek*, 29 June 1981.

84. *Time*, 29 June 1981.

85. *Time*, 20 October 1958.

86. *Center Magazine*, vol. 14, no. 5, September/October 1981.

87. *Ibid.*

88. *Reporter,* 5 February 1959. See also *Newsweek,* 9 April 1962.

89. *Sports Illustrated,* 10 December 1962.

90. *Ibid.*

91. *Time,* 6 April 1962.

92. Charles Moritz, ed., *Current Biography* (New York: Wilson, 1962), pp. 458–60.

93. *New Republic,* 9 April 1962.

94. Fred L. Israel, "Byron R. White," in Leon Friedman and Fred L. Israel, eds., *The Justices of the United States Supreme Court 1789–1969: Their Lives and Major Opinions* (London and New York: Chelsea House, 1969), pp. 2951–55.

95. *Ibid.*

96. *Ibid.*

97. *Ibid.*

98. Robert Shogan, *A Question of Judgment* (Indianapolis, Ind.: Bobbs-Merrill, 1972).

99. Professor Lewis J. Edinger, "Colloquium on Leadership," Columbia University, February 1972. See also Lewis J. Edinger, "Political Science and Political Biography," *Journal of Politics,* vol. 26 (1964).

100. Walter F. Murphy and C. Herman Pritchett, *Court, Judges, and Politics: An Introduction to the Judicial Process,* 3rd ed. (New York: Random House, 1979), pp. 654–57.

101. Alan F. Westin, *The Trial of Martin Luther King,* pp. 234–44.

102. Stephen L. Wasby, *The Supreme Court in the Federal Judicial System,* pp. 175–78. See also David W. Rohde and Harold J. Spaeth, "The Assignment of the Majority Opinion," Chapter 8 in *Supreme Court Decision Making* (San Francisco: Freeman, 1976), pp. 172–92.

103. *Walker* v. *City of Birmingham,* 388 U.S. 307 (1967). There are forty-three pages in this record.

104. Gayle Binion, "An Assessment of Potter Stewart," in *Center Magazine,* vol. XIV (14) no. 5, September/October 1981, pp. 2–5.

105. *Ibid.*

106. *Ashwander* v. *T.V.A.,* 297 U.S. 288 (1936). See separate concurrence by Justice Brandeis.

107. *Time,* 20 October 1958.

108. *Walker* v. *City of Birmingham*, 388 U.S. 307 (1967), 309–11.

109. Gerald T. Dunne, *Hugo Black and the Judicial Revolution*.

110. Fred L. Israel, "Byron R. White."

111. *Walker* v. *City of Birmingham*, 388 U.S. 307 (1967), 318.

112. *Ibid.*, 317.

113. Fred L. Israel, "Byron R. White."

114. *Walker* v. *City of Birmingham*, 388 U.S. 307 (1967), 318–19.

115. See earlier description and analysis of background and pre-court careers of Justices Harlan and Stewart.

116. Glendon Schubert, *Constitutional Politics*, p. 146. See also John P. Frank, *Marble Palace*, pp. 116–19.

117. Gayle Binion, "An Assessment of Potter Stewart."

118. *Walker* v. *City of Birmingham*, 388 U.S. 307 (1967), 316.

119. Henry Abraham, Jr., *Freedom and the Court: Civil Rights and Liberties in the United States*, 2nd ed. (New York: Oxford University Press, 1972).

120. Bob Woodward and Scott Armstrong, *The Brethren: Inside the Supreme Court* (New York: Simon and Schuster, 1979), pp. 147–48.

121. See *Adderly* v. *Florida*, 385 U.S. 39 (1966).

122. Alan F. Westin, *The Trial of Martin Luther King*, p. 284. See also Glendon Schubert, *Judicial Policy Making* (Glenview, Ill.: Scott, Foresman, 1974), pp. 201, 204.

123. *Walker* v. *City of Birmingham*, 388 U.S. 307 (1967), 321.

124. *Walker* v. *City of Birmingham*, 388 U.S. 307 (1967), 349.

125. Richard Kirkendall, "Tom C. Clark."

126. William O. Douglas, "In Defense of Dissent," in Alan F. Westin, ed., *The Supreme Court: Views from Inside* (New York: Norton, 1961), pp. 51–56. Douglas quotes Hughes: "A dissent . . . is an appeal to the brooding spirit of the law, to the intelligence of a future day, when a later decision may possibly correct the error into which the dissenting judge believes the court to have been betrayed."

127. *Walker* v. *City of Birmingham*, 388 U.S. 307 (1967), 324–27.

128. *Ibid.*, 335–37.

129. *Ibid.*, 339.

130. *Ibid.*, 338–41.

131. Leo Katcher, *Earl Warren*.

132. *Walker* v. *City of Birmingham*, 388 U.S. 307 (1967), 325–26.

133. James F. Simon, *Independent Journey: The Life of William O. Douglas*.

134. *Walker* v. *City of Birmingham*, 388 U.S. 307 (1967), 335.

135. *Ibid.*, 346.

136. See previous description and analysis of Justice Brennan's pre-court career and background experiences.

137. *Walker* v. *City of Birmingham*, 388 U.S. 307 (1967), 347.

138. *Ibid.*

139. *Ibid.*

140. *Ibid*, 343, 347.

141. *Ibid.*, 330.

142. *Ibid.*, 330–31.

143. *Ibid.*, 331, n.8.

144. *Ibid.*, 334.

145. See previous description and analysis of Justice Fortas's pre-court career and background experiences. See also Robert Shogan, *A Question of Judgment*.

146. *Walker* v. *City of Birmingham*, 388 U.S. 307 (1967), 315.

CHAPTER 4

TO WIN AND YET TO LOSE

IMPACT ANALYSIS OF A SUPREME COURT DECISION IN A HOSTILE COMMUNITY

Systems theory as applied to the judicial process ends with the impact stage. While the output stage focuses on the judiciary's handing down of the actual case decision and is studied primarily by examining the written opinion of the Court, the impact stage is more complex and involves a number of different elements. A Supreme Court decision naturally has an impact on the actual parties in the case; it decides *for* one and *against* the other. However, this does not always mean that an issue is really settled or that a case is closed. Enforcement of a case decision must occur before that decision can have any impact or influence. Moreover, even if complete compliance with a Court order is secured in the *particular* case decided, this does not mean that automatically a new rule of law will be accepted and applied everywhere. Contestants in similar cases will immediately argue that their situation is so different from that decided by the Court that the decision does not apply to *them*. Lower courts—both federal and state—may interpret the Court decision so as to render it powerless or at least to rob it of any bite or sting. The general public may choose to close its eyes to the decision, thus forcing the Court to decide still another case. Local law-enforcement agents may decide to adopt policies of avoidance, evasion, and delay, and thus prevent a Court decision from having any real or far-reaching impact.[1]

For a Supreme Court decision to have real impact it must meet a number of standards. First, the decision must be so clear that no one could pretend to doubt what the Court had actually said.

Second, the decision needs to be backed by a united Court, speaking in one opinion. Dissents and separate concurrences can rob a decision of its power and provide opponents with the argumentative ammunition necessary to avoid, evade, and delay compliance with that decision. Third, the legitimate authority of the Court to make the decision must be beyond question; the general public must believe that the Court is the proper agent for making the decision and that it has the right to order them to do something they really don't want to do. Fourth, the decision must be enforced by the various individuals, agencies, and groups who have the power to carry out a Court decision. Finally, knowledge about the Court's decision must become widespread through publicity.[2]

It is extremely rare for all of these conditions to be met. However, one might suppose that a Court decision would at least be enforceable against the parties involved in the controversy. Surely there could be no question of the necessity of compliance here. Yet such is not necessarily the case. It is possible to win your case before the Supreme Court and still lose: legal history is replete with examples of the inability of the Court to force compliance even from the parties to the case.[3] One of the most dramatic of such incidents is a Texas case of the late 1930's and early 1940's, the Bob White case (*White* v. *State of Texas*, 310 U.S. 530, 1940). To understand how Bob White's apparent case win before the Court was nevertheless actually a case loss in the end, it is necessary to consider the case in its entirety—from the opening legal battles to the dramatic *coup de grace* that closed it.

A Case of Negative Impact: *Bob White* v. *Texas*

The case opened in the small southeastern Texas town of Livingston, the county seat of Polk County. Livingston had a population of approximately 3,000 in 1937. On August 10 of that year, Mrs. Ruby Cochran, the wife of W. S. Cochran and the mother of two little boys, was raped in her own home by an unknown assailant. Mr. Cochran, a wealthy plantation owner and businessman, was absent from his home that evening, and Mrs. Cochran had been alone in the house except for her two sons—one eleven and the other thirteen. The two boys were asleep in their downstairs bedroom when Mrs. Cochran retired to her bedroom on the second floor of the house. Early in the night she heard some "peculiar noises"; she reached for her pistol, which was in a nearby nightstand, and immediately found herself under attack. Screaming and struggling, she attempted to jump out of her upstairs window, apparently forgetting that it was screened. Although she could not see her assailant in the dark she later testified that he was armed with a knife (she cut her hand on it), was barefooted, had very offensive breath, and was undoubtedly a Negro.

The following day, a manhunt began in Polk County and approximately fifteen blacks in the vicinity of the Cochran home were rounded up and taken to the county courthouse and ultimately to the Polk County jail. Among those apprehended was Bob White, an illiterate black farmhand. At the time he was taken into custody he had been engaged in picking cotton on a plantation located about ten miles from Livingston. Although no warrants were issued and no charges were filed, these black men were kept in the Polk County jail for six or seven days. During this confinement the local sheriff noticed that Bob White was "impatient, restless, and would eat but little, while the others ate heartily." A few nights after the confinement, local police officers had Mrs. Cochran enter a room in a nearby private residence, and the suspects were brought to an adjoining room one at a time and required to repeat the statements used by her assailant during the attack. The dialogue was as follows:

> Mrs. Cochran: Don't you know what the Cochrans will do to you?"
> Assailant: "I don't care what they do to me; I don't care what happens to me."

Mrs. Cochran stated that Bob White's voice was, in her opinion, the same as that of the person who assaulted her. However, she could not identify Bob White in any other manner because there had been "no light burning" in her home at the time the crime was committed.[4] Nevertheless, Texas Rangers then carried White from the jail to a remote wooded area, whipped him, and demanded that he confess. He was warned not to speak about this treatment. Later, one Texas Ranger admitted in court that White had been taken out of jail and interrogated in the woods. The ostensible reason given was that the jail was crowded. Another Ranger testified that White had been kept in handcuffs and that the interrogation had occurred many times—so many that he could not remember the exact number. When White was not being interrogated, the sheriff kept him by himself in the jail and "kept watching him and talking to him." Finally, White was removed to the Jefferson County jail at Beaumont, Texas. Although no reason was given at the time, it was later claimed that the move was essential for White's own protection from mobs. It did not, however, protect him from law-enforcement officials. The sheriff had interrogated White for about an hour and a half before taking him to Beaumont. White was accompanied to the jail in Beaumont by local police and the Polk County prosecuting attorney; Texas Rangers also went and were allowed access to the eighth floor of the jail in Beaumont, where White was interrogated from 11:00 P.M. to 3:30 A.M. At about 2:00 A.M. White "began to cry" and finally agreed to confess. The confession was then typed and was witnessed by two citizens of Beaumont. White signed with his mark since he was unable to write. Only then were charges formally filed. From the time of his arrest up to and including the signing of the confession Bob White had had no lawyer, no charges had been filed against him, and he had been out of touch with friends or relatives.[5]

Bob White and Trial I: The Texas District Court

The case went to trial in District Court, Livingston (Polk County) Texas in late August of 1937. District Court Judge W. B. Browder had appointed a local attorney to represent White. Under the Supreme Court ruling handed down in *Powell* v. *Alabama*, 287 U.S. 45 (1932), it was necessary for the accused to have an attorney in a state prosecution that carried a death penalty. Rape was considered one of the most serious of all crimes in Texas at this time, and the rape of a white woman by a black man was far more serious than even premeditated murder. Given this view, therefore, it came as no surprise when the local attorney withdrew before the case was tried. However, Bob White was fortunate in two respects. First, his family—although very poor—was able to scrape together one hundred dollars for an attorney's retainer. White's widowed mother, uncle, brothers, and sisters pooled their slim resources to accumulate this sum. Second, a Houston attorney, J. P. Rogers, became interested in the case and agreed to accept the retainer from the family and to represent White in court. Rogers was apparently shocked by the withdrawal of the appointed counsel and he had a personal commitment to fair legal procedures. After seeing White and listening to his story, Rogers became convinced that the police had accused the wrong man. Rogers apparently also believed White's account of his movements on the night on which the crime was committed. Because White was unable to read or write he had always had to live on a farm doing manual labor; this was what he had been doing on August 10, the day of the crime. In fact, White had spent the entire day picking cotton on the plantation of the brother-in-law of the victim, Mrs. Cochran. (The Cochran brothers owned large adjoining plantations along the Trinity River in Polk County.) White claimed that he was exhausted after his work and returned to his mother's home and went to sleep on the front porch. This alibi was supported by black witnesses whom Rogers questioned. Rogers also hoped that the NAACP would become involved in the case and would finance the cost of White's defense.[6] These three factors—Rogers's belief in due process, his belief in White's innocence, and his hope for pecuniary reward—combined to provide White with an attorney, and not a state-appointed one.

Difficulties Experienced by White's Attorney

However, Rogers had a difficult time in court. His objections to the state's use of White's confession were overruled by Judge Browder. His attempts to force the state to produce some of its own evidence also failed. For instance, Rogers knew that plaster casts of the footprints discovered around the Cochran home had been made, but the state did not introduce them as evidence. The state also refused to introduce fingerprints that had been made. In spite of the fact that Rogers had a subpoena issued for the fingerprint expert, the state would not allow him to take the witness stand. Rogers also had to cope with numerous procedural problems before the trial began. For example, the court was not in session in Livingston during August; the judge was holding the regular term of court at Conroe, Texas. Nevertheless, the judge hastened back to Livingston and called a special term of the 9th District Court. Rogers insisted that this court was without jurisdiction because a judge could not hold court in two counties at the same time. However, his motion to that effect was overruled. Rogers also sought a change of venue due to the open hostility shown by the community. This motion was likewise overruled, and his request for a continuance to put more time between the crime (August 10) and trial (August 30) was denied. As a result, according to Rogers the jury was prejudiced and the trial nothing more than "mob action." Rogers had secured affidavits to prove White's alibi. However, he was unable to file them because blacks were warned not to appear at the courthouse on the day of the trial. Only a few black witnesses whom Rogers had subpoenaed appeared, and they were placed in the grand jury room under heavy guard. When these witnesses were called to take the stand, they were so frightened that Rogers could barely get any testimony from them. Rogers, who had practiced criminal law in Texas for twenty-two years, was dismayed by these actions. He later referred to Polk and Montgomery counties as "foreign countries" and stated that he had "risked his life" to go there to defend Bob White. Several white spectators attempted to pick a fight with him on the stairs of the courthouse. Moreover, the black chauffeur who drove Rogers by car from Houston to Livingston was threatened by heavily armed men. He was so thoroughly intimidated and frightened that he quickly departed from Livingston, leaving Rogers to get back to Houston as best he could when the trial was over.

On Appeal: The Case Before the Texas State Court of Criminal Appeals

The trial ended quickly and with no surprises. White was found guilty as charged and sentenced to death. Rogers, however, refused to give up. He took a partner, former Judge R. C. Roland, and the two attorneys prepared to appeal to the highest state court, the Texas State Court of Criminal Appeals. The newly reorganized Houston branch of the NAACP became aroused, decided that White was being made a scapegoat, and agreed to try to raise funds for his defense. Because of many demands on their funds, they approached the national organization for money to pay Rogers and Roland, who had requested a fee of $1,500. C. F. Richardson, President of the Houston branch, also wanted a black attorney, W. J. Johnson, to be designated as "advisor." The national organization hesitated to commit funds at first. The local Houston branch, working with the Dallas branch, managed to raise a sufficient amount to underwrite attorneys' fees for briefing and presenting the case to the Texas Court of Criminal Appeals. They also engaged Peden, Johnson, and Peden, a well-established firm located in the Citizens State Bank Building in Houston. Local NAACP officials had decided that Rogers and Roland needed expert help. Attorney Robert F. Peden interviewed Bob White at the Harris County jail, where he was confined in April 1938.[7] Peden reported to the local NAACP officials that it was his belief that White had not been given due process of law, that he was innocent of the crime, and that his life could ultimately be saved, although it would mean a long and bitter fight. White's attorneys were therefore surprised and delighted when the Texas State

Court of Criminal Appeals reversed the decision of the district court in a *per curiam* opinion rendered on April 6, 1938. The court noted the hostile environment in which White had been tried; they also noted that local authorities had failed to act properly when White's attorney attempted to file his bill of exceptions. Attorney Rogers had compiled the list of complaints and citations of errors that, in his opinion, rendered the district-court decision void. To appeal to the higher court White's attorney had to file such a bill of exceptions. However, Rogers had been given the run-around by the district-court judge and other local officials. When Rogers went to file his bill the judge engaged in a series of maneuvers to frustrate him. First, Rogers was told that he must go to Conroe, Texas, to see the judge. When he arrived the judge declared that the matter was not in his hands since the list of errors had been sent on to the district attorney. The district attorney in turn claimed that he no longer had the bill of exceptions, having forwarded it to Z. L. Foreman, the private prosecutor in the case. All of this was done apparently to prevent Rogers from being able to file the list of complaints, exceptions, and errors in time to meet the legal deadline. The Texas State Court of Criminal Appeals also ruled that the language employed by the private prosecutor, Z. L. Foreman, was "prejudicial in its nature." In his argument to the jury, Foreman had exclaimed, "Gentlemen, look at this courtroom; it is crowded with Polk County people demanding the death penalty for Bob White." The Texas State Court of Criminal Appeals found, therefore, that such actions had deprived Bob White of due process of law, and they reversed the lower court's decision. Having lost in his trial in the district court, White was now the winner in his appeal to the Texas State Court of Criminal Appeals. But the case was far from over and White still remained in jail. It was now June 1938, about ten months after the commission of the crime and the arrest of Bob White.

Bob White and Trial II: Texas Seeks an Error-free Trial

During the summer and fall of 1938 the state of Texas moved again to bring Bob White to trial. A change of venue brought this second trial to Conroe, Texas, the county seat of Montgomery County. Although the small county of San Jacinto (total population under 5,000) separated Polk and Montgomery counties, both of these counties were in the same judicial district. Moreover, the district-court judge who would preside over the new trial in

Montgomery County was the same one (Judge W. B. Browder) who had presided over the first trial in Polk County. Thus a change of venue had not secured any real change.

The events in the second trial moved rapidly. A grand jury was empaneled and White was indicted again. A petit jury was selected and the case went to trial. Attorneys for White during his second trial and appeal were J. P. Rogers; the firm of Peden, Johnson, and Peden (represented by Jay M. Johnson); and S. F. Hill—all of Houston. The national NAACP organization had decided to lend aid to the local Texas branch in the spring of 1938, although the national body refused to commit itself to the $2,500 fee requested by the Peden firm.[8] It was all to no avail. Once again the jury convicted White of rape and sentenced him to death. Again White's attorneys appealed to the Texas Court of Criminal Appeals. They argued that there had been systematic exclusion of blacks from the jury and that this violated equal-protection and due-process guarantees of the Fifth and Fourteenth Amendments. White had not had an impartial jury of his peers.

Conviction and Appeal Again: The Highest State Court Refuses to Reverse

However, this time White's attorneys were unsuccessful in their appeal. On March 22, 1939, the highest state court held that White had not been deprived of a fair trial merely because there were no "persons of African descent" on the grand jury that indicted him or on the trial jury that convicted him. The court held that White lacked proof of purposeful discrimination in the jury selections. In addition, this time the state court upheld the prejudicial remarks made by the prosecutor. The private prosecutor, Z. L. Foreman, was a personal friend of the Cochran family. He intensely resented the efforts of "outside" attorneys, viewing them as agitators. During his address to the jury he attacked White's attorneys, claiming, "It doesn't make any difference to Mr. Johnson and Mr. Rogers what happens to Mrs. Cochran. As far as they are concerned their innocent Negro should be turned loose." The tone of Foreman's remarks indicated sarcasm and contempt for White's attorneys. Nevertheless, the Texas Court of Criminal Appeals refused to reverse on this ground because the trial judge had "clearly instructed the jury to disregard these remarks."[9]

In addition, the court accepted medical testimony that showed that Mrs. Cochran had had intercourse with someone during the night of August 10, 1937, but the court did not require the state to produce evidence concerning the presence of venereal disease. Since Bob White was suffering from such, evidence that Mrs. Cochran had *not* been infected would have been a point in his favor. The doctor's grudging admission that there was no way to show whether the sperm had come from a white man or a black man was insufficient to be of any help in White's defense. The medical testimony was far from conclusive. In a different setting and environment, all of it would probably have been excluded.

Finally, the court allowed the confession to be used in White's conviction, even though White had insisted from the opening of the first trial that the confession had been forced. The Court of Criminal Appeals pointed out that the trial judge had allowed defendant's attorneys to make their objections to the use of the confession and had then instructed the jury "not to consider the confession . . . unless they believed . . . that [it] was made under a proper warning, freely and voluntarily, and not under any fear, duress or coercion, fraud, persuasion, promise of immunity, or any other improper influence." This was sufficient protection of defendant's rights according to the Texas State Court of Criminal Appeals.

Appealing to the United States Supreme Court: Problems in Securing *Certiorari*

Having lost in both courts at the state level, White's attorneys (primarily J. P. Rogers and Judge S. J. Hill) prepared a writ of *certiorari* and an affidavit *in forma pauperis* to file with the United States Supreme Court. However, neither Rogers nor Hill were licensed to practice before the Court. Therefore, they secured the assistance of another Houston attorney, Carter W. Wesley, who represented Bob White on the petitions. Wesley was a well-known black attorney licensed to practice before the Court. Rogers and Hill asked Wesley to sign all papers as associate counsel, which he did. Wesley could appreciate the sufferings and problems of Bob White, because he himself had been brutally beaten by a Texas highway patrolman.[10]

The petitions did not reach the Supreme Court until one day after its adjournment—June 6, 1939. This meant that the Court would not consider the applications until the fall term. Bob White had been scheduled to die in the electric chair on June 2, 1939, and had been moved to Huntsville, Texas, and placed in the death cell. However, the state of Texas agreed to a stay of execution until the Supreme Court could act on the petitions. On November 13, 1939, after reviewing the *certiorari* petition, the Court stated that "upon examination of the papers herein submitted" they could find "no ground upon which such a writ should be issued." Apparently the NAACP was not surprised at the Court's action. Thurgood Marshall, now Special Counsel for the NAACP, pointed out that Texas legal procedure required that all motions attacking such matters as indictments, grand jury jurisdiction, and jury selection had to be raised *before* a change of venue was sought. In the Bob White case venue was changed from Polk County to Montgomery County before the motion was made concerning the exclusion of Negroes from the grand jury. Consequently, the Texas State Court of Criminal Appeals had held that the motion came too late. According to Marshall the Supreme Court was extremely reluctant at this time to interfere with questions of procedure in a state court where state law was clear, specific, and non-discriminatory on its face.

A New Precedent for *White*

It was at this point in the fall of 1939 that the NAACP and White's attorneys found themselves in a dilemma concerning the course of action they should follow. They wanted to ask the Supreme Court to reconsider but were unsure of the grounds they could use. Rogers felt that perhaps more evidence could be uncovered if there were time. He therefore concentrated his efforts at the local level and made an impassioned plea to the Board of Pardons and Paroles, asking them to commute White's death sentence into life imprisonment. He hoped that this would give White's friends a chance to find the guilty party. However, the board denied his appeal. In addition his appeal to the Governor for executive clemency also failed and White's execution date was set for March 2, 1940. Rogers was therefore completely unsuccessful in his efforts. However, a new option had opened at the national level. There had been pending in the Supreme Court at this time another case that in many respects was almost identical to the *Bob White* case. It had come to the Court from Florida and involved the rounding up of blacks as suspects in an atrocious crime, a week of questioning (including an all-night session), and forced confessions. The attorneys in this case, *Chambers* v. *Florida*, 309 U.S. 277 (1940), focused dramatically on these pre-trial proceedings and the Supreme Court had responded with a unanimous opinion reversing the state convictions. The Court was thoroughly aroused, and, in a biting opinion by Justice Black, described the methods used in the *Chambers* case as "smacking of the rack, the thumbscrew, and the wheel." Bob White's attorneys had also raised the issue of his forced confession. They had done this from the beginning of his first trial and had retained it in every subsequent trial and appeal. However, their initial emphases had been on the lack of an impartial jury—because the jury had not included blacks—and on the hostility of the community that made a fair trial impossible. The *Chambers* decision had not been handed down until February 12, 1940, and White's attorneys had to work quickly now to take advantage of this decision. In a meeting of the Executive Committee of the Houston branch of the NAACP, a black attorney, F. S. K. Whittaker, who was the Chairman of the Legal Redress Committee, proposed filing an amended motion to the petition for *certiorari;* the amended motion would focus on the forced confession. In particular, Whittaker wanted to highlight White's claim that he had been taken out of jail on four successive nights, carried to the woods, handcuffed around a small tree, and beaten by Texas Rangers whose intent was to secure his confession.[11] The local NAACP decided that this was an appropriate strategy and told Whittaker to go ahead. He succeeded in getting a stay of execution until March 15; on March 11 he secured a second stay, which moved the execution date to April 4, 1940. Both the Governor and the Board of Pardons and Paroles cooperated at this point. Whittaker then went to Austin, Texas, and paid to have the records of White's case sent from the Texas State Court of Criminal Appeals to the Supreme Court.

The Supreme Court Reverses: White's Confession Was Forced

In less than three weeks the Supreme Court did a complete turnaround in the *Bob White* case. On March 25, 1940, it vacated its order of the previous November, in which it had refused to hear the case. Now, the Court not only granted the motion for leave to file a petition for rehearing, but it also granted the motion for leave to proceed *in forma pauperis*, it granted the petition to file for a writ of *certiorari, and* it reversed the judgment of the Texas Court of Criminal Appeals (*White* v. *Texas*, 309 U.S. 631, 1940). Citing the *Chambers* decision as precedent the Supreme Court directed the state of Texas either to set White free or convict him in a proper trial without the use of the confession.

This about-face by the Court could not have occurred in all likelihood had Chief Justice Hughes not intervened as he did. The papers that Johnson and Rogers had submitted were "meager" according to Hughes's personal account. However, the petition submitted by Whittaker caused the Chief Justice to sense that an injustice had been done. He sent for the records from the two trials in the Texas District Court and the records of the Court of Criminal Appeals. These records revealed that Texas Rangers *had* used third-degree methods, and Hughes recommended a rehearing. The Supreme Court then took the case and summarily set aside the conviction—without hearing argument.

Texas fought back. The Attorney General of Texas and the state's Appellate Criminal Attorney petitioned the Court to hear oral argument and to allow the state to present its views. These two irate Texans had called on Chief Justice Hughes personally and accused the Court of arbitrary conduct. Hughes had politely suggested that they file a petition for rehearing. This was done, and on May 20, 1940, the case was argued before a Court composed of Chief Justice Hughes and Justices McReynolds, Stone, Roberts, Black, Reed, Frankfurter, Douglas, and Murphy.[12]

Bob White's attorneys before the Supreme Court were F. S. K. Whittaker and Carter W. Wesley, both of Houston.[13] Both men were black. Whittaker presented the oral argument, concentrating on the coerced confession. He took only thirty-five minutes of the time allocated to him.[14] Texas, on the other hand, engaged in lengthy and ingenious arguments. For example, Texas insisted that since White had denied having made the confession and the jury that convicted him had known that he had denied making it, then his conviction by the jury had obviously *not* been based on the use of the document. However, the case records that the Supreme Court now possessed overwhelmingly convinced the Court to overturn the state conviction of Bob White unanimously.

Thus on May 27, 1940, seven days after the oral argument, Justice Black, speaking for the entire Court, cut through the contorted arguments advanced by the attorneys for the state of Texas and stated that use of the confession in the trial had deprived White of procedural due process guaranteed by the Fourteenth and Fifth Amendments. *White* v. *Texas*, 310 U.S. 530 (1940), was a stinging indictment of "Texas justice"; Texas was now specifically charged to convict White only through constitutional means.

What the Court Actually Said and Did in the *Bob White* Case

Popular opinion often fails to understand the nature of decision making by the Supreme Court. The Court is primarily an *appellate* court; only a fraction of its cases come under original jurisdiction. The majority of the cases that the Court hears have been argued in at least one lower court. The Court reviews the record of these proceedings when it decides whether to hear the case or not. That record provides the foundation for the action the Court will take in a case. In the *Bob White* case, contrary to some elements of popular opinion, the Court said nothing about guilt or innocence. It could not do that; in fact, no appellate court could. The issue before the Court was the narrow question, "Did Bob White have a fair trial with all the guarantees of due process of law?" That question the Court answered with a resounding "No!" after reviewing the record. The record showed clearly that White had been held without a lawyer, had been systematically interrogated, and had, in all likelihood, been beaten by Texas Rangers to extract his confession. Such a confession should not be used to convict White; it violated the guarantees of the Fifth Amendment that state courts as well as federal courts were required to abide by the Constitution's prohibition against compelling a person to be a witness against himself. It is true that originally the federal Bill of Rights was binding only on the national government. Chief Justice John Marshall had stated this clearly in *Barron* v. *Baltimore*, 7 Peters 243 (1833). The founding fathers had believed that states could be relied upon to protect civil liberties under their own state constitutions. However, time revealed that minorities received little protection under the state documents. After the Civil War and the passage of the Fourteenth Amendment in 1868, the Supreme Court slowly began to require states to provide some of the guarantees listed in the Bill of Rights. Generally the Court required that the protection demanded be so essential that justice could not be secured if the individual were denied this right. The process of choosing fundamental rights was known as selective incorporation and was described by Justice Cardozo in *Palko* v. *Connecticut*, 302 U.S. 319 (1937). Gradually the Court moved to extend to state court trials most of the federally protected rights and liberties.

Hostile Reaction in Texas: The Supreme Court under Attack

Yet public opinion, particularly in Texas, could not comprehend what the Court was actually saying and doing in the *Bob White* case. Public opinion in Texas was firmly convinced that Bob White was guilty. He had had two court trials and had been convicted by two juries. Moreover, he had confessed! How the confession had been secured was not significant. Indeed, few people knew the actual details. The Texas newspaper coverage of the case had not included any information about White's interrogation by the Texas Rangers. A hostile public believed that the Supreme Court had declared Bob White to be innocent and had used fancy legal footwork to set him free.[15] The state was now forced to seek a third trial if it wished to convict Bob White. Since the state courts were under orders to conform to higher-court requirements for an "error free" trial, there was no issue of "double jeopardy." Anger against the Supreme Court's ruling mounted in Polk and Montgomery counties. However, much of the anger of the prosecutors was due to the fact that they knew how weak the case was without the confession. Would it be possible to secure a conviction that could withstand judicial scrutiny?

Trial III: Texas Tries Again to Convict White

It was June 1941 before the state was finally ready to move into a new trial and to begin the process of jury selection. It was now almost four years from the date on which the crime had been committed and the first trial held in August 1937. Tuesday, June 10, 1941, dawned bright and hot in the small southeastern town of Conroe, Texas, thirty-seven miles north of Houston. In the Montgomery County Courthouse the jury was being selected for the third trial of Bob White. The cast of characters was almost identical to that involved in the first and second trials. Judge W. B. Browder was again the presiding judge; Z. L. Foreman, whose inflammatory language in the first trial had alienated even the Texas State Court of Criminal Appeals, was still the special prosecutor. White's attorney, J. P. Rogers, was again conducting the defense. Present also was the husband of victim Ruby Cochran, W. S. ("Dude") Cochran. A flashy and arrogant man, Cochran was held in awe by local Negroes, who called him "Mr. Dude"—a title apparently derived from his large land holdings and mercantile business as well as his social status.

Bob White, now thirty-one years old, slumped in his chair; he was quiet and withdrawn.[16] However, he was not quite as alone as he had been before. His wife of three years was present in the back of the courtroom. Ruby Lee had married Bob White in June 1938 at the prison where he was then confined; for three years she had stood by her husband, asserting his innocence. Bob White's mother—Martha White—had also stood by her son; she too was present that fateful June 10, although she was not allowed into the courtroom. She was permitted to wait in a downstairs room in the courthouse. There were a number of local lawmen from Montgomery County in the courtroom: Sheriff Grover Mostyn, Deputy Sheriff Herschel Surrantt, two other deputy sheriffs, and Montgomery County Prosecutor W. C. McClain.[17]

Murder in the Courtroom:
The Supreme Court Is Overruled

The selection of the jury was difficult: few people in Conroe were unbiased in their opinions. In fact, out of a panel of one hundred white veniremen who had been summoned as possible jurors for the trial, only nine were found to be acceptable. When the ninth juror was accepted it was already 12:05 P.M. and it was obvious that a recess would have to be called until another panel could be secured and three more jurors selected. As the ninth juror was being led to join the other eight, "Dude" Cochran suddenly appeared inside the bar that separated the jury and the prisoner from the spectators. He produced a .38 caliber pistol and, holding it three inches from Bob White's head, fired a single shot that "ploughed its way through the Negro's brains, coming out of his right ear." Bob White died immediately.[18] "Dude" Cochran, with the overwhelming approval of the local populace, had reversed the Supreme Court. White's win in that court had now become a loss. White could never receive that fair trial or due process essential to the Anglo-American system of law. The Supreme Court had not been able to enforce its mandate on a hostile community.

There were slightly different reports concerning actual behavior within the courtroom that day. One black newspaper, the *New York Amsterdam Star-News*,[19] told its readers that Cochran had simply "walked into the district court" and shot White. The *Conroe Courier*[20] (the local white newspaper) stated that "W. S. Cochran of Livingston (husband of the victim) whipped out a .38 caliber pistol, advanced close to the Negro and fired one time. A bullet went through White's head and he died immediately." The *New York Times* of June 11 said that "Cochran jumped to his feet." The *Chicago Daily Tribune* of June 11 based its account on the statement of White's attorney, J. P. Rogers, who was sitting near Bob White and who had just been questioning the ninth juror. Rogers said that he saw Cochran walk into the courtroom with a pistol in hand. "I thought he was bringing the gun in as evidence," Rogers said. "He walked down and leaned over to within a foot of the defendant. There was one shot, killing him instantly." Ruby White, in a sworn affidavit of her eyewitness account, declared that she saw Cochran "get up" but had not paid any attention until she heard the gun shot.[21] However, the *Pittsburgh Courier* of June 21 quoted Mrs. White as saying that she noticed "Dude" Cochran "get up from his spectator's seat between his two brothers" and walk toward her husband. "There was a sudden explosion like a bomb, and Bob's head slumped to one side, but he did not fall over," she said.

One thing seemed clear, however. Cochran had obviously come to the courtroom deliberately armed to take the law into his own hands. One black newspaper (the *Chicago Defender* of June 21) asserted that Cochran had planned the crime the night before and had boasted, "I'll end this damn thing tomorrow with my .45; to hell with this rotten court foolishness." Moreover, no one had attempted to stop Cochran. Black newspaper and NAACP officials later claimed that some form of conspiracy must have existed between Cochran and court officials and that the reason no one attempted to stop Cochran was because the officials knew of his plan and deliberately made it easy for him to implement it. An examination of the movements of the sheriff and his deputies seemed to lend credence to this theory. Apparently on Monday, the first day of jury selection, the sheriff and his three deputies were in the courtroom the entire time and no more than one ever left at a time. On Tuesday, the day of the murder, the sheriff and his three deputies brought Bob White into the courtroom at 10:00 A.M. Just before 12:00 P.M. the sheriff and two deputies left the courtroom one after the other until only one deputy, Mr. Herschel Surrantt, was left. At exactly 12:00 P.M. Deputy Surrantt left the room. At that point Cochran carried out his crime. The sound of the gun caused Sheriff Grover Mostyn to rush back into the courtroom.[22]

As the shot rang out, the courtroom burst into pandemonium: blacks broke for the rear doors fearing that it might be the "beginning of a wholesale reign of terror" on the black population; whites, on the other hand, "scrambled to the front railing to shake hands with and congratulate Cochran."[23] According to one account this latter group included court officials and jurymen.[24] The judge apparently remained seated—quite calm and showing no emotion.[25] One newspaper reported that he remarked, "Well, gentlemen, I guess that ends it."[26]

When the excitement had diminished, Cochran walked over to the table of the special prosecutor and quietly handed his gun to his friend, Z. L. Foreman. He then surrendered to Sheriff Grover

Mostyn, who had rushed into the courtroom upon hearing the commotion. Cochran was taken into custody and escorted immediately to the nearby office of Judge J. W. McDaniel, a local justice of the peace. He was booked on a technical charge of murder and immediately released on a nominal bond of $500 posted by his longtime friend, J. L. Pitts, a wealthy Conroe oilman.[27] This took only a few minutes, after which Cochran left the courthouse and met his wife, who drove him to their home in Livingston.

Conroe had always prided itself, however mistakenly, on its belief in the orderly process of the law and adherence to the requirements of a law-and-order society.[28] Thus there was no question of Cochran's going scot-free or escaping the formalities of accusation, charge, and trial.

White's Murderer: "Not Guilty!"

Exactly six days after "Murder in the Courtroom"[29]—Monday, June 16, 1941—W. S. Cochran was brought to trial. Again the scene was familiar. It was still Judge W. B. Browder's courtroom. There was a local jury of "twelve good men and true."[30] However, the state prosecutor, District Attorney W. C. McClain, behaved in an unusual manner. Instead of seeking a conviction of Cochran for the murder of White, McClain urged acquittal. In his address to the jury McClain stated that "the guilty person got justice" when White was shot to death. "I have always said that I would never ask a jury to do anything that I wouldn't do myself," McClain continued. "If I were on the jury I would not hesitate a minute to find the defendant not guilty." Cochran hardly needed a defense given this type of prosecution. McClain's speech generated hearty applause. The jury filed out and returned in two minutes with a verdict of not guilty. Handshakes followed, with judge, jurors, murderer, and prosecutor being almost overwhelmed with congratulations from the audience. The whole trial had taken less than three hours.[31]

Obviously, the white population of Polk and Montgomery counties agreed with McClain's view "that the guilty person was justly disposed of." The formalities of the law had been followed with respect to the arrest and trial of Cochran, and a jury verdict of acquittal allowed Cochran to walk away a free man, never to be charged again. Local white newspapers assured their readers that no issue of race hatred had been involved and that there was no question of White's guilt. Indeed, reading the local account in the *Conroe Courier* of June 12 and 19, one would have found it impossible to make an unbiased and educated judgment based on the *Courier's* summary of the events from August 1937 to June 1941. For instance, the *Courier* declared that bloodhounds had run White down. Testimony in court proceedings, however, stated that the dogs, although used, were unable to track anyone down. A footprint found under the window did not yield sufficient scent. In addition, the local paper stressed the fact that no reign of terror had erupted. Conroe had remained calm, and blacks had continued to "loiter" in their usual places around the courthouse and in the business district one block from the courthouse.[32] In fact, general satisfaction over the killing of Bob White was apparent in the business district, according to the *Courier*.[33]

Public Opinion and the Supreme Court: Texas Blames the Court

Moreover, as the local white press analyzed the course of events, it was the fault of the Supreme Court that Cochran had had to shoot White to secure justice. One major point stressed in Cochran's trial was the fact that "every effort possible had been used to obtain punishment of Bob White for his most heinous crime,"[34] and that justice had not been obtained through the channels of court procedure. The *Conroe Courier* told their readers that White's victory in the first trial had been due only to a technicality—namely, the fact that the prosecutor had used "inflammatory" language. In the second trial, White's victory came because the "Supreme Court of the United States believed that statement of Bob White [that his confession was obtained under duress] against the statements of seven white men who stated that Bob White's confession was voluntary and not forced." The *Courier* declared that "*incontrovertible* proof of Bob White's guilt" was to be found in his confession. The paper rejoiced that the verdict in the Cochran trial had finally closed "one of the ugliest cases in the history of the local courts." Justice, according to white Texans, had finally been secured in spite of the Supreme Court.[35]

Black Americans' Perception of the Power of the Supreme Court

Black newspapers throughout the country saw this for what it really was—"Texas justice"—a deliberate and open defiance that summarily reversed a clear decision of the Supreme Court and showed contempt for that tribunal.[36] The *Pittsburgh Courier* called the Cochran acquittal an "open rape of the Goddess of Justice in the Temple of Law and Order, under the very noses of her oath bound guardians and defenders."[37] For blacks everywhere it seemed that law and justice, at least in Montgomery County, had become a "puny, cowering thing; a whimpering tuck-tail creature ready to cringe anytime at the boot-toe of any bullying outlaw who chooses to take things in his own hands."[38] The *New York Amsterdam Star-News* declared that Cochran had single-handedly reversed a decision of the Supreme Court and had manifested cold-blooded contempt for law.[39] Moreover, this seemed to prove that neither the law itself nor the Supreme Court could protect the Negro in Texas. Texas law failed even "to protect the prisoner in open court before the bar of justice."[40]

The *Baltimore Afro-American* declared that a lynching spirit was not confined to mobs of poor whites and irresponsible hoodlums in the South; the *Bob White* case proved that "jury, prosecutor, and the Bench of Justice itself showed a spirit of lawless violence."[41] The *New York Amsterdam Star-News* declared that the "will to murder," to take the law away from those sworn to uphold it, was present not only in the minds of "poor crackers" but was shared by the wealthy and influential members of Dixie's bourgeoisie. The *Star-News* then illustrated their point by quoting some of the reactions of whites. One was quoted as saying, "The Nigger didn't deserve a trial"; another, "The judge made Cochran's bond too high. He should have released him on his word. Don't he own all the land around here?"[42]

Moreover, it was the consensus of the black papers that Cochran's acquittal demonstrated contempt for the Supreme Court itself as well as for the orderly process of law and justice.[43] The *Crisis* concluded that the United States government had no power in the South and that "the Constitution and the Bill of Rights had no force or meaning south of the Mason-Dixon line." In fact, it appeared to the editor of the *Crisis* that in Texas "the Government resided in the hands of the local peace officer and the local judge. The United States Supreme Court was powerless."[44]

Black newspapers did not try to determine the guilt or innocence of Bob White. Their first concern was that White had not had a fair trial and their second that Cochran had not been properly judged and penalized for his brutal murder of an unarmed man. They demanded a meaningful prosecution of Cochran. The *New York Amsterdam Star-News* declared that the only action that would lessen the "blemish on the name of Texas and the escutch-

eon of justice" would be the uncompromising prosecution of
Cochran.[45] The *Chicago Defender* insisted that Cochran's punishment was necessary to show white people in the South that they
could no longer "take the law into their own hands."[46] The *Defender* portrayed Cochran as a "barbarian" who, along with
others of his type, needed to understand that civilized society
would not tolerate interferences with the administration of justice or a wanton disregard for due process of law. Cochran, said
the *Defender*, should be charged with both first-degree murder
and contempt of court. And, in a graphic cartoon, the *Defender*
portrayed the "murderer Cochran" acting out his contempt of the
Supreme Court through his resort to the "Law of the Jungle" and
his abandonment of the principles of "Equal Justice Under
Law."[47]

Appeals to the Political Branches of Government

Black newspapers urged the federal government to become involved. One editor told his readers that unless a federal issue
could be raised there would be no hope of bringing Cochran to
justice in a town and country that he and his family controlled
and where the prosecutor was a personal friend.[48] To this end
black editors advised their audience to write their Congressmen,
their Senators, the Department of Justice, and the President himself. At the same time the black newspapers themselves stepped
up their pressure for a stronger anti-lynching law. Although such
legislation had been pending before Congress for some time, it
was aimed at mob violence, which was defined as "three or more
people involved in a lynching." Since Cochran had acted alone,
the legislation would have been ineffective in bringing him to
justice. The newspapers urged Congress to pass stronger legislation so that (as one phrased it) "Bob White may not have died in
vain."[49] They also beseeched President Franklin Roosevelt to intervene personally to see that Cochran was justly punished.

Editorial after editorial insisted that American democracy could
not tolerate Cochran's obvious contempt for law and justice; to
allow Cochran to go free was simply to put ammunition in the
hands of fascist governments.[50] One paper dramatically summed
up this point by stating that the persecution of Jews in Nazi Germany did not equal in "frightfulness or terror the murderous assault upon Bob White in the courtroom at Conroe, Texas, and the
freeing of his fiendish murderer in two minutes."[51]

The NAACP, which had believed that Bob White was going to

be released after the Supreme Court had declared use of the confession unconstitutional, now began to work feverishly alongside the black newspapers in an effort to arouse the public conscience and to motivate the federal government to intervene. Walter White, national secretary of the NAACP, sent a telegram to Robert H. Jackson, Attorney General of the United States. Dated June 11, 1941, the telegram reported the murder of Bob White in the Conroe courtroom. The NAACP then urged the Department of Justice to investigate under both Section 47, subsection 2, and Section 48 of Chapter Three, Title Eight of the United States Code Annotated. NAACP officials, including their special counsel Thurgood Marshall, had decided that their best argument lay in convincing the Justice Department to act under the conspiracy clause of the Civil Rights Act. They decided not to specify immediately in writing the forms of conspiracy they alleged. However, they did agree on two possible counts, which they hoped to use as soon as they received some feedback from the federal officials. They charged first that there was some agreement between the court officials and Cochran that permitted him to walk into the courtroom without concealing his revolver and to go up and shoot White to death without any interference by the court officials who were sworn to protect his person and his civil rights. Their second charge was that there was probably some sort of an agreement permitting Z. L. Foreman, Cochran's intimate friend, to be made special prosecutor of White.[52]

Other organized black groups followed the leadership of the NAACP. A. Maceo Smith, Secretary of the Texas Conference of the NAACP and an executive in the Texas Negro Chamber of Commerce, sent a personal letter on behalf of his organization to Assistant Attorney General Schweinhaut, appealing to him to take action in "one of the most flagrant breeches of the dignity of our court in the history of Texas."[53] Schweinhaut had previously met Rev. M. H. Jackson of the NAACP and had apparently impressed this black minister with his sincere concern for the rights of minority groups. Smith enclosed newspaper clippings to impress the lurid details of the crime on Schweinhaut.[54] Some black leaders suggested that the Supreme Court cite Cochran, the judge, *and* the prosecutor for contempt of court and impose a heavy prison term—perhaps twenty years. There was one case precedent—the case of a Negro who had been lynched while his case was pending in the Supreme Court on a capital writ of *certiorari*. In the *Bob White* case, however, the matter was not pending before the Supreme Court when White was murdered. The case had been sent back to Texas on the mandate of the Court, and this had changed the jurisdiction back to the Texas courts. Thus federal governmental officials were unwilling to attempt any action this way, and Thurgood Marshall agreed that there was no strong legal precedent for such an approach.[55]

Black groups sent letters not only to politicians but also to prominent journalists and editors. These included such notables as George Britt of the *New York Evening Post*, Arthur Hayes Sulzberger of the *New York Times*, Freda Kirchway of the *Nation*, Bruce Bliven of the *New Republic*, and Walter Mills of the *New York Herald Tribune*. A lengthy telegram was sent by the NAACP to more than twenty prominent persons describing the murder of Bob White and asking each to issue a statement expressing their reaction. Among those to whom the telegram was sent were Senator Tom Connally of Texas, former Vice-President John N. Garner, James F. Byrnes, Wendell Willkie, Mrs. Ogden Reid, Dr. Nicholas Murray Butler of Columbia University, Chancellor Harry Chase of New York University, Professor Robert Hutchins of the University of Chicago, Dr. Luther Weigle of Yale University, Walter Lippman, Senator Robert F. Wagner, Vice-President Henry Wallace, and William Allen White. All these were white people. The telegram, dramatic and emotional, read as follows:

WESTERN UNION   12 JUNE 1941

WILL YOU WIRE COLLECT FIFTY–WORD OPINION ON SHOOTING BOB WHITE, NEGRO, IN CONROE, TEXAS, TUESDAY BY W.S. COCHRAN, HUSBAND OF WOMAN WHITE WAS CHARGED WITH CRIMINALLY ASSAULTING IN NINETEEN THIRTY SEVEN. CAREFULLY CHECKED FACTS ARE THESE: FINGERPRINTS AND FOOTPRINTS TAKEN BY SHERIFF NOT OFFERED IN EVIDENCE BY STATE.... WHITE WAS TAKEN FROM JAIL FOUR SUCCESSIVE NIGHTS BY POLICE OFFICERS AND BEATEN UNMERCIFULLY. AFTER FIVE DAYS OF TORTURE HE SIGNED STATEMENT UNDER THREATS OF LYNCHING. STATEMENT PREPARED BY Z. FOREMAN, INTIMATE FRIEND OF COCHRAN WHO LATER NAMED SPECIAL PROSECUTOR OF WHITE. ALL NEGROES DRIVEN FROM TOWN DAY OF TRIAL, INCLUDING WITNESSES WHO COULD HAVE TESTIFIED THAT WHITE WAS AT HOME AT TIME OF ALLEGED ATTACK. FEW NEGRO WITNESSES CALLED WERE HELD UNDER ARMED GUARD AND WERE TERRORIZED BY HOWLING MOB OUTSIDE COURTHOUSE. CONVICTION WAS FLAGRANT VIOLATION [OF] EVERY PRECEPT OF CONSTITUTIONAL GOVERNMENT.

TEXAS COURT OF APPEALS REVERSED LOWER COURT
AND ORDERED NEW TRIAL. SECOND CONVICTION WAS
REVERSED BY UNITED STATES SUPREME COURT, NINE-
TEEN FORTY. AT COMMENCEMENT THIRD TRIAL TUES-
DAY LAST COCHRAN WAS PERMITTED TO WALK INTO
COURTROOM WITH PISTOL PLAINLY TO BE SEEN AND
SHOOT WHITE WITHOUT MOLESTATION. COCHRAN THEN
RELEASED UNDER RIDICULOUSLY LOW BAIL OF FIVE
HUNDRED DOLLARS. WE WOULD DEEPLY APPRECIATE
OPINION FROM YOU AND OTHER LEADERS [OF] AMERI-
CAN OPINION REGARDING THIS, ESPECIALLY IN RELA-
TION TO OUR PRESENT EFFORTS TO ARM TO DEFEND DE-
MOCRACY ABROAD.

> Walter White, Secretary
> NATIONAL ASSOCIATION FOR
> ADVANCEMENT OF COLORED PEOPLE

NAACP Secretary Walter White also personally wired details to
Harold Ickes, Secretary of the Interior. The NAACP official cited
the courtroom murder of Bob White as "an additional tragic reason" for Ickes to attend the 32nd annual NAACP convention,
which was set to meet June 24–29, 1941, in Houston.[56]

The NAACP was not successful in generating a tide of positive
public sentiment. Many of the notables contacted were "out of
town" and hence "unable to respond" to the NAACP's telegrams.[57]
A few did, however. Wendell Willkie, columnist Dorothy Thompson, and Robert M. Hutchins of the University of Chicago all responded, calling the murder "outrageous" and a violation of all
democratic principles.[58] The editor of the *Raleigh* (North Carolina)
News and Observer, Jonathan Daniels, wrote a biting editorial in
which he compared the local trial-court judge to a "lynching judge
personified." Editor Daniels declared that mob lynchings were less
heinous than the "official condonation of murder in justice's hall
itself" by a judge sworn to uphold civilized, orderly justice.[59] William Allen White, editor and owner of the *Emporia* (Kansas) *Gazette*, also wrote a widely publicized editorial in which he charged
that the United States could not "point with a clean finger" at
Hitler and his "gangster justice" in Germany as long as crimes
such as the Bob White murder went unpunished.[60]

The presidents of the YMCA and the YWCA also condemned the
shooting of Bob White, while the chancellor of New York University expressed his "deep distress."[61] W. Spencer Robertson was
president of the Young Men's Christian Association at the time.
His telegram in response to the Bob White murder was especially

interesting due to what was probably a typographical error. He declared that Cochran's action showed "DEFIANCE OF HUGH-EST COURTS OF STATE AND NATION." Robertson probably meant "highest," but the substitution of a "u" for an "i" makes for interesting speculation, given the fact that Charles Evans *Hughes* was Chief Justice at this time and was known to "run" his Court. Certainly, Cochran's action directly violated the opinion handed down by the Hughes Court and challenged its authority and power.

However, public sentiment in general could not be aroused sufficiently. Too many other issues preoccupied Americans. Walter White complained to Edward L. Bernays that it was extremely difficult to get publicity for cases involving Negroes like Bob White. Walter White demanded an explanation as to why the New York papers had not published either of the two press releases issued by the NAACP. He asked Bernays, "Was it our failure to include more of a résumé of the case? Or did the ousting of Nazi consuls blanket the news too much?"[62] Concern over Bob White was overshadowed by pending threats of riots in many American cities; full-fledged American entry into World War II was only six months away. The Department of Justice reviewed the situation and refused to act. Assistant Attorney General Wendell Berge, writing for Attorney General Robert H. Jackson, told NAACP officials that after careful consideration the "Federal Government does not believe that it has any jurisdiction over the issue." The Department of Justice interpreted the conspiracy section of Chapter Three of the United States Code, Section 47(2) and Section 48, to mean that "the only basis for federal intervention lies with the individual whose rights have been violated. The Federal Government cannot initiate action." In short,

> the jurisdiction of the Federal Government in civil rights matters is limited to rights secured by the Constitution and laws of the United States. The instant matter [the killing of Bob White by Cochran] appears to involve a murder, and as such is within the exclusive jurisdiction of the State of Texas.[63]

Still, the verdict of the Supreme Court could have emerged triumphant had local officials refused to condone the actions of "Dude" Cochran. Eyewitness accounts showed clearly that the murder was premeditated; Cochran had come armed to the courtroom. Yet state prosecutors made no meaningful attempt to convict and punish Cochran. Indeed, they rushed to acquit him. They not only condoned his actions, but applauded them. The trial and acquittal of Cochran by the state of Texas ultimately left the Supreme Court powerless. Murder is a state crime, as the Justice Department pointed out, and there were no powerful civil-rights laws in 1941 that the federal government could invoke and use to bring Cochran to justice.

The NAACP delegates, who met together in Houston for their 32nd annual convention just fifteen days after the White murder and nine days after the Cochran acquittal, could only listen with sympathy to the plea of Ruby White, the widow of Bob White. Her dramatic, yet simple, eyewitness description of the murder and her story of the events from 1937 to 1941 cut deeply into the emotions of the delegates crowded into the auditorium of the Good Hope Baptist Church in Houston. The convention took up a collection of one hundred dollars for her personally and began its legal battle to bring Cochran to justice.[64] But it was to no avail. The case was closed. "Texas justice" had overruled a United States Supreme Court decision. Bob White had won his case before the Supreme Court, but for him it was the same as though he had lost.

Nevertheless, the story was, and is, not completely ended. In the years that followed, the Supreme Court continued to hear case after case in which blacks were deprived of their constitutional rights. As the Court continued to speak out against such deprivations, the political branches of the government—the Congress and the President—began to stir also. The true meaning of due process of law and a fair trial—those constitutional principles set forth in the Fifth and Sixth Amendments—would begin to emerge triumphant over vigilante justice. Examination of the feedback stage of the judicial process illustrates that today's loser can become tomorrow's winner.

NOTES

1. Albert P. Blaustein and Clarence C. Ferguson, Jr., in Theodore L. Becker and Malcolm M. Feeley, eds., *The Impact of Supreme Court Decisions*, 2nd ed. (New York: Oxford University Press, 1973), pp. 100–9.

2. Walter F. Murphy, *Elements of Judicial Strategy* (Chicago: University of Chicago Press, 1964), pp. 92–93.

3. See *Worcester* v. *Georgia*, 6 Peters 515 (1832), for one example. President Andrew Jackson upheld the state and challenged the Supreme Court to implement its decision. Jackson reportedly said, "Well, John Marshall has made his decision, now let him enforce it." For a detailed discussion see Charles Warren, *The Supreme Court in United States History*, 2 vols. (Boston: Little, Brown, 1922), vol. 1: "The Cherokee Cases and President Jackson," pp. 729–79.

4. See court record *White* v. *State of Texas*, 117 S.W. 2d 450 (1938); see also court record *White* v. *State of Texas*, 128 S.W. 2d 57 (1939).

5. See court record *White* v. *Texas*, 310 U.S. 530 (1940).

6. Correspondence, NAACP Files, Group II, Series L (Addenda), Container 31, Manuscript Division, Library of Congress, Washington, D.C.

7. *White* v. *Texas*, 117 S.W. 2d 450 (1938).

8. Charles H. Houston to Roy Wilkins, 22 July 1938, NAACP Files, Group II, Series L (Addenda), Container 31, Manuscript Division, Library of Congress, Washington, D.C.

9. *White* v. *Texas*, 128 S.W. 2d 51 (1939). The decision was handed down on March 22, 1939, and the Court refused a petition for rehearing on May 17, 1939.

10. *Pittsburgh Courier*, 21 June 1941.

11. Correspondence, NAACP Files, Group II, Series B, Container 55, Manuscript Division, Library of Congress, Washington, D.C.

12. See Merlo J. Pusey, *Charles Evans Hughes* (New York: Macmillan, 1951), vol. 2, p. 727. See also Edwin McElwain, "Chief Justice Hughes," *Harvard Law Review*, vol. 63, no. 1, p. 25. Chief Justice Hughes had lived up to his reputation as a civil libertarian. Hughes also demonstrated his "passion for facts," which had won him a reputation as a legal investigator.

13. F. S. K. Whittaker replaced the two white attorneys, J. P. Rogers and S. F. Hill, for purposes of oral argument as well as the appeal.

14. After the arguments Chief Justice Hughes invited Whittaker to an informal interview in his office at his home. Whittaker later stated that he found Hughes to be a "very congenial and scholarly man, pleasant and easy to talk to." F. S. K. Whittaker to Thurgood Marshall, 31 May

1940, NAACP Files, Group II, Series B, Container 55, Manuscript Division, Library of Congress, Washington, D.C.

15. *Conroe Courier*, 12 June 1941.

16. *Ibid*. See also *Pittsburgh Courier*, 21 June 1941.

17. *Pittsburgh Courier*, 21 June 1941. Bob White and Ruby Lee first met in November 1936.

18. For various accounts of the murder see *Conroe Courier*, 12 June 1941; *New York Amsterdam Star-News*, 14 June 1941; *Chicago Daily Tribune*, 11 June 1941; *Pittsburgh Courier*, 21 June 1941; *Detroit Tribune*, 5 July 1941; *Chicago Defender*, 21 June 1941; *Baltimore Afro-American*, 16 June 1941, *New York Times*, 11 June 1941.

19. *New York Amsterdam Star-News*, 14 June 1941.

20. *Conroe Courier*, 12 June 1941.

21. The sworn affidavit of Ruby White, widow of Bob White, was made on June 28, 1941, and can be found in the NAACP Files, Group II, Series B, Container 214, Manuscript Division, Library of Congress, Washington, D.C.

22. NAACP Files, Group II, Series B, Container 214, Manuscript Division, Library of Congress, Washington, D.C.

23. *Pittsburgh Courier*, 21 June 1941.

24. *Ibid*.

25. Affidavit of Ruby White, NAACP Files, Group II, Series B, Container 214, Manuscript Division, Library of Congress, Washington, D.C.

26. *Chicago Defender*, 21 June 1941.

27. *Conroe Courier*, 12 June 1941; *Pittsburgh Courier*, 21 June 1941; *New York Amsterdam Star-News*, 14 June 1941.

28. *Conroe Courier*, 19 June 1941.

29. *Baltimore Afro-American*, 16 June 1941. The title "Murder in the Cathedral" is a takeoff on the T. S. Eliot play *Murder in the Cathedral*.

30. *Baltimore Afro-American*, 28 June 1941.

31. *New York Amsterdam Star-News*, 21 June 1941; *Chicago Defender*, 21 June 1941. See also correspondence from Walter White, Secretary of the NAACP, to W. Spencer Robertson, Chairman of the National Council of the YMCA, NAACP Files, Group II, Series B, Container 214, Manuscript Division, Library of Congress, Washington, D.C. Several black newspapers reported that a banquet was given for Cochran after the trial and that Mrs. Cochran was showered with flowers. *Chicago Defender*, 21 June 1941.

32. *Conroe Courier*, 12 June 1941.

33. *Conroe Courier*, 19 June 1941.

34. *Ibid.*

35. *Ibid.*

36. *Pittsburgh Courier*, 21 June 1941.

37. *Ibid.*

38. *Pittsburgh Courier*, 28 June 1941.

39. *New York Amsterdam Star-News*, 14 June 1941.

40. *Ibid.*

41. *Baltimore Afro-American*, 28 June 1941.

42. *New York Amsterdam Star-News*, 14 June 1941 and 21 June 1941.

43. *Baltimore Afro-American*, 28 June 1941.

44. *Crisis*, vol. 48 (1941), p. 215.

45. *New York Amsterdam Star-News*, 14 June 1941.

46. *Chicago Defender*, 21 June 1941.

47. *Ibid.* The motto "Equal Justice Under Law" is carved around the top of the United States Supreme Court Building in Washington, D.C.

48. *New York Amsterdam Star-News*, 14 June 1941.

49. *New York Amsterdam Star-News*, 21 June 1941.

50. *Chicago Defender*, 21 June 1941.

51. *Detroit Tribune*, 5 July 1941.

52. NAACP Files, Group II, Series B, Container 214, Manuscript Division, Library of Congress, Washington, D.C.

53. A. Maceo Smith to Assistant Attorney General Schweinhaut, 14 June 1941, NAACP Files, Group II, Series B, Container 214, Manuscript Division, Library of Congress, Washington, D.C.

54. See correspondence between Walter White and William H. Hastie, 11 June 1941, NAACP Files, Group II, Series B, Container 214, Manuscript Division, Library of Congress, Washington, D.C.

55. See correspondence between Thurgood Marshall, Special Counsel, NAACP, and Edward Kaylin. NAACP Files, Group II, Series B, Container 214, Manuscript Division, Library of Congress, Washington, D.C.

56. Walter White to Harold L. Ickes, 11 June 1941, NAACP Files, Group II, Series B, Container 214, Manuscript Division, Library of Congress, Washington, D.C.

57. Walter White to Edward L. Bernays, 17 June 1941, NAACP Files, Group II, Series B, Container 214, Manuscript Division, Library of Congress, Washington, D.C.

58. NAACP Files, Group II, Series B, Container 214, Manuscript Division, Library of Congress, Washington, D.C.

59. Jonathan Daniels, "Judge Lynch Himself," *Raleigh* (North Carolina) *News and Observer*, 12 June 1941.

60. William Allen White, "The Texas Case," *Emporia* (Kansas) *Gazette*, 18 June 1941.

61. W. Spencer Robertson to Walter White, 13 June 1941; Mrs. Henry A. Ingraham to Walter White, 19 June 1941. NAACP Files, Group II, Series B, Container 214, Manuscript Division, Library of Congress, Washington, D.C.

62. Walter White to Edward L. Bernays, 17 June 1941, NAACP Files, Group II, Series B, Container 214, Manuscript Division, Library of Congress, Washington, D.C.

63. Wendell Berge to Walter White, 25 June 1941, NAACP Files, Group II, Series B, Container 214, Manuscript Division, Library of Congress, Washington, D.C.

64. *Detroit Tribune*, 5 July 1941. NAACP officials had asked Ruby White to speak to convention delegates on Wednesday, June 25, 1941. She stated her firm belief in her husband's innocence and then described her last meeting with him. Neither one had been able to understand why White was being brought to trial after the Supreme Court decision. According to Mrs. White, her husband had stated that he was innocent, but that he "had rather die than go through the torture . . . of the last years."

CHAPTER 5

ALL IS NOT LOST

HOW FEEDBACK COMMUNICATIONS
AFFECT THE JUDICIAL PROCESS

The impact of a Supreme Court decision may reverberate for some time, setting counteractions into motion. An immediate reaction occurs almost simultaneously with the communication of the decision to those most immediately affected. Ultimately both the decision and its growing impact will be communicated to more groups and individuals. This communication of the decision and the reactions to it produce what judicial-systems theorists refer to as feedback.

The forms of feedback are many. Whatever the form, however, the purpose is to communicate to the Court a perception of what the Court has done or has failed to do. Generally, the communication of these perceptions will take the form of a new or revised input into the judicial system, which often results in another case for the Court to decide. Feedback, as a result of these communications, thus ultimately leads to positive or negative responses by the Justices.[1] One authority has described the feedback process in the following manner:

> Within a judicial system, feedback can be conceptualized as the communication through formal and informal channels to the judicial authorities of compliance or non-compliance to authoritative output, changes in the level and kind of support, and attempts to limit the authorities and redefine the boundaries of the system. Litigation fed into the system in response to past court decisions is a major form of feedback for a judicial system.[2]

The Supreme Court decisions in *Frohwerk* v. *United States, Minersville* v. *Gobitis, Walker* v. *Birmingham,* and *White* v. *Texas* had varying degrees of impact upon the system. The responses to these decisions would be communicated to the Court as subsequent litigation ensued. The Court would be asked to reconsider the issues raised by the past case in yet another form or context and to re-examine its decisions. This feedback process would ultimately convert the causes apparently lost in the earlier cases into causes won.

Subsequent Court Litigation Relating to the Constitutional Issues Raised in *Frohwerk*

Frohwerk v. *United States* has never been overturned. Jacob Frohwerk lost in his attempt to have freedom of speech and press designated as absolute freedoms that government could not limit. Following the Supreme Court decision in 1919, Frohwerk accepted his sentence of ten years' imprisonment, and on May 31, 1919, he entered the Federal Penitentiary at Fort Leavenworth, Kansas. However, prison records show that his sentence was reduced to "one year and one day," and he actually served only a little over seven months. He was paroled on January 10, 1920.[3]

The controversial issue of regulation of speech and press had really only begun, with Frohwerk's case being one of the early, pioneer cases. Between 1798 (the Alien and Sedition Laws) and 1917 (the Conscription and Espionage Acts) Congress had not passed laws infringing the exercise of First Amendment freedoms. Thus the Supreme Court had not been called on to decide cases in this area. State cases involving civil liberties could not reach the Supreme Court during this period; the Court's jurisdiction was not perceived to extend to state violations of civil liberties until much later. Infringement of freedom-of-expression cases became staples of Court business and a source of frequent controversy after *Frohwerk*. That case decision along with *Schenck* and *Debs* generated other cases, and the feedback cycle was set in motion as different groups sought modification of the ruling.

During the period following World War I the Supreme Court was forced to grapple with many cases testing the reach of governmental power over fundamental freedoms. In the same year that *Frohwerk* was decided, *Abrams* v. *United States,* 250 U.S. 616 (1919), came before the Court. It raised some issues that were similar to those in *Frohwerk*—the publication of material detrimental to the war effort. The charge was that petitioners sought to "incite, provoke, and encourage resistance to the United States" during World War I and conspired to "incite and advocate curtailment of [war] production."[4] Using the same clear-and-present-danger test that had been applied in *Frohwerk*, the Court also found the plaintiffs in *Abrams* guilty. However, Justice Holmes, the author of the test, and Justice Brandeis dissented because their examination of the issues failed to convince them that a sufficient danger existed. As case followed case, it became increasingly evident that the Justices' clear-and-present-danger test was not a mechanical formula that could settle all questions. Thus the Court found itself in the 1920's and 1930's struggling to articulate clearly and apply evenly the clear-and-present-danger test. It did this through a case-by-case approach, moving incrementally—two steps forward, one step back. In each case the Court considered questions of time, place, and manner: who said what, when, and how.[5]

As a result, decisions of the Court were difficult to predict due to the number of divergent facts and the multiplicity of cases. In 1925 in *Gitlow* v. *New York*, 268 U.S. 652 (1925), it appeared that the clear-and-present-danger test had been expanded to allow states to pass laws designed to regulate subversive speech that might tend to create a danger to the life of the state. However, while upholding this New York statute directed against overthrow of government by force and violence, the Court also held that the Fourteenth Amendment incorporated the guarantees of the First Amendment, and states were prohibited from infringements of individual rights of speech, press, and assembly. In addition, Justices Holmes and Brandeis were again in dissent—this time due to the legislative definition of clear and present danger.

Two years later in *Whitney* v. *California*, 274 U.S. 357 (1927), the Court upheld the conviction of a socialist who had been indicted under California's Criminal Syndicalism Act. Yet in this case the Court acted on technical and procedural grounds dealing with its own powers and jurisdiction. Thus the constitutional issue of freedom of speech and association was played down. Moreover, by 1930 the Court had begun to strike down convictions secured under state espionage-type statutes. On the same day that the Court upheld the conviction of Whitney under the California law in spite of her First Amendment claims, it also held unconstitutional an application of a Kansas version of criminal-syndicalism legislation. In *Fiske* v. *Kansas*, 274 U.S. 380 (1927), a unanimous Court held that Fiske, an Industrial Workers of the World (IWW) organizer, had neither done nor said anything that could be understood as advocating violent overthrow of government.

Thus within eight years after the *Frohwerk* decision the Supreme Court indicated support for individual rights under the First Amendment and placed a limit on state actions that infringed these constitutional guarantees. Moreover, the Court continued to move in the direction of finding greater protection for rights of speech, press, and association. In *Dejonge* v. *Oregon*, 299 U.S. 353 (1937), the Court again set aside a state conviction of a man charged with helping conduct a Communist Party meeting. Chief Justice Hughes found this to be in violation of First Amendment rights of assembly, given the fact that there had been no violence nor teaching of violent methods of governmental overthrow. In *Herndon* v. *Lowry*, 301 U.S. 242 (1937), the Court also reversed a state (Georgia) conviction of a black organizer for the Communist Party. The state had not proved that Herndon had ever advocated forcible subversion. Thus his constitutional rights of free speech and assembly had been denied.

In these three cases of the late 1920's and 1930's—*Fiske, Dejonge,* and *Herndon*—the Court began to articulate the "contours of political discussion and agitation required by First Amendment values."[6] In all three cases the Court ruled for the individual's right to freedom of speech and association, discounting the state legislature's determination that dangers existed that had to be controlled through laws restricting First Amendment rights. Moreover, by the late 1930's Jacob Frohwerk's claim that freedom of speech and press was absolute had won at least a limited victory, as the Court began to speak about the preferred position of these freedoms.[7] Justice Benjamin Cardozo, speaking for the Court in *Palko* v. *Connecticut*, 302 U.S. 319 (1939), used dicta to reach out and affirm the doctrine that freedom of speech was a fundamental liberty and indispensable to nearly every other right. Without it there could be no ordered liberty, the essence of a responsible democratic society. In addition, the belief that the Court itself must perform the special duty of guardian of First Amendment rights was clearly articulated in *United States* v. *Carolene Products*, 304 U.S. 144 (1938). In the first and second paragraphs of Footnote Four Justice Harlan F. Stone spoke of the First Amendment as having levied a specific prohibition against governmental encroachments and claimed for the Court a special role in protecting rights of freedom of speech and press.

The 1940's, however, saw the country plunged into World War

II, which brought limitations to the exercise of freedom of speech and press. The passage of the Smith Act in 1940 made it an offense to advocate overthrow of government by force and violence or to belong to a group that had this as its goal. Thus on the national level again there appeared legislation similar to the Conscription Act and the Espionage Act (plus the various amendments), which had generated the *Frohwerk* case during World War I.

Prosecutions under the Smith Act expanded primarily during the Cold War period of the late 1940's and 1950's. In *Dennis* v. *United States*, 341 U.S. 497 (1951), the Court upheld the convictions of Communist Party organizers. However, the opinions in *Dennis* gave a good indication of the Court's dissatisfaction with the clear-and-present-danger formula. The two separate concurrences and the two dissents in *Dennis* demonstrated the struggle within the Court to find a more meaningful standard for coping with the problem of individual liberty versus governmental powers of regulation.

The Court during this period was expanding its use of a balancing strategy to determine the acceptable limits on freedom of speech, press, and association, especially when these involved mainly political issues that affected governmental existence and politics. The Court basically decided that political speech, especially during wartime emergencies, was less entitled to protection than other types of speech—for example, the propounding of religious doctrines. This was demonstrated in *Cantwell* v. *Connecticut*, 310 U.S. 296 (1940), in which the Court, after closely examining the facts, reversed the breach-of-the-peace conviction of a Jehovah's Witness. The Court found "no clear and present danger of riot [or] disorder." However, the use of certain words or terms known as "fighting words"[8] could be prohibited, even if used by a religious leader. The Court affirmed the conviction of another Jehovah's Witness for using such terms in *Chaplinsky* v. *New Hampshire*, 315 U.S. 568 (1942). This did not mean, however, that states were free to create dragnet-type statutes designed to expand state control over any speech they found abrasive; the Court made this very clear in *Terminiello* v. *Chicago*, 337 U.S. 1 (1949), demanding state protection for the individual exercising his constitutional rights of freedom of speech.

The late 1950's saw the Court become increasingly aware that there had to be protection even for the speeches one violently disliked. In cases such as *Yates* v. *United States*, 354 U.S. 298 (1957); *Scales* v. *United States*, 367 U.S. 203 (1961); and *Noto* v.

United States, 367 U.S. 290 (1961), the Court attempted once again to find new tools and techniques appropriate for balancing the individual's First Amendment freedoms against legitimate governmental restraint. The Court tried to refine its balancing or weighing process by fitting each case's facts into a model. Individual rights of freedom of speech, press, and assembly would be placed on one side of the model's judicial scale, while on the other side would be the legitimate powers of the state or national government to protect its existence or implement valid police powers to provide for the health, education, welfare, safety, and morals of its citizens. In case after case the Court undertook to propound the acceptable limits upon freedom of speech, while giving it a preferred position whenever possible.

The 1960's and 1970's brought to the Court innumerable First Amendment cases, and it continued its incremental and piecemeal approach, seeking to preserve liberty and uphold authority at the same time. The Vietnam War created special problems, as draft protestors attempted to exercise their First Amendment right of speech to criticize the draft and even to burn their draft cards (*United States* v. *O'Brien*, 391 U.S. 367, 1968). Cases involving individual freedom of speech became more political in nature, as agitation against the war increased. Flag-defacement (attaching peace symbols to the United States flag) cases occurred across the country and ultimately reached the Court in *Spence* v. *Washington*, 418 U.S. 405 (1974). There the Court majority ruled in favor of the exercise of individual rights even in this emotionally charged area. The use of printed obscene words to describe the draft created still another kind of problem, which the Court confronted in *Cohen* v. *California*, 403 U.S. 15 (1971). In a six-to-three vote the Court upheld the right of the individual to his freedom of expression.

Despite a half century of talk about absolute rights, preferred positions, and balancing, a coherent, comprehensive, consistent framework for First Amendment protection has not yet emerged. There is no simple solution. Complex issues can seldom be solved by mechanical formulas. The Court continues to struggle with the problem raised by *Frohwerk*. This case helped to generate a long series of cases exploring the limitations upon First Amendment rights. Each Court decision ultimately generated still another case. Agitation against the draft has been a recurrent problem in our history; governmental officials are often under public attack; and the questions of personal liberties versus governmental restraints that *Frohwerk* raised live on in cases today.

It can be argued therefore that although Jacob Frohwerk lost his case, his cause was not lost. Indeed, in the years following *Frohwerk* the Court developed the preferred-position doctrine for First Amendment rights. By 1964 Justice Brennan could write that the country had a "profound national commitment to the principle that debate on public issues should be uninhibited, robust, and wide open, and that it may well include vehement, caustic, and sometimes unpleasantly sharp attacks on government and public officials" (*New York Times Co.* v. *Sullivan*, 376 U.S. 254, 1964).

The Flag-Salute Requirement Challenged Again

The eight-to-one Supreme Court decision in *Minersville* v. *Gobitis* did not settle the controversy over the flag salute. Instead, the issue spread to other states, more groups were drawn into the dispute, and bitterness increased. Finally, three years later, the same problem made its way back to the Supreme Court.

The *Gobitis* decision generated an enormous amount of feedback. Criticism was widespread, both from the academic world and from leading newspapers across the country. The press focused its attention on Justice Stone's dissent, and 171 newspaper editorials supported his minority position.[9] In addition, law-review articles overwhelmingly supported Stone and criticized the majority decision. Legal scholars, professors, lawyers, educators, Justice Department officials, and respected religious leaders protested the Court's decision. Justice Frankfurter found his opinion under attack from former supporters and friends, including Eleanor Roosevelt. Liberals everywhere were shocked and dismayed by Frankfurter's reasoning.[10] Justice Stone, on the other hand, received highly complimentary letters from the legal and academic world. Men who had been close friends of both Frankfurter and Stone almost unanimously repudiated the former and extolled the latter. Stone was commended for his legal opinion and moral courage in standing alone. He was deeply gratified by such a response, and in a large file he carefully accumulated newspaper clippings praising his dissent.[11] These came from both large cities and small towns across the country. Stone's dissent in *Gobitis* ultimately would be hailed as "his finest achievement."[12]

However, *Gobitis* also generated increased persecution of Jehovah's Witnesses. Additional states passed compulsory flag-salute laws, and more children were expelled from local schools. In part this was due to the intensity of the religious propagandizing characteristic of this sect. Jehovah's Witnesses insisted on the right to distribute their religious leaflets and tracts on street corners and door-to-door, ringing doorbells and seeking donations as they went.[13] They also organized parades and held open-air religious meetings in public parks.[14] Their members were eager to be martyrs and willing to accept arrest. Moreover, they were also ready to take each case to court, and their legal office was dedicated to defending them before the judicial branch. Jehovah's Witnesses were not disheartened by those decisions that they lost. They pressed new cases forward with even greater zeal. In addition, they monitored the Supreme Court closely, noting the attitudes and voting behavior of the Justices.

Thus, when Jehovah's Witnesses lost a case testing the validity of municipal occupational-licenses taxes as applied to their door-to-door selling of books and tracts, they were not dismayed. They focused not on their loss of the case but on the fact that they had been only one vote short of winning. The Court split five-to-four in *Jones* v. *Opelika*, 316 U.S. 584 (1942). The four dissenting Justices argued that distribution of religious tracts and books accompanied by requests for donations was not "selling"[15] literature as part of one's occupation. The dissenters in this case included the new Chief Justice, Harlan F. Stone, the lone dissenter of *Gobitis*. He was now joined by Justices Black, Douglas, and Murphy. The potential but non-functioning bloc in *Gobitis* had emerged in *Jones* v. *Opelika*.

Jehovah's Witnesses were not only elated at the appearance of this four-man bloc, they were also gratified by the majority's refusal to cite *Gobitis* as the controlling precedent in *Jones* v. *Opelika*. A careful reading of the majority opinion written by Justice Stanley Reed revealed that the majority had actually "distinguished" *Gobitis*.[16] This had probably been necessary to keep a bare majority together. In fact, Reed's opinion also seemed to indicate that he or someone in the majority found *Gobitis* to be an "embarrassing precedent."[17]

Finally, the fact that the Witnesses were jubilant even over a loss in *Jones* v. *Opelika* was due to a special, extraordinary dissenting opinion written by Justices Black, Douglas, and Murphy. In their dissent these Justices completely ignored all of the case issues raised in *Jones* v. *Opelika* and instead apologized for their *Gobitis* vote. This was a most unusual procedure, given the fact that the Court majority had gone out of its way to avoid reliance on *Gobitis* in their *Jones* v. *Opelika* decision. Jehovah's Witnesses believed that these Justices had experienced a conversion to the truth and were inviting the initiation of another flag-salute case.

The Court personnel changes also contributed to the optimism of the Witnesses. When Chief Justice Hughes retired in 1941, Justice Stone was elevated to Chief Justice. Stone's position on the Court was filled by Justice Robert Jackson. In the fall of 1942 Justice Byrnes resigned after only one term. His short stay on the Court undercut the value of his vote in the *Opelika* case. In addition, he was replaced by a known liberal, Justice Wiley Rutledge of the District of Columbia Court of Appeals. Rutledge's position on the application of licensing laws to the evangelizing activities of Jehovah's Witnesses was already known from his decision in a lower-court case. In fact, Rutledge was on record as being opposed to both the *Gobitis* decision and the majority holding in *Jones* v. *Opelika*.[18]

Jehovah's Witnesses decided, therefore, to ask the Supreme Court to re-hear the *Opelika* case and also to consider a similar case, *Murdock* v. *Pennsylvania*, 319 U.S. 103 (1943). On February 15, 1943, the Court agreed to do this. The legal staff of Jehovah's Witnesses was naturally elated. They believed that Chief Justice Stone and Justices Black, Douglas, and Murphy would now be joined by Justice Rutledge and a minority of four would be transformed into a majority of five. They were correct.

The Supreme Court reversed its ruling in *Jones* v. *Opelika* less than one year after deciding it and also ruled in favor of Jehovah's Witnesses in *Murdock* v. *Pennsylvania*. A new Court majority of five found that "religious literature [that] is 'sold' by itinerate preachers . . . does not transform evangelism into a commercial enterprise."[19] Three Justices also believed that freedom of religion had been infringed by the municipal ordinances that had been applied against the evangelizing efforts of Jehovah's Witnesses.

This change of position by the Court was a stimulus to Jehovah's Witnesses who wanted to secure a different Court ruling on the flag-salute issue. Their strategy had consistently involved the legal arena; case losses were generally fed back into the system in the form of new cases. Unable to mobilize support for their cause within either the executive or legislative branches of government, Jehovah's Witnesses turned eagerly to the Court, seeking to impress upon that body its need to perform a guardianship role by preserving First Amendment freedoms for religious minorities. They were never lacking in members who were willing to become parties to a suit challenging local and state laws. As a result, there was no difficulty in securing another flag-salute case. The two daughters of Walter Barnette of Charleston, West Virginia, had been expelled from the West Virginia public-school system for failure to comply with the state flag-salute law. This would become the basic case through which the Witnesses' legal office would seek to secure reversal of *Gobitis*.

The Barnette children, like the Gobitis children, had won their case in lower court. Although the state of West Virginia was not enthusiastic about continuing the suit, the State Board of Education decided to appeal rather than readmit the children and pay court costs. The case was accepted for oral argument before the Supreme Court in March 1943. On June 14 the Court overruled *Gobitis* and, by a vote of six to three, upheld the preferred position of freedom of religion. Justice Robert Jackson was assigned the task of writing the majority opinion, which was joined by Chief Justice Stone and Justices Black, Douglas, Murphy, and Rutledge. Justices Black and Douglas also wrote a strongly supportive separate concurrence to indicate their complete reversal from their *Gobitis* vote and to emphasize their commitment to religious freedom. Justice Murphy also wrote a separate concurrence designed to add weight to the preferred position now accorded freedom of religion. Two Justices—Reed and Roberts—noted dissent, but they did not write opinions. Only Justice Felix Frankfurter, the author of the *Gobitis* opinion, wrote in dissent.[20]

Thus the judicial alignment that had appeared to prevail in *Minersville* v. *Gobitis* radically altered in the *Barnette* case. Frankfurter's spiteful dissent in *West Virginia State Board of Education* v. *Barnette*, 319 U.S. 624 (1943), revealed a deep and bitter Court split. Frankfurter had lost any pretensions to leadership of a liberal bloc. In addition, his intellectual superiority had ceased to overawe his colleagues. He could no longer command either Douglas or Murphy, who, from this time on, did not look to him for leadership.[21] Moreover, the rhetoric used by Justice Jackson would come to be regarded as a masterpiece of judicial thought, quoted by laymen and scholars alike. A profound impression was created by one paragraph in particular, in which the Justice wrote:

> If there is any fixed star in our constitutional constellation, it is that no official, high or petty, can prescribe what shall be orthodox in politics, nationalism, religion, or other matters of opinion or force citizens to confess by word or act their faith therein.[22]

Thus the negative feedback generated by *Gobitis* resulted, within the short space of three years, in the overturning of that precedent. The flag-salute controversy within this context was settled. A case was lost in *Gobitis;* a cause was won in *Barnette*.

Walker Revisited: The Court Takes Another Look

The *Walker* opinion was an aberration from the moment it was handed down. Decided outside of the environment that had created it, the case reached the Court during a period of rising hostility toward civil-rights agitations. Moreover, a short time later additional cases would be decided quite differently.

In November 1968 the Supreme Court again faced one of the key issues in *Walker*—the *ex parte* injunction. The case raising this issue was *Carroll* v. *President and Commissioners of Princess Anne*, 393 U.S. 175 (1968). A unanimous Court held that injunctions that restrained the exercise of First Amendment freedoms could not be issued *ex parte* where it was "possible to notify the opposing parties and give them an opportunity to be heard." Although petitioners in *Carroll*, unlike those in *Walker*, had not disobeyed an injunction but had taken their case immediately to court, the *Carroll* holding nevertheless indicated that states and local governments would have to demonstrate their overriding need to limit First Amendment rights. The burden of proof thus rested on the state or local officials and not the individual demonstrators. The *Carroll* decision clearly demonstrated that the *ex parte* injunction that had been issued against the civil-rights leaders in *Walker* was unconstitutional. There had been ample opportunity for the attorneys of the city of Birmingham and those representing the black ministers to argue the question, "Should the court issue a restraining order to halt the planned Good Friday and Easter Sunday demonstrations?" There was no need for an *ex parte* injunction, since both parties were available to debate the issues.

In addition, the Supreme Court reached an entirely different decision in a case closely associated with *Walker*. *Shuttlesworth* v. *Birmingham*, 394 U.S. 147 (1969), involved Rev. Fred Shuttlesworth, who had attempted to secure the parade-demonstration permit in the *Walker* case. The city of Birmingham had charged Shuttlesworth in a separate case with violation of the Birmingham parade ordinance. He had not secured a demonstration permit. Convicted in the trial court, Shuttlesworth had been sentenced to ninety days' imprisonment at hard labor and a fine of seventy-five dollars. Shuttlesworth thus faced difficulties on two fronts: first, the general charge of violating the court's *ex parte* injunction in the *Walker* case; and second, the specific charge of violating the city's parade ordinance.

The issues that attorneys for the civil-rights leaders in *Walker* had sought to bring to the notice of the Supreme Court were recognized by the Court in *Shuttlesworth*. For example, Justice Stewart writing for the majority (as he had also done in *Walker*) stated that the Birmingham parade-demonstration ordinance was invalid on its face *and* as it had been applied. According to Stewart it conferred too much arbitrary power on the City Commission and allowed its members to act as censors in violation of the First Amendment. Stewart also held that picketing and parading even in a case of this nature were methods of expression entitled to First Amendment protection.

The attempts of Mrs. Hendricks and Rev. Shuttlesworth to secure the permit were now considered appropriate by the Court and sufficient to prove that they had made a good-faith effort to comply with the law. The Court focused particularly on the telegram that Shuttlesworth had sent to Public Safety Commissioner Connor.

There were no dissents in the *Shuttlesworth* case. Justice Black noted a limited concurrence in the result. Justice Harlan wrote a separate concurrence because he could not agree with parts of Stewart's opinion that seemed to indicate a "right to ignore a permit requirement" if it was, in the "opinion of citizen," being administered unconstitutionally. For Harlan, the critical fact in *Shuttlesworth* was that Alabama did not provide for a system of speedy judicial review and that the desired date for the demonstration would have been long past before Shuttlesworth could have secured a court ruling. Harlan recognized that "no effective relief could [have been] obtained by Good Friday." Moreover, Harlan concluded:

> Since the right to engage in peaceful and orderly political demonstrations is, under appropriate conditions, a fundamental aspect of the 'liberty' protected by the Fourteenth Amendment, . . . the petitioner [Shuttlesworth] was not obliged to invoke procedures which could not give him effective relief.[23]

Chief Justice Warren and Justices Douglas, Brennan, White, and Fortas joined Justice Stewart's opinion without comment. Justice Thurgood Marshall, who had replaced Justice Tom Clark, did not participate in the decision.

Justice Stewart attempted to distinguish *Walker* from *Shuttlesworth*. In a footnote he stated that the legal and constitutional issues in the two cases were different, since a court injunction had been issued in *Walker*. Nevertheless, the *Walker* decision had been modified within a two-year period by these decisions in *Carroll* and *Shuttlesworth*.

Although the civil-rights demonstrators had lost their attempt to have the Birmingham parade-permit ordinance declared unconstitutional in the *Walker* case, they succeeded in *Shuttlesworth*. Moreover, the misuse of *ex parte* injunctions to preclude consideration of an unconstitutional ordinance was recognized and rendered no longer appropriate as a result of the *Carroll* opinion. The decision of the Court in *Walker* had rested on such a technical and narrow issue—disobedience of a court order—that its future application as precedent was limited from the beginning.[24]

The cause of the civil-rights demonstrators in *Walker* was also won in a larger sense. The ending of the segregated lunch counters had been the main purpose of the Birmingham demonstrations during April 1963. Ultimately, those who marched and picketed against this practice would win: the Birmingham merchants and businessmen desegregated their department-store lunch counters.

Bob White Did Not Die in Vain

The courtroom murder of Bob White made it impossible for him ever to have a fair trial in which evidence could be tested impartially to determine his guilt or innocence. The jury acquittal of his murderer, Cochran, seemed not only to foreclose the issue of impartial legal trials for blacks but also to approve vigilante justice. However, a wider examination reveals that the Court, already sensitive to gross miscarriages of justice of this type, was beginning to hold states accountable for providing Fourth, Fifth, and Sixth Amendment guarantees for blacks.

The Supreme Court under the leadership of Chief Justice Hughes had begun the process of carefully scrutinizing *in forma pauperis* petitions and expanding their docket to include more civil-liberties cases. It was said of Hughes that he could sense cases in which civil rights had been violated and there had been a miscarriage of justice.[25] Even before the 1940 decision in *Bob White* Hughes's Court had dealt with the infamous *Scottsboro* cases. In these three cases the Supreme Court reversed rape convictions of defendants who had been tried without an attorney by a biased jury in a hostile environment.[26] The Supreme Court insisted upon guarantees of procedural due process for these young black men: the right to "meaningful"[27] counsel and the right to a jury-selection process devoid of racial discrimination. The Supreme Court's heightened scrutiny of confessions was obvious in *Brown* v. *Mississippi*, 297 U.S. 278 (1936), where murder convictions had been based solely on confessions obtained through beatings of black suspects by local deputy sheriffs. Brown, the Negro defendant, had been whipped with a leather belt to which was attached a heavy metal buckle. Another Negro was "semi-hanged" twice and also beaten. This had been done in order to secure the confessions necessary for conviction. Chief Justice Hughes, speaking for a unanimous Supreme Court, ruled that such involuntary confessions violated the Fifth Amendment and concluded that, "The rack and torture chamber may not be substituted for the witness stand."[28]

The Supreme Court's awareness of the lack of procedural safeguards, particularly for black defendants, increased throughout the 1930's and 1940's. The decision in *Chambers* v. *Florida*, 309 U.S. 277 (1940), which had provided the basis for reversal in the *Bob White* case, was but another step in a growing succession of case decisions in which the Court moved into a guardianship role with respect to black defendants. However, the Court could do nothing in cases where blacks had been lynched by private citizens, not state officials, who took the law into their own hands and administered summary punishment. Under the existing interpretation of the Constitution there was no national power to punish or prevent private acts of discrimination. Owners and operators of private businesses could choose to refuse service to blacks without violating any federal law. Vigilante actions could only be punished by the state legal system.[29]

The Court had interpreted the Fourteenth Amendment to mean that states could not deny certain fundamental rights to citizens. However, there was a very clear distinction between state action that deprived individuals of their civil-rights guarantees and private actions. The Court itself could regulate and make rulings in cases of state action. This had been demonstrated in the *Scottsboro* cases, in *Brown* v. *Mississippi*, in *Chambers* v. *Florida*, and in *Bob White*. On the other hand, many Supreme Court Justices did not believe that the Court or Congress could prevent acts of private discrimination.

The problem of congressional power to reach private acts of discrimination was an old one. After the Civil War several Congresses had enacted various Civil Rights Acts, culminating in the Civil Rights Act of 1875, which made it a crime to close places of public accommodation (inns, theaters, railroad cars) to individuals on the basis of their race. However, the Supreme Court in the *Civil Rights Cases*, 109 U.S. 3 (1883), had ruled that the Constitution did not give Congress the power to pass such a law; thus the

Civil Rights Act of 1875 was declared unconstitutional. As public concern for freed blacks retreated in terms of social, economic, and political priorities, Congress made no further attempt to legislate in the field of civil rights. In fact, except for some minor voting-rights legislation, Congress did not pass a major civil-rights law between 1875 and 1964. As a result, during this period private acts of discrimination were under the jurisdiction and power of the state governments.[30]

Federal legislation making it a federal crime for anyone to dispose of another summarily on the basis of race and color was desperately needed. It was also essential that such legislation be clearly within the power of Congress to enact. Throughout the 1940's and 1950's various attempts to secure anti-lynching laws died in Congress. Only time and a growing public awareness and sensitivity would finally combine to make possible the passage of the Civil Rights Act of 1964 and supplementary amendments in 1968. Miscarriages of justice in cases like *Bob White* and televised news showing police brutality toward black demonstrators finally penetrated the American consciousness.

The new legislation, designed to rectify such wrongs, was quite similar to that which Congress had enacted in 1875. Would the Court also find the Civil Rights Act of 1964 unconstitutional? This question concerned many of the legislators who helped draft the new statutes. They therefore sought to anchor the legislation in a recognized power of Congress—power over interstate commerce—so that the Court would find it to be constitutional.[31] Congress in 1964 was ready to put an end to state deprivations of civil rights and under Title IX of the Civil Rights Act of 1964 provided for federal intervention in cases claiming denial of equal protection. The act contained some of the following provisions:

18 U.S. C. § 241. *"Conspiracy against rights of citizens.* If two or more persons conspire to injure, oppress, threaten, or intimidate any citizen in the free exercise or enjoyment of any right or privilege secured to him by the Constitution or laws of the United States . . . ;" or "If two or more persons go in disguise on the highway, or on the premises of another, with intent to prevent or hinder his free exercise or enjoyment of any right or privilege so secured . . . they shall be fined not more than $10,000 or imprisoned not more than ten years or both; if death results, they shall be subjected to imprisonment for any term of years or for life," 18 U.S. C § 242. *"Deprivation of rights under color of law.* Whoever, under color of any law, statute, [or] ordinance . . . subjects [another] to the deprivation of any rights . . .

protected by the constitution or laws of the United States . . . on account of . . . his color, or race . . . shall be fined not more than $1,000 or [imprisoned] not more than one year or both; and if death results shall be subject to imprisonment for any term of years or for life."

As a result of these provisions it would be possible for the national government to reach private as well as state interferences with constitutional rights. Congress was ready in 1964 to write *finis* to private vigilante justice. The Supreme Court had been moving in this direction even before the passage of the 1964 Act. Obviously the federal legislative, executive, and judicial branches wanted to provide protection for minority rights when states refused to do so. However, the Supreme Court needed to find a way to allow Congress to do this. Could the Court find such a grant of power to Congress in the interstate commerce clause? If not, could it be found in the Fourteenth Amendment?

In the period following the passage of the Civil Rights Act of 1964 the Court would struggle with this problem. Two cases particularly illustrate this and indicate that while the Court (as well as Congress) was keenly aware of the necessity of federal intervention to secure civil rights for blacks, it was not an easy task to find a source of power for such intervention.

United States v. *Guest*, 383 U.S. 745 (1966), involved the attempt of the federal government to prosecute six white men for the shooting death of a black man in the vicinity of Athens, Georgia. Two of the six defendants had been prosecuted for this murder in a Georgia state court, and the local jury had returned a verdict of not guilty. Under the provisions of the Civil Rights Act of 1964, however, it was possible for the federal government to institute a suit in federal court and ultimately to secure the conviction of the murderers.

United States v. *Price*, 383 U.S. 787 (1966), arose out of a widely publicized murder of three civil-rights workers near Philadelphia, Mississippi, in 1964. The defendants included the sheriff, the deputy sheriff, a policeman, and fifteen private individuals. The federal government charged these eighteen defendants with a conspiracy that involved releasing the victims from jail at night, intercepting and killing them, and disposing of their bodies in a dam under construction nearby. This was summary punishment that deprived the three civil-rights workers of their Fourteenth Amendment rights without due process of law by persons acting under color of the laws of the state of Mississippi. The Supreme

Court held that the defendants had acted exactly as charged; the national government's power to act under the Civil Rights Act of 1964 could at last prevent state obstructions.

Although these two case decisions did not settle all the questions relative to the source of Congress's power, the decisions did clearly indicate that the Court would no longer tolerate the kind of "Texas justice"[32] that had failed to give Bob White the full benefits of his constitutional rights and that, in addition, had failed to seriously prosecute his murderer. Thus, it could finally be claimed with a certain degree of assurance that Bob White had not died in vain and that the cause of equal justice under law had finally prevailed.

Epilogue

A complete understanding of the Supreme Court's powers and limitations is gained by a thorough analysis of all stages of the judicial process—input, conversion, output, impact, and feedback. Decision making does not take place in a vacuum. It is affected by the legal environment and its personalities, the climate of public opinion and its shifting attitudes and beliefs. Analyses of cases lost before the Court as well as those won can increase our understanding of the role that the Supreme Court plays both as actor and reactor within our governmental system.

The four cases analyzed not only reveal the various factors that affect the total decision-making process but also clearly highlight the new role that the Supreme Court has been increasingly playing since the 1930's. The problems associated with individual rights have grown and now comprise nearly two-thirds of the Court's business.[33] The Court's struggles with issues of freedom of speech, religion, assembly, and press as well as with the rights of procedural due process are illustrated in *Frohwerk*, *Gobitis*, *Walker*, and *Bob White*.

The idea that the Court would play an active and positive role in the area of civil rights and liberties had been clearly articulated by Justice Stone's Footnote Four in *Carolene Products*. Stone had insisted that the Court had a duty to carefully scrutinize actions that restricted the political processes designed to protect minorities. If a statute or action clearly abridged one of the freedoms guaranteed in the Bill of Rights and made applicable to states by the Fourteenth Amendment, then the Court was charged with the duty of declaring it unconstitutional. Any action that made it difficult for "discrete and insular" minorities to work successfully within the system to secure their constitutionally guaranteed rights was also to be subjected to exacting judicial scrutiny.[34]

Stone had specifically stated that the Court should play this role when a particular "religious . . . , national . . . , or racial minority" was involved. *Gobitis, Frohwerk, Walker,* and *Bob White* presented the Court with these groups: Jehovah's Witnesses were definitely a religious minority in *Gobitis*; German-Americans were a "national" or ethnic minority in *Frohwerk*; the civil-rights leaders in *Walker* and Bob White himself were members of a racial minority that had been subjected to centuries of invidious discrimination. The Court under Footnote Four had claimed power to exercise close judicial scrutiny over legislation and action that affected these specific groups, and it had invited those so situated—who fitted into these categories and found the ordinary political processes unresponsive—to appeal to the Court as their guardian. In all of these cases the individuals did make this appeal, and the Court was called upon to make a judicial determination, deciding who was to win and who to lose.[35]

However, it is essential to avoid oversimplification. It is not enough to state that Jacob Frohwerk lost when the Court ruled against him or that Bob White won when the Court ruled for him. To do this would be to focus on only one level or stage in the process of decision making. Moreover, as illustrated in each case, different variables assumed varying degrees of importance in contributing to the long range significance of each case. The input stage in *Frohwerk* assumed great importance through the choice of the attorney; the judicial interaction at the conversion stage played a significant role in the decision that the Court reached in *Minersville* v. *Gobitis;* the judicial attitudes developed over time and triggered by individual perceptions of events were critical to the Court's decision (output) in *Walker;* the impact stage highlighted in *Bob White* showed the power of public opinion to reverse a Court decision. Each case generated new demands and the feedback cycle operated to systematically channel these demands back into the system. The judicial process is thus seen in its totality—ongoing with incremental changes. Ideally, such changes will ultimately produce that highest goal of a fair and orderly judicial process in which the guarantees of the Constitution come alive through the system.

NOTES

1. Charles H. Sheldon, *The American Judicial Process: Models and Approaches* (New York: Dodd, Mead, 1974), pp. 168, 194, 195.

2. Sheldon Goldman and Thomas P. Jahnige, "Systems Analysis and Judicial Systems: Potential and Limitations," *Polity*, vol. III (Spring 1971), p. 353.

3. Fort Leavenworth, Kansas, United States Penitentiary, Documents and Records, 1919–20.

4. *Abrams* v. *United States*, 250 U.S. 616 (1919).

5. Gerald Gunther, *Constitutional Law: Cases and Materials*, 10th ed. (Mineola, N.Y.: Foundation, 1980), pp. 1124–31.

6. *Ibid.*, pp. 1148–53.

7. *Ibid.*, pp. 1103–17. Alfred Bettman, Special Assistant to the Attorney General, was not convinced that Jacob Frohwerk had violated the Espionage Act, although Bettman helped to prepare the government's case. He later wrote that he had personally believed from the beginning that Frohwerk's articles were protected by the First Amendment's guarantees. See note 31 in article by Fred D. Ragan, "Justice Oliver Wendell Holmes, Jr., Zechariah Chafee, Jr., and the Clear and Present Danger Test for Free Speech: The First Year, 1919," 58 *Journal of American Legal History 27 (1971)*.

8. *Ibid.*, pp. 1219–21.

9. Stone Papers, vol. 81, Manuscript Division, Library of Congress, Washington, D.C.

10. Joseph P. Lash, *From the Diaries of Felix Frankfurter* (New York: Norton, 1975), pp. 68–69.

11. Stone Papers, vol. 81, Manuscript Division, Library of Congress, Washington, D.C.

12. Alpheus T. Mason, *Harlan Fiske Stone: Pillar of the Law* (New York: Viking, 1956), p. 809.

13. *Lovell* v. *Griffin*, 303 U.S. 444 (1938). See also Gerald Gunther, *Constitutional Law: Cases and Materials*, pp. 1200–2.

14. *Cox* v. *New Hampshire*, 312 U.S. 569 (1941).

15. *Jones* v. *Opelika*, 316 U.S. 584 (1942), *vacated*, 319 U.S. 103 (1943).

16. Glendon Schubert, *Constitutional Politics: The Political Behavior of Supreme Court Justices and the Constitutional Policies That They Make* (New York: Holt, Rinehart and Winston, 1964), pp. 224–25. "The technique of distinguishing precedents is . . . [a] discretionary tool of adjudi-

cation that the court can and does use to avoid following inconvenient precedents, and at the same time to avoid creating the impression that it is fomenting instability in the law by frequently overruling its own prior decisions. The court usually . . . [does this] by limiting it [the case] to its own special facts."

17. David R. Manwaring, *Render unto Ceasar: The Flag Salute Controversy* (Chicago: University of Chicago Press, 1962), pp. 198–201.

18. *Ibid.*, pp. 202–3.

19. *Jones* v. *Opelika*, 316 U.S. 584 (1942), *vacated*, 319 U.S. 103 (1943).

20. *West Virginia State Board of Education* v. *Barnette*, 319 U.S. 624 (1943).

21. James Simon, *Independent Journey: The Life of William O. Douglas* (New York: Harper and Row, 1980), pp. 11, 206–9. See also William O. Douglas, *The Court Years: 1939–1975* (New York: Vintage, 1981), pp. 44–48, and Joseph P. Lash, *From the Diaries of Felix Frankfurter*, pp. 68–69.

22. *West Virginia State Board of Education* v. *Barnette*, 319 U.S. 624 (1943).

23. *Shuttlesworth* v. *Birmingham*, 394 U.S. 147 (1969).

24. Professor Alan F. Westin holds a different view. He believes that the Court rendered a broad decision in *Walker*. See Alan F. Westin, *The Trial of Martin Luther King* (New York: Crowell, 1974), pp. 286–88.

25. Alice Fleetwood Bartee, "Judicial Biography and the Judicial Process" (Ph.D. dissertation, Columbia University, 1976), pp. 269–70. See also Merlo J. Pusey, *Charles Evans Hughes* (New York: Macmillan, 1951), vol. 2, pp. 711–17.

26. *Powell* v. *Alabama*, 287 U.S. 45 (1932); *Norris* v. *Alabama*, 294 U.S. 587 (1935); *Patterson* v. *Alabama*, 294 U.S. 600 (1935). See Dan T. Carter, *Scottsboro: A Tragedy of the American South* (New York: Oxford University Press, 1971).

27. *Powell* v. *Alabama*, 287 U.S. 45 (1932). In his opinion for the Court, Justice Sutherland noted that "the trial judge . . . said that he had appointed all the members of the bar for the purpose of arraigning the defendants and then of course anticipated that the members of the bar would continue to help the defendants if no counsel appeared. . . . On the morning of the trial . . . [a] Mr. Roddy (a Tennessee lawyer) stated to the court that he did not appear as counsel, but that he would . . . appeal along with counsel that the court might appoint. . . . Under the[se] circumstances disclosed, we hold that defendants were not accorded the right of counsel *in any substantial sense*. . . . [Italics added.] Defendants did not have the aid of counsel in any real sense."

28. *Brown* v. *Mississippi*, 297 U.S. 278 (1936).

29. Gerald Gunther, *Constitutional Law: Cases and Materials*, pp. 978–1042.

30. *Ibid.*, pp. 1028–30.

31. *Ibid.*, pp. 195–204.

32. Jonathan Daniels, "Judge Lynch Himself," *Raleigh* (North Carolina) *News and Observer*, 12 June 1941.

33. Gerald Gunther, *Constitutional Law: Cases and Materials*, p. xxiii.

34. *United States* v. *Carolene Products Co.*, 304 U.S. 144 (1938), 152, n. 4.

35. There is an ongoing controversy over what Stone actually intended to do in the footnote. Justice Lewis F. Powell has asserted that Stone did not mean for the term "discrete and insular minorities" to reach beyond the areas of race, religion, and nationality. See Lewis F. Powell, Jr., "*Carolene Products* Revisited," 82 *Columbia Law Review* 1087 (1982). Professor Louis Lusky asserts that Stone meant for the term to be more expansive than this. However, Lusky maintains that Stone was only inviting discussion in the footnote and did not intend for it to be a formula to govern Court action. See Louis Lusky, "Footnote Redux: A *Carolene Products* Reminiscence," 82 *Columbia Law Review* 1093 (1982).

GLOSSARY

Adequate-and-Independent-State-Grounds Doctrine
A doctrine that the Supreme Court uses to determine which cases to review. Applying the doctrine, the Court declines jurisdiction over cases that do not contain a federal issue and that have been decided in a state court on the basis of state law that is sufficient to dispose of the cases.

Amicus Curiae
A Latin phrase meaning "friend of the court." Individuals or groups that are not direct parties to a case may request the privilege of filing an *amicus curiae* brief to provide the court with additional arguments and information. The court and the parties to the case may refuse such assistance.

Appellant
The party who takes his or her case to a superior court to secure review of a lower court's decision.

Ashwander Rules
Seven principles listed in the concurring opinion of Justice Brandeis in *Ashwander* v. *TVA*, 297 U.S. 288, 346–348 (1936), which state grounds used by the Supreme Court in declining to hear cases within its jurisdiction.

Brief
A written statement prepared by the attorney arguing a case in court. It consists of a statement of the case facts and citation of applicable law.

Central Powers
The World War I alignment of Germany, Austria-Hungary, and the Turkish Empire.

Certiorari, Writ of
A device originating in common-law practice, by which a superior court requires a lower court to send up a case record. The Supreme Court uses it as a discretionary device to choose the cases it wishes to hear.

Civil Rights Acts of 1875 and 1964
The 1875 act contains, among other provisions, a public-accommodation section to prevent discrimination on the basis of race in inns, theaters, and railroads. The Supreme Court ruled this section unconstitutional in the 1883 *Civil Rights Cases*, 109 U.S. 3 (1883). The 1964 Civil Rights Act contains a similar public-accommodations provision, based mainly on the commerce clause and giving the federal government power to punish owners and managers who refuse services on the basis of race.

Clear-and-Present-Danger Test
A test first stated in *Schenck* v. *United States*, 249 U.S. 47 (1919). The Supreme Court used the test to hold constitutional certain governmental restrictions on freedoms of speech and press that were deemed necessary to prevent serious and immediate dangers to the existence of the state.

Complaint, Bill of
The plaintiff's initial pleading, which frames the issues in the suit.

Compact Theory of American Government
The belief that the United States Constitution was a contract (or compact) made between the national government and the state governments. According to this theory, if one party breaks the contract, the other is no longer bound by it. An alternate theory states that the Constitution represents an agreement made between the people, not the states, and the national government.

Concurring Opinion
A case opinion filed by a Justice who agrees with another opinion, perhaps the majority opinion, and wishes to state his or her own reasons for agreeing.

Consent List
A list, prepared by the Chief Justice with the aid of his law clerks, of cases that he considers frivolous and lying outside Supreme Court jurisdiction. Sometimes referred to as a "dead" list, a petition can be removed to a "discuss" list by the request of any one Justice. If, following discussion, four of the nine Justices vote to hear the case, it will be scheduled for oral argument. Otherwise, the Court will summarily refuse to hear the case.

Court-Packing Plan
An attempt by President Franklin Roosevelt in 1937 to replace those Supreme Court Justices who had declared some of his New Deal programs unconstitutional. Roosevelt proposed additions to the Court for every Justice over the age of seventy. He planned to appoint Justices who agreed with his social and economic theories.

Deposition
A legal process to obtain the sworn testimony of a witness outside of court.

Dicta
Expressions of principle in a court's opinion that go beyond the facts before the court and exceed the judgment it made. Such expressions are not binding in subsequent cases.

Discrete and Insular Minorities
Entities entitled to special judicial protection, according to Justice Harlan F. Stone in *United States* v. *Carolene Products Company*, 304 U.S. 144 (1938). The phrase was designed to cover those who were separated and isolated from the majority and thus not capable of mobilizing empathy groups to support them.

Dispositive
The quality of settling a matter finally and definitively. A state law is dispositive of an issue in a case if the law settles the issue finally, other laws, rules, and regulations notwithstanding.

Distinguishing Cases
A method used to point out differences between a case precedent and a current case. This allows a court to bypass the precedent rather than to overrule it.

Double Jeopardy
A Fifth Amendment prohibition against a second prosecution after a first trial for the same offense.

Elastic Clause (Necessary-and-Proper Clause)
Article I §8 cl. 18 of the United States Constitution gives Congress the power "to make all laws which shall be necessary and proper for carrying . . . [out] . . . the foregoing powers." Some construe this grant narrowly, while others argue that it is an additional grant of power to Congress.

Exceptions, Bill of
A formal written statement of a party's objections to the rulings of a judge during a trial. To establish the bill's accuracy, the objections, along with the factual circumstances on which they are based, must be clearly stated and the bill must be signed by the judge. Its purpose is to place the disputed rulings in the court record for purposes of appeal.

Error-free Trial
A trial devoid of mistakes of fact and law.

Error, Writ of
A method of appeal by which an appellate court orders a lower court to send up a case for review of alleged mistakes made by the lower court. This method is no longer used by the Supreme Court.

Ex Parte Hearing
A judicial hearing with only one party present.

Ex Post Facto Law
A law passed after the commission of an act, making the act—which was legal when it was committed—illegal.

"Freedom Riders"
Groups of blacks, supported by white civil-rights advocates, who in the spring and summer of 1961 purchased bus tickets for interstate travel in the South. Their purpose was to show that Supreme Court decisions ordering desegregation of vehicles and terminals were not being enforced. The "Freedom Rides" were organized by SCLC and CORE and generated great hostility, particularly in Alabama. Federal-government intervention became necessary to maintain order.

Game Theory
A method of analyzing power relationships. In the judicial process, game theory is used to study leadership roles and judicial decision making by focusing on power relationships in a court.

Habeas Corpus
A Latin phrase meaning "you have the body." The purpose of a writ of *habeas corpus* is to bring a party before a court to assure that no one is "restrained of his liberty by due process."

In Forma Pauperis
A Latin term meaning "in the manner of a pauper." It is the no-cost method used by indigents to sue in court.

Injunction
A court order directing someone to do something or refrain from doing something.

Intent
Design, determination, or resolve with which a person acts. Intent can be charged if the actor desires to cause certain consequences and is relatively certain that his or her act will lead to them.

Justiciable Issues
Controversies that are within the proper jurisdiction of a court and appropriate for judicial resolution.

Mandamus, Writ of
A Latin phrase meaning "we command." It is a court order commanding a public offical to perform a certain act.

Moot Action
An action no longer presenting a justiciable controversy because the issues involved have become dead.

Per Curiam
A Latin phrase meaning "by the court." A *per curiam* decision is one that all the Justices support; generally, no name is attached to the written opinion in the case.

Preferred-Position Doctrine
The belief that First Amendment values are entitled to special protection by a court. The doctrine is based on the idea that freedom of thought and freedom of speech are necessary for every other form of freedom.

Prior Restraint
The act of preventing the publication of a book, article, or other printed matter before it is published. The First Amendment to the United States Constitution prohibits such actions.

Ripe Case
A case that is ready for review because the controversy has "jelled" sufficiently. Courts decide the issue of ripeness on a case-by-case basis under the authority of Article III of the United States Constitution.

Rule of Four
A tradition of the Supreme Court whereby a vote of four Justices assures a grant of *certiorari* and the Court agrees to hear the case so appealed.

***Scottsboro* Cases**
Powell v. *Alabama*, 287 U.S. 45 (1932); *Norris* v. *Alabama*, 294 U.S. 587 (1935); and *Patterson* v. *Alabama*, 294 U.S. 600 (1935). In these cases the Supreme Court reversed attempts by the state of Alabama to convict a group of young blacks of rape. The issue raised in *Powell* was that the conviction violated the Sixth Amendment's guarantee of counsel. The Supreme Court asserted for the first time that state-appointed counsel was necessary in a case involving the death penalty. In *Norris* and *Patterson*, the issue raised was that of racial discrimination in jury selection. Due process of law, guaranteed by the Fourteenth Amendment, had been violated by the state's actions.

Selective Incorporation
The process used by the Supreme Court to extend the civil liberties of the federal Bill of Rights gradually to cover state proceedings. This became possible only after the passage of the Fourteenth Amendment in 1868. States originally were not bound by the Bill of Rights. Civil liberties within a state depended upon the state constitution.

Smith Act
A federal statute punishing the advocacy of the overthrow of the government by force and violence.

Standing to Sue
The legal right to sue another party in court. The petitioning party must show that a legal injury would result unless a lawsuit is permitted. The party must have a sufficient stake in an otherwise justiciable controversy to obtain judicial resolution of the case.

Stare Decisis
A Latin phrase meaning "let the decision stand." This is a court policy whereby once a court has laid down a principle of law as applicable to a certain set of facts, it will adhere to that principle in all future cases with the same facts.

State Police Power
The power given to the states in the Tenth Amendment to the United States Constitution. It includes the right of the states to pass laws for the protection of its citizens' health, education, welfare, safety, and morals.

Supremacy Clause
Article VI cl. 2 of the United States Constitution declares that the Constitution and all laws made under it, as well as treaties, shall be superior to state laws.

Systems Theory
A framework for selecting, organizing, and analyzing data, adopted by David Easton in the 1960's for the study of political systems. It seeks to investigate the "authoritative allocation of values" in the system. The judicial process can constitute a system by itself. Models show relationships among the parts of the system: inputs, conversion, outputs, impact, and feedback.

Temporary Restraining Order
An emergency remedy issued by a court to prevent any action until the trial court can hear arguments.

Veniremen
Members of a panel of jurors summoned to make up a jury. They are to be good, lawful, and not kin to the parties in the case.

Venue, Change of
The removal of a suit begun in one county to another. It is usually granted if the court believes that due to prejudice a defendant cannot receive a fair trial in the area where the crime occurred.

Vigilante Justice
Punishment administered summarily by a group organized to suppress and punish crime when the legal processes are not functioning.

INDEX